You've Got a Great Past Ahead of You

You've Got a Great Past Ahead of You

How Women Can Expand Their Work Options

Patricia E. Berne, Ph.D.   Judy Dubin   Sherri Muchnick

The Bobbs-Merrill Company Inc.,   Indianapolis/New York

Copyright © 1980 by Patricia E. Berne, Judy Dubin, & Sherri Muchnick

*All rights reserved, including the right of reproduction
in whole or in part in any form
Published by The Bobbs-Merrill Company, Inc.
Indianapolis   New York*

*Designed by Jean Callan King
Manufactured in the United States of America*

First printing

Library of Congress Cataloging in Publication Data
Berne, Patricia E
  You've got a great past ahead of you.

  1. Vocational guidance for women. I. Dubin,
Judy, joint author. II. Muchnick, Sherri, joint
author. III. Title.
HD6058.B527   650.1'4'088042   80-683
ISBN 0-672-52658-1

This book is dedicated to
our husbands
Richard, Richard, and Ron
whose support and encouragement and pride, as well as
good humor, continued throughout the writing of the book
and to our children
Jason, Brendan, Amy, Jennifer, Marc, and Adam
who we hope will find satisfaction in their work,
and a comfortable integration of work into their lives

Acknowledgments

We gratefully wish to acknowledge the many women we have worked with during the past five years. First, we wish to thank the many women who shared their hopes and sorrows, plans and disappointments—their lives—with us while participating in the women's interest programs at St. Louis Community College at Meramec and at the other institutions where we have taught classes. Secondly, we are grateful to those women who have come to us as private clients and have helped us to an ever better understanding of the variety of options for women as well as their desires for the future. And thirdly, we acknowledge our families and many, many friends who have encouraged us to continue our writing and our work.

Contents

You've Got a Great Past Ahead of You

Introduction

❧

WOMEN WORKING. How could such a simple two-word phrase be controversial? But it is. This book is for all women who are struggling with the issue of work and how they can fit into the "world of work." It speaks to women who plan to work, immediately or in the sometime future, as well as to the women who are presently employed.

It is for women who have labored at home with husband and usually children and who now "need" to become gainfully employed—from desire or economic necessity. It is for the woman who once had a job—nursing, teaching, typing, selling—and who now chooses to return to work and to perceive it as a career, employment that she will enjoy, and that will allow her a sense of fulfillment, pride, and personal accomplishment. She may or may not plan to return to the same type of job she once held, but by describing her job as a career, she will be indicating a new investment of self and an increasing awareness of her future possibilities.

This book is also for the woman who has never been employed, who left high school or college to marry and have a family and who has now worked herself out of the job of raising her family. She may feel quite successful, but still she asks, "Who am I today and where am I going tomorrow?" In this book women will learn how to bridge this gap and ease their transition into the formal world of work.

CAREER CHANGING. The very thought can be paralyzing. This book will be helpful to the woman who is currently employed but who wants to plan for a change. She would like to be involved in a new or different work setting. She may want to move into a job that is more challenging, more fulfilling, or more lucrative. She may feel the need for more flexibility within her job as she reexamines its demands upon her time. She may want to redesign the interplay of her work with other aspects of her life.

STAYING IN TRAINING. Does stepping out of the work force mean losing out? This book supports women in their decision to take a sabbatical from their formal work without jeopardizing their chances of returning. Whether preparing to have children, planning for new career directions or taking time for personal development, anxiety about how she'll return can be replaced by positive steps that will help her maintain contact with the work world. Although staying in training may not require major time commitments, it does mean a conscious effort to seek ways of assuring continuity and growth within her work life. Twenty minutes of jogging daily will not prepare one for the Boston Marathon, but it does make the decision to run seriously at some future time a possibility.

This book is written to help women, all of us, explore and define the role of work in our lives. We have many choices and options. Awareness of these choices and options will help us gain control and power over our distinctly personal work patterns—over our lives.

Desire for growth and change is the greatest commonality among the groups of women for whom this book is written. Women are becoming increasingly aware of their desire for expanded options and life styles. Although they have been bombarded with expectations that they join the labor force, there is a great absence of information about alternative work/career patterns that help integrate work into the different stages of a woman's life. But even as we may be ready to embrace the expanding horizons opening to women today, we frequently experience a fear of change, though we may not admit it. We are hesitant to take risks, for we may not succeed. We often lack self-confidence in untried situations. We are plagued by negative statements to ourself: "Nobody will hire me; I'm too old, too young, too fat, too dumb, too *me*."

Statistics show that the majority of women will spend an average of twenty-three years employed outside the home. The number of women who are employed has increased by 3.2 million since 1970. About 41% of women now work and about 60% of families depend on two wage earners. In addition, one of every seven families is headed by a woman. Research, however, on work patterns of women has done little more than chart statistics on numbers of women employed in various occupations and their salary levels. Work on the life stages of the adult

2

has usually linked the adult woman's developmental stages with the life cycle of the family. Only recently have theories been offered to describe the patterns of how a woman integrates the many facets of her life—career aspirations, marriage, family, community participation. Even in the midst of the feminist movement in the 1960s, an acknowledged authority on the stages of adult development, Erik Erikson, still held that the only true generativity of a woman is childbearing.

More recent researchers such as Eli Ginzberg, Marjorie Fiske Lowenthal, and Bernice Neugarten are seeing evidence that a woman's need for fulfillment and generativity does go beyond childbirth. Prior to the twentieth century, these needs of hers were met within the family life cycle, in that she was physically and psychologically essential to its survival. A woman's need for identity and generativity was fulfilled through physical activities such as tilling the soil, reaping the harvest, spinning the wool, chopping the wood. She was also teacher, nurse, social worker, conservationist, nutritionist, engineer, accountant, and designer for her family and often for her community. For good or for ill, the mechanization and socialization of the twentieth century has limited the need for this work, and as John Dewey in the 1920s decreed, "in forty years time, women will be the greatest untapped natural resource of our country." That time is now.

It is now clearer than ever before in history that while most women do have a life cycle that interacts with that of her family, each woman nevertheless has one of her own. But as women, we are presently moving along an uncharted course—we must believe that we can take responsibility for our own future directions.

Studies on women and work have described the work patterns of women in the twentieth century as "discontinuous," as moving in and out of the paid labor force to have and to raise children. The term "discontinuous" assumes that all work must be done in a formal context in order to "count" and to be part of a continuous career pattern. This view of career patterns does not allow a woman to perceive "nonpaid" employment as part of her work continuum. A new perspective can allow her to use this time for regeneration and reenergizing, leading her to new growth and new horizons.

If you were to take a survey of the next twenty women you

meet, you would encounter many variations in their work patterns. With each woman you would see different patterns of growth and change in the "work" which they are doing. Some women will also be more conscious than others of the changes that have taken place in their lives. However, we firmly believe that women's work patterns are kaleidoscopic rather than discontinuous: our phases of life shift one into the other and each segment of time integrates the past elements into the future possibilities. In each block of time the components of our kaleidoscope are arranged in different configurations. We can participate in designing these configurations in order to gain power and control over our lives. We can turn our kaleidoscope. Our active involvement in designing our own future life of work will help smooth our transition periods. By choosing what will predominate in each stage of life that we are moving toward, our life/work pattern becomes wonderfully continuous.

To begin turning our own kaleidoscope, we need to reassess how we define words that may have a controlling effect on decisions about our future. First consider the word "work." When you say the word work, what do you see? What kind of images does it conjure up? Negative ones? Feelings of triumph or anxiety? Something to be sought or avoided?

One woman, Anne, shared with us that she defined work, primarily, as something done to earn money. It should be directly related to her educational preparation and usually requires a great deal of personal energy. Anne was enrolled in a class for women who were preparing to get a job. Her overriding fear concerning the "whole ordeal" of seeking employment outside the home resulted from her feeling that she "had not worked" in fifteen years. However, when she began describing what she had been doing during that time, it was clarified that in addition to raising children and caring for a home, Anne had been involved in many community activities. She had initiated a baby-sitting co-op in her neighborhood, had helped raise money for the symphony, was a creative Girl Scout leader and had organized and participated in a monthly book discussion club. The other women in the group saw Anne as having done an enormous amount of work in the last fifteen years.

As Anne was able to expand her definition of work, and count these experiences as relevant, she began to see herself as having been continuously involved in *working*. Her anxiety then centered around the common fears and difficulties involved with job hunting. She could then evaluate her fifteen years of experience in terms of organizational and management skills that would be valuable to many potential employers. She saw that she was able to initiate, plan, and reach goals. Anne may need additional education or training to enter a new work environment. However, her focus became *how* to best acquire these new skills and information so necessary to become comfortable and competent with her work choice. Then Anne came to see herself as an individual who had been involved in a continuous work pattern. Anne radiated self-assurance as she began to anticipate new work opportunities. In reality, Anne had not changed any aspect of her experiences. New *perceptions* about what she had accomplished had increased her options multifold.

Women who are at the point of returning to the labor force usually see themselves as being different from women who are involved in changing careers; but they often share a number of conflicts and concerns.

Karen had been working as a highly skilled chemical research assistant for the last twelve years, and as a result of her job being gradually phased out, she needed to plan for a job change. When she was asked to describe the specifics of her job, it was evident that her title was preventing her from detailing the many complex responsibilities of her job. She was a "research assistant" and saw herself as only fulfilling the functions outlined in her official job description. Karen defined her work primarily as a "technician who carries out experiments under the direction of a supervisor, and who keeps careful records of the results of the tests." However, continued supportive questioning helped her to more accurately appraise her work. Expanded awareness of her daily work enabled her to add that she had devised a complex, detailed record-keeping system, had independently determined which experiments to replicate, and almost effortlessly taught herself how to work with computers. She had clearly shown initiative in her job and demonstrated skills beyond what had been expected of her.

The reevaluation process helped Karen to become aware of what made her job particularly satisfying to her. She enjoyed being precise, working with her hands, and making independent decisions, and she wanted to pursue her fascination with the area of computers. It seems hard to believe that this incredibly competent woman perceived so few career options for herself.

Closer inquiry led to the discovery that her lack of education beyond high school was an important source of her concern. The company's policy was to promote those with college degrees, leaving her to believe that she had no hope for advancement within the company. When Karen changed her self-statements to "I am skilled at . . . , I thoroughly enjoy . . . , and I have learned. . ." she began to feel that she was certainly employable, and became excited about changing jobs. She gained enough confidence to go to her present employer and request that she be given a different title, one that more accurately described her responsibilities. Acquiring a title change was Karen's first step toward taking responsibility for exploring and increasing her work options. In the midst of career changing, Karen, like the job seeker, needed to reevaluate past experiences in order to plan for the future. She had to step back, and turn her kaleidoscope, in order to see her experiences in a new perspective.

And what about the woman who is neither seeking to return to the work force nor to change jobs? She is examining the issue of taking a sabbatical from her work in order to have children, explore new directions, test out a fantasy, or follow a personal star. She asks herself: "Will I be bored (or boring)?" "Can I afford to take time out (can I afford not to)?" "Will our life style change?" (Of course!) "Is this what I want to do or what I think I should do?" "Can I stay current in my field (I'm sick of asking all these questions)?" She feels pulled by conflicting roles, wanting to be the perfect "modern woman." Is there time for everything?

Ellen is struggling with those questions. She married Tom right after graduation from college and worked as a special-education teacher while completing a master's degree in counseling. Now at twenty-seven, Ellen and Tom have decided that they want children in their lives. But Ellen is concerned about how this time out will jeopardize her future chances in this tight job market.

And Wendy, through hard work, has moved up in a publishing company and wants someday to become a children's book editor. She is also clear about her desire to have children and be home with them in their early years. How can she at the same time maintain close contact with the multifaceted world of publishing so that she does not lose out on her dreams?

Can these women approach time away from work in a planful, purposeful way? Can they see this "time out" as part of the flow of life, an important stage in their lifelong process of growth and change? The challenge then becomes *how* to carve out small, though erratic, bits of time. You can have lunch with a former co-worker. Attend a workshop. Subscribe to a journal. Expand your curiosity about other people and their work. Now you have the time. . talk with someone at a cocktail party about her work, to someone next to you on a plane, at a doctor's office, at a P.T.A. meeting. Be bold! Take a chance! Create new opportunities!

Today more and more women are choosing to work and choosing their own work; some from desire, some from necessity. But the potential variety of life/work patterns is boundless. Each woman, however, must first get in touch with her feelings and her current situation before she can begin to plan for her future. The options are endless . . . the patterns ever changing in an exciting array of configurations that will grow and change as she grows and changes in her self-awareness. We must all learn how to turn our own kaleidoscope.

We would like to take away the pressure that you should conform to any one life/work pattern. We will deal with the many different ways to design your life/work pattern and will present the tools and the process whereby the kaleidoscope will never remain static for you.

This book, then, is an affirmation of the possibilities that exist for women in the world of work; for those who are reentering the work force, entering it for the first time, planning to change careers or choosing to stay home for an extended period of time. We are encouraging you to search for your own pattern, to design it, and to take responsibility for your future.

Getting Through Your Barriers to Growth and Change

❦

Definitions à la *Webster*

Change: to cause to become different; alter, convert
Power: ability to do; capacity to act; authority; sway; influence
Success: a favorable or satisfactory outcome or result
Security: a sense of safety; certainty; freedom from doubt
Risk: the chance of injury, damage, or loss; hazard

These are common, ordinary, everyday words. Within the realm of all of our vocabularies. But these words have become emotion-laden because of the messages we bring to them from our personal experiences. The instant we hear them, they become subjective. Our statements to ourselves (our self-statements) will limit our perceptions—and ultimately our options.

The goal of this chapter is to examine how each of us has developed our own individual set of responses to words which, by definition, do not have emotional connotations. Careful scrutiny of how our responses to each of these words may have been influenced or distorted by our unique personal experiences, can be a freeing process. Becoming conscious of *why* we may be responding to the word "power" with disdain or distaste can help us evaluate in a more objective fashion how we would *like* to respond to the word "power." A broader awareness of how we have limited our responses and consequently restricted our options, can help to enlarge our horizons, expand our perspectives, and enhance our growth. For the purposes of examination, we will talk about these words independently, although they are clearly interrelated.

CHANGE

A fallacy to which many of us hold is that we must be unhappy in the present situation if we are seeking a change for the future.

We have spoken to many women who feel ambivalent, and almost defensive, about wanting to make a change in their lives. These women are visibly relieved when they hear other women also expressing a desire for change, although they may have been happy with what their lives have been to this point. We are all aware of our physical changes as the years pass and we take it for granted that our circumstances will change as well. We may marry or not. We have more or less money. We may or may not have children. We move, leave old friends and make new ones. It is only natural then that our needs will change as well. What is important at one point in our life isn't necessarily our main focus at another stage.

A modern philosopher-psychologist, Klaus Riegal, feels that the natural state of the person is not that of rest, but rather unrest. For from the unrest comes the energy to be creative, to grow. So discontent need not be the same as being unhappy or even mean that I must change everything around me. Rather I can view it as an indication that I desire a new way of being creative; I desire another challenge in my life; I want to add to my life; not necessarily detract from what I already have and have done. That is another way of looking at change. When I desire change, I may be wanting to add another dimension to my life. I do not necessarily desire to radically alter it (however, at times radical alterations may be necessary). Rather, I may be wanting to redesign the present elements in order to allow for a new dimension in my life.

In support of this different view of change, probably the most frequently asked question throughout our lives is, "Who am I?" or, "Who are you?" At different points in our lives we find that one or another aspect of ourselves is the main focus of our questioning. As an adolescent we may frequently answer with, "daughter," "sister," "student," "girlfriend," or "athlete." A few years later the answer to the same question differs. We may now say "wife," "mother," "neighbor," "lawyer," "teacher," "volunteer," or "friend." And as time moves on and many of our dreams become fulfilled or as we take the old ones out to take a new look at them, we change the question, itself, ever so slightly. We may say, "Who do I want to be?" or, "Who am I, in addition to all the answers I have given before?" At this point, we feel that we are embarking upon that uncharted sea: the future.

The healthiness and normality of the recurring question "Who am I?" among both men and women has been documented by at least four current-day psychologists. There is agreement among the following four researchers that the specific focus of the question is to some extent age-related, although past experiences also play a part in the type of answer we are seeking. What I have done in the last twenty or forty or sixty years is as important as the fact that I am twenty or forty or sixty years old. But speaking generally, there are a number of age-related similarities.

During our late adolescence and early adulthood, we are searching for an identity apart from our family of origin. We are exploring the possibilities of what we want to be "when we grow up." The next period of life finds us with much physical energy, enabling us to concentrate on becoming what we "want to be," a period of initial creativity that is consistent with our reaching out to form our own union with another or with a group of others.

The next period, that of middle age, is concerned with the question, "Who *else* am I besides 'what I have become'?" There is also a greater preoccupation with "time" and with fulfillment of myself as an individual. And the last segment of life is more leisurely; time is spent exploring the question, "Who am I in *this world*?"

In the last part of this century, psychologists have become very curious about the stages we pass through as adults. They have attempted to chart some of the patterns of growth and change of adulthood. Such studies give us a better understanding of the kind of events going on in our lives during the numerous times we ask the question, "Who am I?" and strive to answer it.

Listed here is a brief comparison of the results of research of four major psychologists in the field of adult development. These people were among the first to give as much serious consideration to adulthood as many others have given to the stages of childhood and adolescence. These studies center around the relationships of adults to one another. To date, there are no studies on the career paths of women, only those of men. So when we want to look at adult developmental stages of women, we must use the studies that look at the differences between men and women as they relate to one another and to the world around them.

Among all of the researchers there is general agreement that at about the age of forty-five there is a period of great reexamination of our lives. Whether or not we do so consciously, we begin to look at what we have done or accomplished to that point, and then to assess if we want to make any changes in the future direction of our lives. Have we missed something in our life that we now want to do or have or accomplish "before it is too late"? We also begin to look around and ask ourselves the question, "What am I leaving behind me to future generations?" And as "young people" in their mid forties begin to have serious illnesses, we may ask, "If I had a year to live, is this how I would want to spend it?"

At first these questions may seem morbid and perhaps unnecessarily serious, but it is about this time when we become aware that time no longer stretches ahead endlessly. We begin to realize that there are some limits to what we may have planned for our future. We reassess those things that have value for us, and try to include them in our lives. The woman who has happily spent many years at home raising her family may begin to say, "What am I going to do now; what new meaning is there in my life?" Or the woman who has decided not to marry may now take

	18–25	25–45	45–65	65–80	80
Charlotte Bühler: 1935	Tentative seeking of role in society	Self-realization in career, marriage, family	Critical self-assessment	Self-fulfillment	Regression to satisfaction of basic needs
Erik Erikson: 1952	Seeking self-identity	Seeking intimacy	Seeking generativity, contribution to society	Seeking integration of the meaning of life	
Bernice Neugarten: 1968	**time since birth** Time stretches forth, there is time to seek and do everything; achievement oriented	**time left to live** Time is limited, can only finish a few important things. Sense of life cycle and inevitability, increased freedom and home satisfaction	**reexamination** stocktaking, conscious self-utilization		

	18	25	45	60
Marjorie Fiske Lowenthal: 1975	**Women** Negative self-concept, dependent	**Women** Complex life style. Warm, lacking energy, jealous of activities of husband	**Women** Last child gone. Negative self-concept. Unhappy, increased marital problems. Critical of husband. Simplistic life style	**Women** More positive self-concept. Competent, less dependent. Frank, more assertive
	Men Insecure Discontented	**Men** Expansive Risk-taking	**Men** Life narrowed and focused. Sense of orderliness. Plateau in job. Strain, boredom, potential problems	**Men** Concern for companionship, nurturance, mellow. Self-protective, avoiding strain
				Both Renewed interest in spouse

a look at her career path and think about what she wants to leave behind as her legacy. Or she may decide it is time to develop other interests, and put less energy into her career.

Generally speaking, these researchers have found that the first part of our life is spent in finding a place for ourselves in the society we live in, and the second half is more concerned with seeking personal self-fulfillment and spending time on those things that are of greater value to us. We begin to see ourselves within the great scope of the life cycle.

Marjorie Lowenthal has also spent time studying the different preoccupations or concerns of men and women of the same age. She has drawn some conclusions that indicate that men and women have different developmental paths.

She feels that during the earlier part of a woman's life, she is more inward-directed. Generally speaking, she is seeking security, and attributes setbacks more to personal failures than to the natural give-and-take of living. The woman's life tends to be more complex, also, in that she has strong concerns in many areas, including career, family, and/or community affairs. At this time, men seem to be more focused in their energy output—primarily toward career. That is not to say that they are not concerned with family and community, but their energies are not focused in as many directions as the woman's are. One can see where there may be the frequent need for men and women to resolve their differences.

There comes a point at which a shift in focus occurs. Women move toward becoming more concerned with self-fulfillment within the larger world. They become more expansive in their interests. They are more self-confident and seek to be competent in many areas. At about the same point, men begin to step back somewhat from their careers and become more concerned with their personal lives and with family concerns. So as the man begins to seek nurturing, the woman is moving away from that need. Again, there is the need to be aware of the different paths and to try to reconcile the different points of view when necessary.

The specifics of this study aside, we can gain freedom simply from knowing that we all have points of change and even crises in our lives. They can be worked through, and all of our life we will continue to grow and learn and reach new understandings of "Who I am."

A good example of the woman who is asking, "Who else am I?" and, "Who do I still want to be?" is Carol. At age forty-five she felt good about her past accomplishments in volunteer organizations and proud of her contributions. But she began reevaluating her work satisfaction and decided that she wanted to begin anew. With a potential business partner she traveled to another city to consult with a woman who had begun a unique and immensely successful tour guide company. Carol returned home, began this business, and entered the world of small businesses. Her company has grown, fills a distinct need in her city, is profitable and gives her a great deal of satisfaction. The outcome sounds too easy and so perfect. But let's look at some of the personal questioning and evaluation that went on before Carol took the leap and made the change.

First of all, Carol knew that because of the prestige she had gained in her own volunteer work and because of the prestige she shared as the wife of a successful businessman, she wouldn't really be happy in an entry-level job, with low pay and little status. So she and her husband agreed that they could afford to gamble with the possible loss of a certain sum of money. (Other couples might decide to spend money on the wife's education as a worthy investment.)

Carol then did some stocktaking of her own assets and experiences that would help her to start her own business. She included her ability to organize, to convince people, her knowledge of interesting and appealing aspects of her city, and her experiences of attending many conventions with her husband. Coupled with a desire for a change in life style, and a desire to get paid for her work, was an assessment of what things are important to her in a job setting as well as a listing of her assets and potential business opportunities. And as with most changes, all was not a bed of roses; unanticipated events always occur. For example, you would assume that if Carol considered starting a business of guiding tours, she herself must have had a good sense of direction or be a whiz at reading maps. Not so. Carol had a terrible sense of direction, but believed that map reading was a skill that she could acquire. And with that statement to herself, she was liberated from the counterstatement just a gasp away: "I can't do this because I have no sense of direction. . . . It will take me too long to learn what I need to know. . . . I'm afraid others will know that I don't know

15

everything about the business. . . . People won't trust me enough to give me their business." Carol said to herself something like, "I'm not yet what I want to become, but I'm on the way and I will learn."

Another aspect of change common to many of us is the fear that in wanting a change we are being disloyal to or unapprecia- tive of what we already have. In fact we may allow ourselves to be pulled into anticipating negative reactions from family and friends. Research has shown some relationship between an anticipation of the outcome of a situation and our behavior in the situation, which often sets the stage for the outcome we anticipated. For example, we might anticipate that a husband or a friend will react negatively when we talk about wanting to make changes in our life. And accompanying our statements about our plans are voice tone, facial expressions, and postures that send a "clue" to the other person. The other tends to give much weight to those nonverbal clues and so may respond as they think we really want them to respond. The final outcome results in our anticipation being realized. By knowing about the relationship between our anticipation, our actual behavior and the probable response of the other, we can learn to anticipate more positive situations for ourselves. We can anticipate that although they may not understand our need for change or even understand how they will fit into our change, they will respect our needs and desires.

Another fact of change of which we must be aware is that when we change, others will also change in some way. For when change is introduced into any system or relationship, the system or relationship does not remain exactly the same. Compare change in a system to having your car's engine repaired. Driving away from the repair shop, we sometimes think, "It sounds worse than it did before I took it in." Why? The engine sounds as though something doesn't belong. What is happening is that the new part and the old parts are trying to adjust to one another. The new part has to become part of the engine's system and the system has to adjust to the new part that is necessary to its continued operation. The same concept is true with people. The woman says to her family, "I want to go back to school, or I want to go back to work." The normal feelings and reactions of the family are, "How do I fit into your plans?" "What is it going to mean for me?" "What am I going to have to do?" Most often these thoughts are not expressed out loud. What frequently comes out is "Okay, but I can't help you; I'm doing as much as I can now." And remembering that each part of the system is concerned with how changes will affect him/her, we can talk with everyone about what the changes will mean; the whole system can negotiate the working out of the changes and can again learn to work together smoothly.

Now a word about being that part of the system that itself does not desire a change. We sometimes, unrealistically, believe that resisting change will keep things the same. But that cannot be. If, in a marriage, either the husband or the wife introduces a change—"going back to work or to school" or "changing jobs or moving to another town"—and then the one initiating the change decides that it is better for the marriage that the proposed change not take place, things in the system do not return to the previous state. Instead the system incorporates the fact that certain decisions *were* made and as the members of the system record that information that creates another dimension of the system. To put it in paradoxical terms, we cannot not change when new decisions are made about our system. If the husband decides not to take a transfer, the wife may consequently feel guilty and they as a couple will feel the results of this guilt. Or if the wife decides to put off returning to work because her husband expresses opposition or apprehension, the husband may feel guilty or anxious about the relationship and again a change has taken place within the system. And for both the wife and the husband the fact that they each have considered their own personal needs means that they each will have to incorporate the new aspects of their emerging selves into their respective lives and into their life together.

Change is such a complex issue that it reaches back into the past as well as forward into the future. In fact it may be its origin in the past that makes some seemingly simple changes difficult. We carry around with us many "messages" from our childhood that should be examined and perhaps updated from time to time. As adults our behaviors often reflect the recorded messages learned as children. One woman, Edith, remembers always hearing the message, "If you are going to buy anything, buy the best." On a recent trip with her husband, she saw a silver ring she liked. She wanted to buy the ring as a memento of their trip; the price was $10.50. She was aware that a part of her rejected the idea of buying the cheap ring, saying it would turn green on her finger; "it's not sterling." She later realized that this particular "tape" continued to be replayed in situations like that of the ring. And through discussion about the socialization process, she saw how she was still allowing these tapes to control her present life without consciously deciding whether or not she wanted them to do so. She made a new decision that although she knew souvenirs like the ring were not going to last forever, she could see them for what they were, mementos to be bought and enjoyed. Without too much effort we all could find past messages that are influencing our future in ways that help or hinder it.

One final point must be made concerning the making of changes. There are definite clues that indicate to us that a change of some sort, however minimal, is a necessity. If we should hear ourselves saying something like, "I hate to get up in the morning because there is really nothing to look forward to," we know that now is the time for some change. A number of women have expressed this growing reluctance to get up in the morning as symptomatic of their feelings that they are no longer needed by their family. The children have become less dependent and their other responsibilities have also lessened. They express it in a number of ways: "I'm tired of 'enjoying myself' shopping or going to lunch"; "I don't know what to do with myself; my house is cleaned by 9:00 A.M!" These statements can be clues to sit down with someone and begin looking at what new possibilities your future could hold, what new dreams you could strive toward.

POWER

"Power" comes from the Latin word which means "to be able." It is the ability to cause, prevent, or influence change. Many women we've talked to seem to feel "powerless." They describe themselves as having been at one time spunky, confident, hopeful, and self-assured, but that was long ago. It seems that many women have forgotten themselves in their responsibilities of career or of being a wife and mother. They may control households and raise children yet they perceive themselves as being powerless and not in charge of their own lives.

It is not uncommon for women to believe that when they

marry they must take their freedom to choose, as well as the control over their lives, and hand it over in a neatly wrapped package to their husbands. Then, bit by bit, they ask their husbands for a piece of it back and if their husbands hesitate or refuse, wives may resent them. They may ask, "Can I go to work?" "Can I go back to school?" "Can I go to the lecture at the museum?" "Can I drive alone in that neighborhood at night?" Or the questions may never be asked, but permission may be denied to do something. ("You can't drive alone in that neighborhood at night; are you crazy?"—the decision is made.) Or, "We can't afford for you to go back to work; it is hardly worth it because of the income taxes we would have to pay." (And so we shelve the idea.) Or, "You should concentrate on one area of interest and not jump around from art to music to dance." (We begin to question our own lack of seriousness rather than seeing that we are exploring, searching—learning where we want to invest ourselves.)

The nature of this kind of communication implies that the husband is his wife's keeper and sets up a "one up" and "one down" positioning between spouses. When the husband objects or questions the soundness of a request, the wife often feels unloved, resentful, and as though she has no choice but to obey. This authoritative position that the husband finds himself in may be as uncomfortable for him as for his wife. It can be a burdensome responsibility to be another person's keeper. It makes him feel responsible if anything goes amiss, if she is frustrated, bored or unfulfilled. After all, he's the one saying, "You can't do _____." Or she tells herself, "If it weren't for him! . . . " How much easier it is to be angry at him than to face up to making choices and taking risks ourselves.

We can learn to ask out loud the questions we are asking ourselves. The question need not be, "Can I go to work?" but rather, "I've been thinking about working, how do you feel about that?" Or, "What problems would my working present that we would need to work out?" In this kind of a discussion the husband is not set up as the "villain" and the wife hasn't cast herself in the role of the poor, helpless, and powerless little girl. Rather, both become partners who then have an opportunity to work out solutions in a mutual way.

An episode from one woman's vacation clarified how ingrained it has become for many of us to ask permission of another to do simple things. One summer, on a family camping trip, the family was uncertain about whether they would stay an extra day. As they left the campsite one morning to do some sight-seeing, the wife asked her husband, "Should we buy some more milk for the morning?" He said, "No, it's not necessary." She said nothing but felt angry and pouted as they drove away. Later when the husband asked what she was angry about, she told him she thought they should have bought the milk. He angrily replied, "You can decide for yourself if you want to spend ninety cents on milk! You asked me what I thought and I told you." It had become natural for her to ask what he thought about something and then to hear his opinion as definitive not as just simply his viewpoint. He clearly did not like the position in which she was placing him. He felt she should say, "I want to stop and buy milk. In case we stay, I'll have it." She began to realize how easy it was not to take responsibility for her own thoughts and preferences. How pervasive is this among women? How does it make us feel about ourselves and the power we have over our lives? This condition of looking to our spouse or another person in authority to decide the simplest questions in our lives seems to be a subtle widespread reaction among women.

Another woman, who found herself in the same position, related that she has not bought herself a new coat in years. Each time she mentioned to her husband how worn her coat looked he replied, "It looks just fine." She never got as far as "asking" if she could get a new coat because she was translating her husband's response to mean, "He doesn't want me to spend the money." It would have been more helpful to her if she had asked him what he meant by, "It looks fine." There are many other possible interpretations of his response. He may have wanted her to feel all right about what she was wearing. He may not have wanted her to worry about her coat because they were just about to go out. However, with her interpretation, her coat grew older and her list of grudges against him grew longer.

As the group discussed the issue of personal power and our own ability to influence change, this woman began to realize that she had not taken any responsibility for the decision to buy the coat or many other things she thought necessary and reasonable. She was not ready to decide to buy a new coat on her own but with the group's support she decided to purchase a new outfit. The next week she walked in wearing an attractive new suit . . . glowing as she told us that she had bought the clothes without consulting her husband. And when she wore them to church on Sunday morning, not only was her husband not angry (as she had feared), but he commented on how lovely she looked. To her, his reaction was shocking in the face of the torment she had put herself through.

Much to her surprise, she began to discover that this seemingly ogreish man had less influence on her doing without things than she did! She had not realized it was within her own ability to influence her life and make her own decisions. She was shocked to find out that this power was always within her, that she had just given it away. This was her first step toward feeling more confident and able to plan what she wanted to do with her time.

Neither the example of the milk nor the woman who needed a new coat are significant in and of themselves. What becomes significant is the pattern that may begin to develop—the insidious process of handing someone else the power over our lives. There may be many times when we would like to consult someone else regarding a decision; but when we remember that the other person is a "consultant," not our keeper, then we are free to weigh their thoughts and expertise, integrating them with our own feelings and desires, and come up with a solution that is stronger, but nevertheless our own.

Sometimes we fail to make choices that would be beneficial to us for fear of displeasing or upsetting others. An author we know was faced with this situation one winter when she took time off from the book she was writing to vacation with her husband in a warmer climate. She was wishing that she could spend time on the trip writing, but she discounted the possibility of writing because she wouldn't have her typewriter with her. Suddenly the light bulb went on. She *could* take a typewriter with her! She then hesitatingly broached her husband, worried about his putting an obstacle in her way: "One doesn't take type-writers . . . you are going to rest"—and, implicitly, "how could you do this to me?" He responded predictably: "Don't be ridiculous, you can't take a typewriter with you to Puerto Rico."

His implicit message, of feeling bad because she would take time from him, was part of his resistance. Another part was that her actions differed from all past vacations. She had changed. He needed time to respond to her changed behavior and to realize that although she had not worked on a vacation before, there had always been some time they enjoyed spending apart—on the tennis courts, in the health club—and that really their vacation was not actually being threatened.

Her tentative response was to let go of the idea; her secondary response was to continue to pursue it—to check into weight allowance on the plane, to decide if she really wanted to spend time writing, and then make her own decision. A small issue? Not really. Particularly because she came very close to giving up the idea because of a mildly negative response from her husband. In how many other cases does she shy away from her own ideas and preferences in deference to others? What effect does this behavior have over her sense of power, sense of self, and sense of independence?

It is the same situation in reverse when the husband enters the domain of the home. The seesaw is reversed. At home, the husband asks the wife to make decisions like, "Which spoon should I use to stir the sauce?" "Should I run the dishwasher now?" The wife feels like saying, "I don't care; you can make that decision." Or when she's sick and he says, "I'll make supper," and then asks twenty questions about preparations, the wife's reaction is, "If you're going to do it, do it and don't ask me so many questions, because then I don't really get a break from cooking." This feeling is not so very different from the husband who feels, "If you want a new coat, please get it and please don't ask me to make another decision today."

The issue of how much power and control we have over our own lives can be very subtle—we may not be aware that we are failing to assume responsibility for our actions, taking the responsibility for our lives. We often play the game of "Fortunately/Unfortunately"—perhaps finding ourselves responding to life rather than having a greater degree of control over it.

Fortunately/Unfortunately

Fortunately, there was a want ad in the *Journal* for a Training Assistant in a small local company but

Unfortunately, my car was in the shop the day of my interview . . . but

Fortunately, my husband was out of town, and I could use his car . . . but

Unfortunately, it had snowed a great deal the night before, and the driveway was impassable, but

Fortunately, there were men plowing my street and I asked them to plow my driveway . . . but

Unfortunately, I had taken my good coat to the cleaners, and had no appropriate coat to wear to the interview . . . but

Fortunately, my mother dropped by and lent me her coat which had a definite "business" look to it . . . but

Unfortunately, by that time, I had missed my appointment.

Versus

Fortunately/Unfortunately ("Take 2")

Fortunately, there was a want ad in the *Journal* for a Training Assistant in a small local company, but

Unfortunately, my car was in the shop the day of the interview . . . but

Fortunately, I had arranged with my husband for him to get a ride to work, so I could use his car that day . . . but

Unfortunately, it snowed a great deal the night before, and the driveway seemed impassable, but . . .

Fortunately, I had insisted on snow tires for both our cars, as well as early snow removal (even at high cost) . . . but

Unfortunately, I had taken my coat to the cleaners . . . but

Fortunately, I had arranged to pick up my coat on my way to the interview . . . so I made it to the interview on time . . . but

Unfortunately, I don't know if I got the job or not, since there were a dozen applicants . . . but

Fortunately, I feel good about the interview, good that I began to conquer my fears about interviews, and next time I won't be so scared. And perhaps I will get the offer.

In "take 2" the woman took responsibility for anticipating the possible obstacles to her job interview working out satisfactorily—and anticipating problems gave her greater control of the outcome. Though the desired result—getting a job—may not be attained in either case, growth had taken place. She acquired self-confidence about the job-hunt process, and a great sense of power over her life. She did not *wait* for everything to happen just right. She planned for the event to be as positive as possible for a first go-around thus having more power and control over her own life.

SUCCESS

Each step forward in work as a successful American regardless of sex means a step backward as a woman . . .
—*Margaret Mead*, Male and Female

Although this statement was made in 1949, the essence of it still remains important today. Cultural attitudes toward appropriate sex roles still limit the horizons of women. Even recent studies among women have verified that we still expect that success in achievement situations will be followed by some sort of negative consequences, such as the loss of femininity. And it continues to be an area of concern to women who are successful in business settings. How can they maintain their desirable feminine characteristics while being successful? Sometimes in the desire not to take away from our femininity we neglect to add to our femininity new descriptors which, over time, would include elements of personal success and achievement.

As one of the exercises in a life/work planning workshop, women were asked to describe someone they considered to be a successful woman. The most frequent responses were:

A friend who raised three fine, independent children after losing her husband at an early age.

A neighbor who retured to school to finish her cc'lege degree after putting it aside to raise two children.

A woman at church who at age fifty became a publisher's representative for children's books and who developed the idea of having book fairs at nursery schools.

A woman who was working in a social service agency and then decided that she really wanted to pursue her first love: training horses.

My niece who decided not to give up her career when she married and had children. She still works and the marriage seems great.

A woman who borrowed five hundred dollars from her father-in-law after her husband's death and began a company that sells beauty products door to door. Now it's the second biggest chain in Texas.

And the list always includes famous women such as Beverly Sills, Eleanor Roosevelt, Barbara Jordan, Pat Nixon, and Helen

Keller. But they primarily named famous women who have had to overcome adversity themselves or who stood by someone else at a time of adversity or were successful after being "pushed" into the public eye. Some women mentioned the gaining of prestige and money as an important criterion for qualifying as a successful person; others felt that making a contribution to society and gaining a feeling of self-satisfaction were paramount to being considered successful. In almost all descriptions of a successful woman, the woman placed herself second or was involved in a humanitarian endeavor. In fact when a workshop participant would offer the name of a woman who was openly oriented to personal achievement and success, the participant usually preceded her remark with a statement such as, "Some people might consider her selfish, but I think that she is successful." However, for all the women who answered the question, success was considered to be the attainment of some particular goal—getting a diploma, raising well-adjusted children, or always being a cheerful listener.

And what do we mean by the standard phrase offered at graduations and marriages, "I wish you all the happiness and success in the world"? To be wished success somehow indicates either that we *will* or *will not* be A Success, as if it is an end product—and we have only one shot at it. Moreover it is the rare person who would consider him/herself A Success. He/she may, however, consider him/herself as successful in specific aspects of their lives: graduating, being made president of a company, buying a car for the first time, getting an interesting job, saving a soufflé, car pooling three children in three different directions on the same day, or making a difficult decision. It is through the discovery and valuing of subsequent successes, however small they may be, that we gain the confidence necessary if we plan to reenter the job market, change careers, return to school or venture in any new direction. On the other hand, when success is seen as only a specific end product, the attainment of that long-range goal may seem impossible and we might too quickly drop out of the contest.

We know that in training children to eat by themselves or to dress themselves, we do not wait until they can do the whole procedure perfectly before we praise them. Rather we break up the process into manageable steps—putting on socks and shoes, using a spoon instead of hands—small successes which can be built upon until they reach the total desired results.

Sue is a thirty-two-year-old woman who used this "small steps" process, which finally led to her successful entry into graduate school. Sue had completed her master's degree when her children were young and was working part-time in her field. But in order to advance, it was necessary that she expand her options by earning a doctoral degree. The prospect of beginning such an endeavor filled her with terror. Her negative self-statements kept her vacillating for two years: "How could *I* get through the statistics courses?" "*Me* write a dissertation, impossible!" "I might not even get accepted into the program." "How embarrassing that would be." "How could I pay for it?" Sue spent almost two years focusing on the obstacles that made the end goal of a Ph.D. seem impossible. She finally was able to break down the endeavor into manageable steps and take them one at a time, actually learning to see the completion of each step as "a success" in itself. She found her confidence and determination growing with each hurdle she passed. She has not reached the end goal, but she is able to feel that the gaining of additional knowledge and expertise in her field is of value whether or not she is actually able to earn the degree. And as we mentioned before, a crucial element in Sue's situation is that she is beginning to *anticipate* success for herself and in this anticipation of success she is doing many things to enhance the probability that she will succeed.

We can amplify somewhat upon this theory of "anticipation training" and use its proponents to help us redefine our behaviors in terms of past and future successes. The word success still puts off some people; they feel as though it can belong to others and not to them. One exercise that we have used in workshops with women has proven helpful in encouraging women to see their past accomplishments as success and indeed to determine and extract patterns from the past that can be used in the future. We ask the women to list at least seventeen things they are "proud of having achieved," no matter how small or insignificant they may seem: running an efficient household, winning a blue ribbon at camp, making an A in a high school math course, having someone ask *me* if I want a job, running a book fair or a church social event. *Anything counts.* Next we examine in detail these achievements, these points of pride. We look at the specific aspects of the event that gave us the most pride and the greatest feeling of success. We look for patterns among these events. For we know that our lives are built upon patterns of behavior—learning new ones, continuing and building upon old ones. We have the woman tell someone else in great detail about her achievements; how she felt, why it was so important to her. Careful attention is given to the adjectives they use in describing the events. Did they say words like "good" or "okay" and "pretty well"? Or did they say "terrific" and "fabulous" and "excellent"? Did they see themselves as being the one who brought about the achievement or did they see themselves as "lucky" or "fortunate"?

The women who took credit for their own achievements also tended to describe the events with strong, positive adjectives. Those same women "anticipated" that given a chance or direction and some additional information and/or education they would also be "proud" of future achievements. The women who saw themselves as "lucky" and tended to use weak adjectives to describe past events found out that in most situations they tend to take a back seat and hope that other people will notice their accomplishments. As one might imagine, they anticipated much more difficulty in deciding upon their future directions and were dubious about whether they would succeed in accomplishing new goals. Working together with the second group of women, we helped them to find new adjectives that were more active and positive but that still accurately described the past. This helped them to describe which behaviors in their past would be helpful to them in achieving in the future. In other words, they learned to identify patterns in the past that they can "anticipate" will remain with them in future situations and those patterns that can be changed, that they are currently "anticipating" will hinder them in future endeavors.

Look at these two ways of describing a real event:

"A few of my friends who had often tasted my cooking asked if I would teach them how to cook. I happened to be lucky enough to have the editor of the local paper take pictures of us and run them in the weekly food section. I experimented with other dishes, because I like to, and even got paid by the paper for doing it."

and

"A number of my friends raved about my cooking, particularly my ability to experiment with dishes and come up with exotic combinations of dishes. They suggested that I conduct gourmet cooking classes in my home. I contacted the local paper, in order to generate some possible business in recipe testing for their food section. I can be accurate as well as creative in my cooking. The work was fun, interesting and even a little scary, but extremely rewarding."

Which description would you have liked to have been your own? Does the second one, filled with positive self-statements, sound unfeminine or bragging? Not at all. It sounds direct, honest, and appropriately appreciative of her own skills and abilities. We are not accustomed to selling ourselves (even to ourselves), but this is a necessary ingredient in finding a place that feels right for us, whether it be in the job market, in school, at home, or in leisure activities.

Another brief example comes to mind of our tendency to minimize our past accomplishments. One woman listed as a success the fact that as a teenager she had won a state ice skating championship. She then decided that gaining the title wasn't really *her* success because her mother pushed her into competitive skating—as though she herself hadn't done the actual skating. She may have felt pushed and so not claim total responsibility for the title, but she could and did decide which of her own behaviors contributed to that achievement and had continued to be present in other situations of success. She no longer totally discounted her very real success.

SECURITY AND RISK

We agree with Webster's definition of security, observing "a sense of safety," but we would like to expand it. Security and risk may well be opposite sides of the same coin. Our security is knowing what we feel we could not or would not want to live without. Knowing the priorities in which we find our base of security allows us to insure that those priorities are maintained. When this is accomplished we then feel the freedom to grow and expand. We must incorporate our priorities into our plans for the future. For some of us, our base of security lies in knowing that we are financially solvent. For others a feeling of security revolves around the family unit or maintenance of health or continuing education.

It is necessary to the growth process that we periodically reflect on that value or values that form the base of our security, to see if they have remained the same or if they have changed in any way. Some will remain the same throughout life and others will probably alter with time and circumstances. For example, some women indicate that before they make any plans for either returning to work or school, they must know that they can still be at home when the children return home from school. That is an important priority to them, and it needs to be attended to and not ignored. But the situation of having young children will change and so will the necessity to have a work or school schedule that allows the woman to be home at 3:30 each day and home during the summer vacation. This fact seems obvious on the surface (everyone knows that children won't always be young), but when we are in the midst of the present situation we may forget that they will grow and we fail to also plan for a future in which we will have more flexibility. We must make choices that are both consistent with our present circumstances and which will also allow us to be prepared for our future circumstances.

When we consider making changes we are also reexamining and possibly realigning our priorities, our base of security. And in fact the process of deciding upon change would probably be smoother if we would directly address the issue of what our priorities are at that particular point in time. Let's take a look at how values like money, leisure, prestige, challenge, or risk-taking are attended to when deciding upon changes.

Joyce is a forty-five-year-old woman who was teaching chemistry part-time at the local high school. The part-time position fit in nicely with her priorities. It was a challenging job. She loved teaching high school students and found that she related well with them. She had enough free time to spend with the family, to clean and keep the house by herself and to prepare all the family meals. To be working in a field in which she was trained was another priority high on her list, while values like prestige, high salary, and opportunity for advancement were, at this time, low on her list of priorities.

Since she was enthusiastic and successful in her work, she

was asked to teach full-time. The decision to take on the additional responsibility was an important one because it meant more time spent in classes and in preparation for them, but it would also mean less time for her home and family. She still wanted to have primary responsibility for meal preparations, even though the rest of the family was willing to help. So before accepting the full-time teaching assignment, she did some experimenting to see if she could accommodate both priorities. She spent a couple of weekends cooking and freezing meals for the following week. This method seemed to be a satisfactory solution to her problem, even though she found out that her sons were heating and eating her homemade pot pies almost as quickly as she put them into the freezer.

Another priority almost always comes into question, even if not consciously, when deciding on change. That is, how do we feel about taking risks? This is a problem faced by men as well as women, even though men, unlike most women, have been socialized to take risks, to live through failure and to try again. One big difference between how men and women approach the taking of risks is that more men tend to initiate situations in which the taking of risks is necessary and more women tend to react or respond to situations in which they must take risks. It is helpful and important that we gain some clarity on how we relate to risk taking—and how we would like to relate to it in the future. Do we tend to seek situations in which risk is involved or do we tend to be a person who "rises to the occasion" and take risks only when inescapable?

Before each of us makes any definitive statement about how we relate to "risk taking," let us add some information from research in social psychology on how we form attitudes about ourselves and others. A social psychologist, Stanley Schacter, has done a number of studies that substantiate his theory that we infer our own attitudes about ourselves from reflecting on our past behavior—just as we infer the attitudes of others by looking at their behavior. When we are asked how someone close to us *feels* about taking risks, we reflect on their past behavior and infer from those situations their attitudes about taking risks. We do the same thing about our own attitudes. If someone were to say to us, "Do you like to take risks?" we would reflect for a minute or two, think of any situations in which we either took risks or avoided them and then answer yes or no. But that is not really answering the question of how do I *feel* about taking risks. I am limiting myself by my past behaviors and therefore inferring an attitude. Rather I need to take a look at where I would include "risk taking" on my list of priorities. In the past I may have taken few risks and now I would like to take more chances, to attempt more things—whether or not I may fail at them. Or I may have taken risks, not really looking at the consequences, and now I may decide that I want to take fewer risks in the future, to be fully aware of all the possible consequences.

As mentioned before, priorities often change as a result of changing circumstances. At one point in time, financial "security" might be very high on the list because of family responsibilities. But as family responsibilities diminish, a challenging job may be more important than having the same degree of financial solvency. This point is well illustrated by a man who recently made a significant job change. He is in his late forties, with only seven years to work before he could take early retirement from a company he has been with since his early twenties. Rather than wait another seven years, he decided to make a change and go with another small company that would hold some new challenges for him.

He and his wife decided that they had enough financial security to accommodate the two of them if the change did not work out well. He would still receive a small monthly income from the previous company when he retired. They own a small piece of land in the country with a house trailer. Three of their four children are independent, and having only one child at home was a much-reduced financial drain.

Another person decided that her financial security was linked to getting a better education. She was in the process of a divorce and her primary concern was that she be allotted enough money to get adequate training for future employment even though it would mean less usable income at present. Still others say, "I must always have X number of dollars in the bank, for only then do I feel secure."

For yet other people, relationships are their security base. "Even though we might end up broke, if you are willing to trust me, and take a chance with me, then I feel that I can take this risk." Or, "I cannot take a risk that will jeopardize the closeness of our family. Being away three weeks out of every month is clearly not a risk I want to take."

What may clearly constitute a risk for one person may for another person be no risk at all. For one woman to sign up for a class in refresher skills at a local college may require an enormous risk. She may envision others laughing at her ineptness at taking notes, writing papers, even asking "appropriate" questions. For another woman, signing up for classes may be a distinct avoidance of risk. It may be easy for her, and be an excuse to herself for not pushing forward into a degree program, which would be quite a difficult challenge to her. If each woman were to take the time and energy necessary to evaluate her responses to risk taking, and in particular the specific risk facing her, she could then decide whether the benefits would outweigh the potential negative consequences.

In both cases it is probable that some sense of personal dissatisfaction in their lives would need to exist, some feeling of a need to change the status quo. After all, risk taking creates an uncertain situation, takes away some comfort, may not feel good at all. The woman who decides to sign up for a refresher skills course may be just dissatisfied enough to take that step. She may be bored with her present job, looking toward a new career, feeling ambivalent about her children growing older, jealous of the satisfaction her husband receives from his work, or feeling a financial pinch and a need to plan for greater financial security. She may have other friends or acquaintances who have taken a similar step and who seemed to have survived in style. The second woman may have no financial need to return to a full-time job, may never have to face the uncertain future that other women have to face. Perhaps however, she would really like to be working at a job that requires further training, and she has been avoiding taking a major step in that direction. When she becomes dissatisfied more often than she is contented, she may decide to risk entering a degree program, to tackle the pressures that accompany that decision, and to throw the status quo temporarily out of whack.

A majority of women will work in the 1980s. Many are single heads of households, or contribute significant, necessary income to the family money pot. Many of these women may not have been fortunate enough to receive a college education, and are locked into low-paying jobs with little hope for much financial growth. One area that is wide open to women, and which offers much higher earnings, is sales. Sales of commercial real estate, advertising space, word-processing systems, copier machines, insurance, motivational travel packages. The list goes on and on. But most women are reluctant to try sales, citing reasons such as, "I would never be able to call on new clients all day long," and, "I don't have a sales personality . . . I would never succeed!"

Underneath those objections are self-statements such as, "I am afraid to call on new clients because I am afraid of rejection" and, "I am reluctant to take that risk because it is so new to me, I have never done anything like it." One woman who really wanted to try sales had a master's degree in French literature, but needed and wanted to earn more money than her teaching job allowed and was struggling with a decision to try her hand at selling custom-designed art prints and originals. For her the risk was not in calling on clients, nor was it in the very small original investment this job would require. For her, the risk was in facing her friends and fellow professionals, and being judged by them.

She perceived sales as much lower status than her present job, and for her to take this step was a major threat to her self-esteem. If they should denigrate her new choice of work, and she felt more anxious and uncomfortable than she already was feeling, it could have a devastating effect on her decision, on her perseverance in her new work, and on her eventual success. To protect herself, she needed to come to terms with her decision, feel good about it, and decide that the risk of her cohorts' possibly negative responses were not going to stop her. Her financial security was at stake, and the risk of *not* taking this step, in terms of financial planning and financial security, was too great. So she plunged ahead, began to feel competent and accomplished in her new profession, and no longer worried at night how she would be able to pay the bills.

With every growth there is a risk. It need not be taking a new job or moving to another town or running for a public office. It may be a quiet, less noticeable risk. It may be the risk of recognizing that you want to change your attitude about yourself or your view of money or your desire for independence. All growth involves change, and change involves a risk—a risk that you may not like the change or will not be able to handle it as well as you had hoped you could.

There are many interpretations for the word "security," and each of us needs to determine our own personal definition.

Consequently, we can then find our *own* security base from which to expand. One woman's security base may be that she feels safe only if there are X number of dollars in the bank. Another may feel secure if she has skills that are always salable such as accounting or audit skills, or as long as she has contacts with companies that may use her on a part-time basis. And still another woman's security may reside in her knowledge of how to farm her own vegetables, fix her own plumbing, and repair the roof if necessary. She may have learned to be a wise consumer, and to barter her services for commodities that she needed. There is power in self-knowledge and self-awareness about our individual needs for security. Taking calculated risks that are carefully planned and executed and continuously reevaluated can have enormous influence on establishing our personal security base.

What Is Your Personal Meaning of Work?

❧

What are the differences between our expectations about work and the reality? What are our responses to the word "work"? What messages did we receive while growing up about work and its place in our lives?

A very young child is playing with building blocks and creating a city, finger painting with intensity, pretending to be a fireman or Superman or Wonder Woman (with the appropriate cape or hat to set the scene). From our perception, the child is just playing. But simply by observing her closely, her facial expressions, her high level of concentration, it is clear that her play is work.

Her work/play involves concentration, imagining, creating, planning, organizing, experimenting, learning, remembering. What may look to us like unplanned, perhaps even totally random involvement with the finger paints, may be careful, planned experimentation in touching, observing, correcting, and changing her work of art. For a child previously afraid to mess her hands, finger painting is hard work at learning that it is okay, even important, to play in this way. For the child building a city, memories about her experiences in a city impact her sense of spatial relations of cars and buildings and people. She has to struggle to manipulate the blocks to stand in a way that makes sense to her, and to learn to move around without knocking down her growing creation.

And what about the child playing dress-up—and her struggle to work through the process of identifying with the adults in her life? If both parents work, she may act like mother in the kitchen and at work too, in an effort to internalize the dual roles her mother is playing in her life. She can begin to learn that mother works away from home, and always returns with love and the anticipation of seeing her. The book *Mommies At Work,* a children's book by Eve Merriam that pictures women in traditional and nontraditional jobs, is an effort to broaden very young children's perceptions about the world of work and to expand a child's perception about other mothers who work. Many of the mothers that children see in their daily lives work either in the home or in jobs immediately familiar to them, such as supermarket checker, sales clerk, beautician. This book attempts to expand children's perception of options by intro- ducing them to women working in jobs they probably don't have an opportunity to observe. It does end with the conclusion that after working all day, mommies look forward to coming home to their children. The idea that is communicated so well is that work is important to these mothers, that it can be exciting and stimulating, and that it usually involves learning; but work does not take up all of their mother's time, nor does she want it to. A great deal of time and energy is saved for the child. Work is presented as an integral part of their mothers' lives. The child who dresses up is working at the important business of learning about mother's roles and mother's allegiances.

As a child, how did you perceive work? Was it something seen as potentially self-fulfilling? Was it stimulating? Was it something seen as necessary to put food on the table? Was it something to "get used to"? When father and mother said, "I have to go to work now," what tone of voice did they use? Did it seem as though they were looking forward to going to work? And if they were anticipating their day, did they *say* they were going to work because they had to, or because they wanted to? How did your mother talk to you about your work as a child, whether it was schoolwork or household chores or preparations for an athletic event? When she (as she undoubtedly did) told you to work hard, did she use a tone of voice that was encouraging and supporting? Or was it more demanding and driving?

One man was asked by his young child why he had to go to work. He answered, "So that you can live in this nice house, have lovely clothes and take piano lessons." Nowhere in that response was there the remotest suggestion that any other reason existed (though undoubtedly there were other reasons for his going to work). In reality this man loved his job, but his somewhat programmed response to his child indicated that he worked because he had to for monetary reasons. And women who work frequently fare no better in passing on their feelings about work. We seem to need to give the illusion that "if I didn't *have* to, I'd never even go."

One five-year-old girl just happened to mention at bedtime: "I am glad that I am a girl, Mommy. When I grow up I will not have to go to work. I can get married and have someone take care of me." That child was the daughter of a woman who worked in a part-time job she loved, doing research at a university. The child's father was a lawyer, loved his work, and totally appreciated his wife's sharing of the financial burden of the family. Clearly, the impact of society on this little girl's perceptions about herself and the world of work was already tremendous. It seemed that the explicit messages at home about the value and importance of work for men and women were already offset by societal messages around her.

Another seven-year-old girl was asked, "Will you work when you grow up?" and answered, "Of course. Everyone has to work." This girl's mother, who happened to work as a housewife and mother, valued and took tremendous pride and satisfaction in this job. She communicated her contentment with her present work to her daughter, along with possible future plans she had to enter the paid labor force. It is important to note the difference in these two girls' expectations of themselves and their future work. The five-year-old will possibly be disappointed if she "has" to work. Her present perceptions are primarily that work is something to be avoided. The seven-year-old, who believes that everyone works, already has an implicit understanding about the pride and accomplishment that can be gained through working. Though she may not always want or need to work for pay, working has become an integral part of her perception about her future. Our past and present expectations and attitudes about work will determine the degree of satisfaction we will experience with the work we choose for ourselves.

MYTH: THERE IS ONE MYTH ABOUT WORK

The first illusion is that we all share common expectations about work, its purpose, the way it is to be woven into our lives. Our responses are influenced and often distorted by the messages and experiences about working that we received as children. There is a wonderful book of essays about working women and the place of work in their lives, called *Working It Out*, edited by Sarah Ruddick and Pamela Daniels. A variety of women, when asked about their response simply to the title of the book, gave an astounding array of responses:

1. "It is about women who have to work and their struggle."

2. "It is about women who have the luxury of working at what they want."

3. "It is about the trials and tribulations of that dog-eat-dog male work world."

4. "It is about the tremendous satisfaction possible from figuring out about work in our lives."

5. "I wouldn't want to read it. It is probably just another women's lib book about women in the paid labor force, a real put-down to those of us who choose to stay home and be wives and mothers."

6. "It is about the intellectual woman who does not really know about us blue-collar and pink-collar workers. We don't stop to ask if we are always satisfied. We work because we *have* to."

7. "I am so tired of books about working by people who don't have the foggiest about the meaning of the word 'work' and the exhausting struggle to make ends meet."

8. "I don't need a book like that. I just do my job in order to get on to the real fun."

These differences in response to the title of the book and its probable contents stem partially from early messages and experiences about work, about why we work, and about what we can expect from our work.

38

These responses indicate to an almost shocking degree just how different our perceptions and expectations about work can be, depending on our early impressions. They clearly show that we see work through our own colored glasses, and even those we work with daily may see it differently.

From these responses we learn that some women have never had positive experiences in their work; that for some, work is monotonous, repetitive, exhausting. We learn that though we talk about a majority of women working, their circumstances are vastly dissimilar, and the fact that they are bringing home a paycheck may be their only common thread. We learn that satisfaction in one's work may not be all that common, but perhaps just an ideal of the upper-middle-class intellectuals and the career guidance professionals who desperately want their clients to reach fulfillment in their jobs. Any assumption that we know another's experience with work, just because they are working, should be dispelled after having read these varying responses.

One freely propagated myth is the myth that work is supposed to be challenging, fulfilling and satisfying most if not all of the time. This belief is perpetuated by the fact that our knowledge of other people's jobs is limited. Often we only see the parts of the job that seem satisfying or exciting. Rarely do we get a glimpse of the drudgery, the detail, the tedious work that may comprise a large portion of the job. Later, much to our chagrin, we may find that our own job includes a large percentage of tasks and responsibilities that do not particularly appeal to us. Having such limited, unrealistic expectations about our future work can have numerous outcomes.

One person in search of a job that would meet the stringent criteria of total satisfaction might find herself frustrated, with a tendency to change jobs often in search of the near-perfect job. Another might elect to stay in her job, all the while quietly chastising her parents and/or society for misleading her, for failing to help her perceive her options more accurately. She may feel angry at having gone to college to learn analytical skills and find herself in an unchallenging job with little potential growth in the foreseeable future. She may perceive the job as having failed her, the system as having misled her, or society as having deceived her. A third person might place the blame for job dissatisfaction entirely on herself. She may think, "I am not as smart as I thought. The job requires more than I can give. I did not do enough research before I accepted the job," and become frustrated, and/or disappointed with herself, feeling like a total failure.

On the other hand, there is the myth that work is *not* supposed to be wonderful, satisfying, creative, challenging, renewing, or energizing. It is supposed to be hard, something to be tolerated in order to get on with the business of living. Some people will choose jobs or trades that are potentially fulfilling, and they may indeed derive much pleasure and satisfaction from their work. If they don't hold the almost impossible expectation of total fulfillment, they may find themselves much more satisfied than the college graduate with enormous expectations.

About the Work World

Each of us has an exceptionally personal view of the work world, from which we tend to generalize to the entire work world. Though most of our actual work experiences are fairly limited, perhaps just to two or three work environments, we often assume one of two different alternative positions. Many women in traditionally female jobs come to believe that the "rest" of the work world is very different. One woman may operate effectively as a social worker in a hospital setting, interacting with patients, families, nurses, agencies, and the administration. But she does not perceive herself as a part of a complex system that in many respects is quite similar to a multitude of other work environments. The housewife and mother who has chosen a career in the home often believes that the work world is entirely different from her world. It seems foreign and frightening, largely because of her lack of recent significant contact or practice in various sectors of that world.

When women are helped to discover the transferability of the skills they so effectively utilize in the home, they can often move into this unknown arena without much difficulty. One such woman in her late forties attended a class for women exploring career alternatives, and learned to "count" her experience at home as valid and useful to potential employers. Her skills in organizing, teaching, and communicating helped her to successfully land a job in the training department of a bank. She responded to training opportunities available to her, eventually moving into middle management. Once she achieved this promotion, she also saw herself as a person clearly capable of coping, learning, and achieving in the labor force.

Most people do the reverse. They generalize that other work environments are similar to theirs. Our lack of broad exposure to the many-faceted world of work may limit our perceptions of the variety and differences among jobs. Another woman, a systems analyst, was astounded at the differences between the work environments in two similar jobs that she held. The first was in a large corporation, where bureaucracy combined with the pressure to meet the company's behavioral objectives contributed to her discontent with her work. The second job, with the same title, was in a smaller company, where she was allowed considerably greater latitude in doing her job. There she was supported and encouraged in such a way that she felt challenged and satisfied. Her first inclination had been to seek a different kind of job. Luckily for her and her second employer, she continued in her chosen field.

MYTH: THERE IS A PERMANENT SOLUTION TO THE QUEST FOR SATISFYING WORK

As young children we are often asked the question, "What do you want to do when you grow up?" Even at a tender age there is a sense that if you don't have an answer, you had better manufacture one that will sound good to the person asking the question. They seem to want to hear "a fireman," "a policeman," "a mother," . . . a *something*. There is the implicit message that there is *one* thing for us to become, rather than developing skills and strengths that we can use in a variety of jobs. And further, once we make a choice we assume that we are supposed to stick with it. The assumption has been that one job will satisfy us all our lives or that longevity with one company is equivalent to success. In the past, people who changed jobs were in the minority. Many people spent their entire work life with one company and never considered leaving the safety and comfort of their job.

The myth that we should find and keep one job that will provide us with permanent happiness is giving way to the emerging belief that a satisfying career is built and invented. Professionals are more frequently called upon to help people equip themselves to switch careers and cope with change. We are beginning to deal with the reality that there may be a decreasing amount of creative energy expended the longer a job remains the same. If we are discontented with the limited growth possibilities within a job, a more logical decision would be to seek a promotion, or make a lateral change to another business or field, or perhaps ask to redefine the scope of the present job. Robin Montgomery, vice-president of marketing at Vidal Sassoon, Inc., was quoted in *Business Week* as saying, "I know so many women who are assistant managers in one industry, but are too scared to switch to another and move up." She continues, "If you're good, you're good anyplace." She has changed employers eight times since 1964, beginning as a manager of a showroom, and working in a variety of industries. She is a good example of the transferability of one's skills, and the great potential for success possible by taking some risks. Too frequently women seem to need extra encouragement to seek a promotion. They may readily take on additional responsibilities without also asking for an accompanying promotion.

Our Perceptions of the Work World . . . Are They Stereotypes?
Most of us have had direct contact with a very small proportion of the multitude of jobs that comprise the labor force. Two problems result from this limited exposure to potential work possibilities. First, there are many jobs—even entire fields—that we never even remotely consider because we do not know which fields have become more sophisticated or which jobs have been phased out. Those women who have not worked for several years are not aware of their existence. And second, we often tend to assume that all persons working in an occupation with which we are familiar are doing the same thing as the one or two personal contacts we may have had. For example, we may have had an aunt who was a secretary, even gone to work with her once as a child. Later when we think of secretaries, we imagine an environment similar to that one, and a job that parallels our impression of our aunt's. With the proliferation of businesses and the increasing trend to more creatively define the responsibilities of secretaries, there are as many variations of job definitions for secretaries as there are for managers in differing work environments.

Likewise, if we know one buyer for sportswear in a

department store, we tend to think that all buyers are involved in similar jobs, and that we possess full awareness of the tasks and expectations of a person who fits the job title "buyer." In reality, the jobs of buyers vary drastically, depending on the degree of responsibility, the area for which they are buying, the work setting, the size of the organization, and the number of years of experience. One situation might appeal to us, whereas another might not, depending on these factors, among others.

It is unreasonable to expect that we can have contact and firsthand experience with great numbers of people in similar jobs, but if we become aware of our tendency to generalize, we can protect ourselves from mentally discarding and discounting many kinds of work that could ultimately appeal and be satisfying to us, if we would learn more about them.

To demonstrate at how early an age children begin to form stereotyped impressions of the work world, we showed a group of eight-year-old girls the photographic documentary *Women at Work* by Betty Medsger depicting women working at many different jobs. The pictures portray a great variety of women at work in their respective job settings. The pictures and the children's responses included the following:

1. Picture of a woman in uniform answering the phone at her desk. Common belief: She is a secretary. (She is a colonel in the Marines in California.)

2. Picture of a woman at the head of a rectangular table, with other women around the table; all are drinking coffee. Most common guess: These are secretaries at lunch. (This woman is the vice-president of a division of General Telephone and Electronics meeting with her staff.)

3. Picture of a woman in a lab, with cans of fruit cocktail next to lab samples. Common guess: She is a cook. (She is a food chemist.)

4. Picture of a woman looking at and handling the complex equipment in an airplane cockpit. Most common guess: She is a stewardess. (She is a pilot for Braniff Airlines.)

Clearly, these children have been exposed to women in traditionally female occupations and, as a result, generalize from their limited experiences to these photographs. If they had carefully studied the pictures, noticing the lab coat on the food chemist, or the uniform on the colonel, they would have realized that these women were working in jobs that were different from what they initially thought. As adults we frequently continue the same pattern. Members in one occupation tend to generalize about members of other occupations, rarely allowing for much divergence from their expectations. People in business assume that social service careers are soft, lack pressure, and require very little accountability. People in social service jobs assume that business people are hard, aggressive, do not know how to communicate, and are only interested in profits. Actually, there are tremendous variations in people and settings within the work world and rarely do they conform to these black-and-white stereotypes. The danger is that our limited exposure to a particular job will dictate our impressions and expectations for years to come.

Situational Factors that Influence Our Stereotypes

We have noted that both as children and as adults we have had limited exposure to people working in different jobs. This lack of direct contact is an important factor in limiting our growth potential. And if we do have direct contact, we rarely take advantage of it by taking the opportunity to learn about someone else's work or their special field of endeavor. Though reading about different careers can be informative, rarely does it give insight into the complexities of a job, into its "guts." As young girls, we were obviously conditioned to believe that we would enter one of the traditionally female work environments, *if* we planned to work. Consequently, as growing children, we did not learn or were not encouraged to "raise our antennae," to take advantage of personal contacts and experiences that would help us to broaden our awareness of the work world.

Your father probably did not say, "Sue, meet Dr. Fox. You might be interested in learning about his job and someday decide to be a doctor." Or, "Meet Mr. Jones. He is an electrician. Maybe you'd be interested in that field." Instead you might have been told, "Sue, meet my friend Dr. Fox. Someday, before you are married, you might be interested in being a nurse or receptionist in his office." However, a second alternative is more probable. That is, "Sue, meet my friend Dr. Fox. Dr. Fox, Sue is very helpful with her younger brothers—takes after her mother!" Sue was not thought of as a potential worker, as a future member of the labor force. She was not encouraged to learn, investigate, question, weigh opinions. In many cases young boys did not receive all that much encouragement to "raise their antennae" either. But their contact with other men working, combined with exposure to media that projected men into various occupations, helped to compensate for a possible lack of encouragement to explore options.

Even career-oriented women face another situational factor that has hindered women's career development. They have had a lack of mentors, that is a lack of people who have expended a great deal of personal interest and energy in an attempt to guide and sponsor women on their career path. In the *Harvard Business Review*, Gerard R. Roche explores the subject of mentors in an article entitled "Much ado about mentors." In the study discussed, six in ten of the successful male executives that were questioned had an average of two mentors in the first fifteen years of their careers. Additionally, those with mentors seemed to follow a career plan more often than those without mentors. And even more significantly, those men with mentors derived greater pleasure from their work than those without.

Though female executives constituted only 1 percent of the total executives queried, all had at least one mentor, and the average number of mentors was three. Seven out of ten of these women executives' mentors were male, largely due to the still small percentages of women in the executive ranks that would qualify to function as mentors.

An interesting point touched on by the article was that many of these successful executives actively sought out mentors, sensing their importance to their future success. Logically, having someone interested in and committed to one's work would have great impact on one's self-esteem and productivity on the job. The cultivation of mentors is a suggested task for women in all areas and at all levels of the labor force. Though it often feels threatening to be the one to initiate contact, and is difficult to ask for help, the payoffs can be more than worth any initial discomfort.

A Career Versus a Job

Women usually think of a job as something done for a finite period of time. A career is usually described as a series of jobs that comprise an overall plan. For many women to say they have a career feels pretentious, but to have a job feels comfortable and acceptable. Webster defines a job as a piece of work, a task, a position of employment. A career is defined as one's advancement or achievement in a particular occupation, a lifework, a profession, an occupation. A job is in the present, and is part of a short-term plan. A career includes the present, the past, and the future, and is a long-term plan. The dictionary definitions do not attach any positive or negative connotations to either word, and neither do we.

But from many women's perceptions both words have acquired a bad reputation. Women who have "just a job" are sometimes perceived by career women as being dilettantes, not really all that serious about their work. Those women who have "just a job" often have the stereotyped impression that women pursuing careers are necessarily aggressive, hardened, driven individuals. A common assumption about having decided to pursue a career is that it must be consuming, and require total devotion. At a moment's notice, she must be prepared to grab her coat and head with a prepacked suitcase (always ready in such emergencies) for the airport. This image is not totally unfounded in some occupational areas, and a strong pattern has been set by men who are committed to developing their careers and their financial security at all costs.

Let us take a moment to look at emerging definitions of life career development and of career consciousness. People involved in developing life career competencies will spend time seriously visualizing themselves in possible life career roles, settings, and events, and then in analyzing and relating these to their present situation. Charles Reich, in *The Greening of America*, published in 1971, states that career consciousness includes "a person's background, education and philosophy. . . . it is the whole man [or the whole woman we might add], his 'head,' his way of life. It is that by which he creates his own life and thus creates the society in which he lives." A career plan involves a continuing process of personal growth in our occupational lives. A person involved in career planning has an impact on her experience in addition to a reaction to it.

What seems to be most important is our perception of the work that we do. Numerous specific tasks or jobs could be perceived as components of a career. And conversely, what we are doing at various times during our work life can be perceived simply as parts of a job when these activities are not seen as part of a continuing process of personal growth in our occupational life.

Most women have not been raised to perceive or to plan their work life, whatever or wherever it is, in terms of a continuing career pattern. Consequently, there is often limited attention paid to its growth and development. They experience much difficulty in defining what their work is and in seeing it as important enough to their lives to warrant long-term career planning.

If we could remove the negative connotations from the words "job" and "career," we would be moving in a positive direction. In order for a woman to be involved and committed to her career development, she does not necessarily have to be working full-time outside the home with total energy output. What is important is that she has a sense of continuity in her perception of her work life. She may choose to be in the labor force part-time, or not at all, but can be continually conscious of and involved with planning for her future. She can still have a career, though she may have taken a sabbatical from the salaried labor force. What is crucial is that she be comfortable in projecting herself into the future, that she continue to make decisions and choices that feel as if they are integrated with who she is and who she wants to become.

THE MYTH OF WOMEN TAKING MEN'S JOBS

Along with the commonly held belief that women are entering a multitude of new professions in great numbers, is the definite implication that women are *taking* men's jobs. Women *are* accepting some jobs that were previously, perhaps, held by men . . . those women who are qualified, that is. The implication that men are going jobless, that women are "snatching" their jobs, is a very strong image and in most cases invalid.

The feelings and perceptions of those in a position to hire are slowly changing. Affirmative action guidelines are influential in precipitating change and in attracting more women to nontraditionally female jobs. Some personnel people are truly committed to helping women meet their potential, to get a fair chance in the job market. But many of these employers hope to fill their positions with only outstanding women. To a disproportionate degree many of the women hired will, indeed, need to prove themselves to be outstanding in their work. Fewer women of average ability can compete successfully with men of average ability for a job (unless a company is under strong affirmative action pressure). When as many women of average ability as men of average ability are hired and retained, real progress will have been made. When we reach that point, it may be valid to perceive women as having taken jobs that men would have had in the past. Clearly, however, simply because men held most of these coveted jobs in the first place does not mean that they still deserve to, or that their needs to work are any more important than the needs of women looking for work.

WHAT IS THE PLACE OF WOMEN IN THE WORK WORLD?

Some people believe that women are entering all areas of the work world in droves, and that there have been significant changes in women entering higher paid, nonblue- and nonpink-collar occupations. A common belief is that the main struggle for women is over. True, there are examples of women entering many nontraditional fields of endeavor. It is also true that women comprise a much larger percentage of the students in law schools and medical schools than a decade ago. But most women are still employed in offices, restaurants, stores, hospitals, beauty shops, factories, schools, and other jobs predominantly filled by women. Within formerly male occupations, still a small fraction of the work force is female. Even in Sweden, where laws favor maternity leave and good child-care centers, this is still true.

Rosabeth Moss Kanter in *Men and Women of the Corporation* states that in 1970 half of all women workers were employed in seventeen occupations, as opposed to half of all men in sixty-three occupations. She also says that, "Men constitute over 96 percent of all managers and administrators earning more than $15,000 yearly, and nearly 98 percent of those earning over $30,000 yearly. In over half of the companies, women held only 2 percent or fewer of the first-level supervisory jobs, including jobs such as manager of secretaries; in three-fourths of the companies, they held *none* of the top management jobs. It looks as if we can negate the myth that women are invading top management. In fact, in many cases, as the statistics show, women are barely represented." One further point seems important. Ms. Kanter explains that even in areas traditionally considered to be "female concerns," the managers are likely to be men.

Part-Time Doesn't Mean Part-Energy

Most jobs in the salaried labor force require a minimum commitment of forty hours per week on the job. Many people working "full-time" believe that "the job" cannot be done without this total consumption of time. There is some movement toward developing flexible time in certain work settings, where employees may work four ten-hour days instead of five eight-hour days. But the total number of hours required usually remains relatively unchanged.

Most women with children continue to bear the primary responsibility of their children, although there is a trend toward greater sharing of child-care responsibilities among some young couples, particularly two-career families. Traditionally, women were able to secure part-time jobs mostly in the service and pink-collar occupations or other traditionally female jobs. That is still the case. Though there are increased numbers of trained women in all occupational areas, and many of whom would like to work less than a forty-hour week, there is a great reluctance by employers to permit this to occur. It is believed that if these women are not serious enough to commit themselves to a "normal" workweek, they cannot possibly do a high caliber job. The additional implication is that all jobs require total time commitment to do them well, and that this time *must* be spent physically at the job site. Those who do work part-time often have to struggle for fringe benefits, since these workers are often perceived as transient and/or even frivolous, only wanting something to do or to fill up their time, or to occupy them temporarily.

There are many women working part-time, however, who are extremely committed to their work. They care deeply, prepare diligently, and can accomplish a great deal perhaps even *because* their day may begin an hour later and end an hour earlier than their male counterparts. Many women who work part-time expend an enormous amount of energy in their jobs.

Their work is as important to them and to their future as to any full-time employees. They learn to utilize their time wisely at work and at home, and work hard to protect their positions. Some universities hire married couples who share a teaching post, although such a phenomenon is still rare. Each is working part-time. Some feel that the university is getting the bargain . . . the dedication and expertise of two persons instead of just one. By midday most people decrease their output and begin to lag. With a replacement person, more can often be accomplished than with one person working the full day.

There are many areas of the business world that would be wise to utilize much more flexible scheduling, to begin to define more jobs that could utilize the great untapped potential in the job market. Often work expands to fit the time allotted to it. If there is a smaller amount of time, efficiently used, much can be accomplished. If women have training, expertise, and experience, then business and industry would be wise to develop ways to utilize their talents, without requiring a full-time commitment.

THE MYTH THAT CORPORATE WOMEN WILL JOB HOP

"It is a commonly held myth about women that they leave jobs more frequently than men," says Helen J. McLane, vice-president of a Chicago-based executive search firm, in the June 11, 1979 issue of *Business Week*. It was feared that women in executive jobs are more likely than men to change jobs in response to chances for advancement and financial growth possibilities. *Business Week* reports this myth to be unfounded: "Perhaps because top managers are unaccustomed to seeing women executives change jobs, they overreact to even a moderate turnover rate," *Business Week* continues. In actuality, the highest rated reason for corporate women to change jobs is the type of challenge in the new job, followed by potential scope of responsibility and finally, opportunity for advancement. Women at these upper levels have been shown to be as responsible as men.

One of the principal barriers to women entering nontraditional jobs and jobs of greater status and responsibility is the perception that women present a greater turnover risk than do men. Perhaps these lingering feelings about women's lack of seriousness and commitment have contributed to the expectation that women at corporate levels cannot be counted on over the long haul.

THE MYTH THAT JOB CHANGING IS EASY FOR OTHER PEOPLE

Both men and women at all levels of employment often find the process of changing jobs frightening, humiliating, embarrassing, difficult, complex, and above all arduous. Upper-level executives desiring to change jobs experience concern about whether they will find another job as challenging, without risking a large salary cut. They share common feelings with other job changers, particularly the feeling of powerlessness in the face of those with the power to hire. Though they may know that they are talented and knowledgeable, having to ask someone to hire them or give them recommendations is cause for frustration and embarrassment, feelings that inhibit their progress in the job-search process.

Women who are being phased out of their present jobs or are considering a career change often assume that other women do not share their self-doubts. They report feelings that others must have significantly more self-confidence and control over the process of job changing. Thus the myth that it is easy to change jobs is clearly a myth, whether changing to a traditionally female job, traditionally male job, a job at a low salary, or one at an executive level.

Searching for a job is a job in itself. Certain processes will significantly decrease the struggle and humiliation and decrease the amount of time spent searching for a new job, but the struggle is still there. Though it is commonly thought that having an advanced degree makes the process easier, such is not necessarily the case. Often these degrees and credentials simply increase the difficulty of finding a job. Being specialized can limit the numbers of job possibilities that can be considered. It is also thought that people with years of experience in a field will have an easy job redirecting themselves, even if they desire to change careers and move into a new field of endeavor. In the eyes of an employer, these years of experience are not always a positive factor. He may wonder how he can adequately motivate and compensate this potential employee. This experienced, well-educated person is faced with the hazards of job searching and career changing, similar to those facing the novice entering or reentering the labor force. In fact, it is possible that the higher the level of skills you have, the less possible that the jobs you seek will ever be advertised.

To combat the insecurity, difficulty, and complexity of the job hunt and career change processes, it is necessary to remain in control, to be in the driver's seat rather than in the passenger seat, where you are waiting for the driver to make a decision about where you will go. The traditional job hunt process includes creating a résumé, responding to want ads, using an employment agency, facing personnel managers, and an inordinate amount of waiting . . . for people to call, to answer your letters and phone calls, to ask you for an interview. Many companies receive hundreds of thousands of unsolicited résumés each year, and have a personnel department for eliminating these people. Richard Bolles in his book on career changing entitled *What Color Is Your Parachute?* referred to one study showing that one invitation was sent for every 245 résumés received. Another company sent out one per 1,188 résumés. For help in reversing this process to one in which a career changer is more actively controlling the process, there are a number of helpful guides which can be found in most bookstores.

MYTH OF "WHEN SOMETHING COUNTS"

A common thought many of us have is: "What I define as 'important work,' others will also define as important work, and have the same high regard for it that I have." This is not necessarily true, any more than the reverse. Someone else may very well have extremely high regard for the work that you do, though you personally may not perceive it as being all that important. One multitalented woman in her thirties was in the process of a career change, and lamented the fact that though she had a great many abilities and strengths, she could not call herself a _____ . If she were a doctor, a lawyer, a producer, a writer, a professional person, she would have felt more successful and self-confident. Even though she did have flexibility for job choices, for she had successfully pursued commercial real estate at a time when few women entered that aspect of the field, she felt that she needed a title in order to feel proud of herself.

On the other hand, a woman who became a sales representative for a computer company felt as if her work really counted. She was proud to be in a field that was growing and was in the forefront of the technological development of our country. A woman stockbroker did feel that her work was really important. She was helping women to enlarge their horizons, learn about investing, and hopefully increase their net worth. But yet another woman stockbroker subsequently left her job because she felt that her work was not important, that it did not count. Though she was well trained and equally as competent as the first stockbroker mentioned, she felt that she was selling something she did not always believe in, and felt that she could be doing something more important elsewhere.

One of the strengths of the women's movement has been that it has opened up hundreds of possibilities for women, promoted new job fields for women, and paved the way for women to think about entering jobs they never would have considered even a decade ago. Another strength is that it has helped remove the stigma attached to being called a "working" mother. It has presented new hope and fresh horizons for the women of tomorrow. But one unfortunate aspect of the women's movement is the discomfort it causes many women due to the emphasis that has been put on working outside the home, the intimation that "working" is the key to status. Consequently many women, especially those who choose to continue working in the home, feel a loss of status, and often feel the need to apologize for choosing to do what is now becoming less and less common. The message they are internalizing is that only when they enter the salaried work force can their work be called important.

Now, although earning a paycheck may be crucial and may also contribute to a sense of self-esteem and accomplishment, it is certainly not a determinant of the worth of one's work. And neither is *not* receiving a paycheck an indication of having *no* worth. Many women are signing up for personal development classes and career exploration classes in response to the societal pressure to go to work. Many women who are most desirous and financially able to stay home with their infants and very young children are being challenged by their friends and the media to consider returning to work. Sometimes these women participate in a series of classes and regain the sense of being comfortable with the decision *not* to work outside the home just now. Often, however, this decision is accompanied by an increased awareness of their strengths and they begin planning their future work options. Sometimes these classes help remove the pressure that may otherwise contribute to a woman making a decision that is not really in her best interests.

Judith Wax, in her book *Starting in the Middle,* expressed disdain over this subtle pressure on nonsalaried women, by depicting a conversation at a dinner party. A man turns to the woman seated next to him and asks her a question about what she does. The comeback, "I have been working as a topless nuclear physicist," in a frantic, if humorous attempt to quickly dredge up something that "counts." Having done that, supposedly, one's status has been removed from the potential critical list to the list of those in stable condition. An appropriate response to the questions "Do you work?" or "What do you do?" could be, "I am involved with _____" or "My newest position is _____" or "I have become interested in _____ ." Actually, the question is often an attempt to break through initial discomfort in search of common ground about which to converse. A much better question would be "What are your special interests?" or "How do you like to spend your time?" Then the implication that only talking about salaried work deserves conversation, is put to rest. And a real attempt to communicate has become possible.

Changing

Your

Perspective

Beginning a career or making new decisions about the meaning of work in our lives often requires changing our perspective. Getting in our way are the negative myths and stereotypes we hold about ourselves, our relationships, and our work. ("It is selfish to be concerned with my own career needs." "One person should fill all my needs, so I should not need to work." "If I take a job and it does not work out I am a failure.") Although we may not even be consciously aware that we hold these beliefs, they are powerful forces that restrain us when we want to change our lives.

We may not be able to control the external barriers, such as a tight job market, other people's attitudes toward working mothers, or the income tax bracket our job places us in. But we *can* gain control over the paralyzing effects of our own myths and stereotypes, because they are fostered and maintained by our own thought processes. Once we realize this we have a tool, and a place to begin.

The first step is to become consciously aware of the myths and stereotypes that influence the choices we make. By doing this, we create an opportunity to update and reevaluate these beliefs. It is then possible to replace them with ideas that help us to grow and to risk change.

A stereotype is based on some degree of truth, but that

element of truth has been generalized to all the members of the category being stereotyped. ("Women are too emotional." "Little boys are just curious by nature." "Men find it hard to express their feelings.")

At some point in our lives we have all been aware of feelings of frustration when having a stereotype applied to us in ways we consider to be unfair. Or we have found ourselves desiring to depart from the following of some "traditional" plan already devised for us. ("Girls don't need an education." "Girls don't know about or can't work mechanical things because their brains don't function that way.")

Might these myths and stereotypes retard growth and inhibit the change in our perspective of ourselves? What makes it difficult is that element of truth contained within the stereotypes, which makes it impossible to completely refute them. These elements of truth can keep us bound to the stereotypes. We are able to point out many exceptions to the set opinions; but these exceptions are often viewed as only that, exceptions. There remain too many people who behave in ways that tend to encourage the stereotypes. The stereotype may actually be true for them or else they have found some incentive to continue behaving in ways that contribute to the continuation of the stereotype. In fact, some people may have to *learn* how to behave in a stereotypical manner. ("Boys don't like girls with brains; I have to remember that.") If we meet or deal with many people whose behavior maintains the stereotype, we may even forget the "exceptions" we have also encountered. We may begin to wonder if, indeed, the stereotype does have some genetic basis, rather than just being culturally produced.

The real problem lies in trying to refute the total stereotype. Rather, we can examine the ways in which we see stereotypes being true of us *and* also, importantly, the ways in which the stereotypes *do not* apply to us. The ways in which we differ from the stereotypes are as "true" as the ways in which we don't differ from them. For instance, we might find that we deal with criticism the following way: "I find it hard not to cry when being criticized—like many women I know—but I also know that I am learning to accept criticism without dissolving into tears." Just as a stereotype has an element of truth, there are also a myriad of ways in which such generalizations do not apply to most of the members of the category being stereotyped. Not being able to balance a checkbook can apply equally to men and women as well as finding that some men and some women are mechanically inclined.

Let's take a look at the stereotype of the middle-class or working-class housewife (in America there are many characteristics shared by each). She is generally depicted as not being employed outside the home, as having to care for the home and family as her primary daily task. She may do some volunteer work at the children's school or the local hospital, or pay weekly visits to parents. She frequently belongs to a bridge club, or to a bowling team, or a health or swim club or goes to a weekly bingo. Barring significant crises, the systems will remain as they are. Children grow up, husbands may change jobs, the wife may do some periodic part-time work, but basically the pattern remains the same and each member knows what is expected of him or her and what expectations they hold for other members of the system.

Then along comes some other factor that affects the system. Economic need can be such a factor or force. The pattern is changed in that the wife now takes on full-time employment. The old stereotypes are no longer the norm, but the *idea* of the stereotype remains, for both the men and the women within the system, and this can cause upset.

For instance, though the two teenagers in the family know, intellectually, that their mother is working now, and that they must contribute more time and energy to cooking, shopping, and cleaning, they still picture their mother in the nurturing, supportive, ever-present role that enveloped them in the first thirteen or fourteen years of their lives. They still expect dinner on the table at 6:00 P.M. and their favorite shirts ironed for their weekend dates. And usually, the mother has some ambivalence about no longer having the time to fulfill all these roles, and about "letting her family down." The children detect her ambivalence, may feel guilty about making unfair demands, but for a while they resent the changes that have occurred.

In likewise fashion, the husband may truly support his wife's decision to take a full-time job and is aware of his anxiety, being relieved by a second income coming into the home. Even so, he may be quite accustomed to having a schedule at home that had been adapted to his work schedule. He may feel some irritation (or at least frustration) at waiting for her to return from working late, and being expected to have dinner on the table for her! And again, the juggling of roles, the change in the way the family had operated up until the change, is difficult for everyone in the family. It takes time to establish a new status quo, to decrease the anxiety about change, and to build a new base for working together.

And the single working woman may find herself liking her job and her frequent promotions, but she may hesitate to tell the men she meets what she does or her actual position in a company. She may still feel that men do not like women to have better jobs than they have. She may be concerned that talk of her job may sound like bragging, and "men don't like women who brag." She may feel that she could "scare" away possible companionship by seeming too successful. So she maintains her own stereotype of how men feel about "successful" women.

Regardless of the entrance of many women into the labor force, the stereotype still persists that women should attempt to successfully perform *all* the duties implicit in the roles of career woman, spouse, and mother. Even among professional women there are strong questions as to the possibility of doing all three *equally* well. That perhaps is the crux of the problem. American women, as a whole, do believe that they *should* be able to do all three well. They even more strongly believe that unless they do all three exceptionally well they are not really "successful." We are not advocating that women should necessarily desire or attempt to maintain all three roles at once: to be a career woman, to be married, and to be a parent. What we are asking you to question is that still prevalent belief that unless a woman fully dedicates herself to each of the endeavors, with equal zeal and energy, she is not successful. Or that she must choose *for* one or two of the roles and *against* one or two roles and that she must maintain her choice once she has made it.

It has not been especially useful for women to hear that "men have always integrated the three roles," for the answer of many women is, "but they've never really done the housekeeping role, because they've had a wife around to do it." Although men may have indeed maintained all three roles of worker, spouse, and parent, their priorities have not been the same. They have rarely assumed the major responsibility of taking care of children and the home, and they have not had years of socialization to combat as they attempt to engage in all three endeavors. In fact they have had years of modeling on how to do all three, with permission to invest themselves in these roles with varying degrees of intensity.

And, unfortunately, a new stereotype is beginning to emerge in descriptions of the "successful" career woman. She is in her early thirties, she has a good education and she is now in a decision-making position in business or industry. Perhaps she is a lawyer or a physician or a stockbroker—basically male-dominated worlds. She is attractive, dresses in classic good taste, is health and body conscious, lives in an apartment or a condominium, takes a couple of well-planned vacations a year and is a gourmet cook. As to the rest of her life, the picture is blurred. No one asks if that woman really exists. In actuality the successful career woman comes in all sizes, has varying amounts of education, lives in all types of housing, and may have careers in the home, in the volunteer force, or in traditional as well as nontraditional female occupations. It almost appears that we are not satisfied with diversity. It seems that when we try to eliminate one stereotype we do so by replacing it with another, equally as binding.

It may be that each of us has within ourself our own "description" of the successful woman. In our mind's eye we see a picture that is neither the old stereotype nor the one born in the '70s, but a personal one. And we want some validation to try to bring that one to fruition.

And what about myths? How do those traditional and convenient beliefs and explanations hinder our ability to change our perspective of ourselves, our goals, our desires, our future careers? Myths are based in tradition. When we question the myths that surround us we are questioning the traditions that may have nurtured and restricted us at the same time. Often within a myth we find elements we want to retain as well as some elements we want to discard. But separating the two, the desirable from the undesirable, is a difficult and arduous task. And we may even find ourselves wondering about the value gained as opposed to the cost of trying to separate the two. It may be tempting, rather, to just maintain the myths or completely discard them.

One myth that typifies the difficulty involved in trying to separate the wanted from the unwanted parts of a myth is that old adage, "A woman's place is in the home." A first reaction may be to "throw out the whole idea. No good can come from perpetuating that myth." But second thoughts set in: "I think that there is something to be said for what a woman can bring to a home." "I don't want to say that a man should have no influence in the home." "There is some sensitivity that a woman brings to a home that we don't want to lose." After looking at the positive aspects of perpetuating the myth, a subsequent reaction may be that what is gained is not worth the loss, so let's not rock the boat. Then we are in the dilemma of wholesale rejection of the statement, which many of us do not want, or a continuation of the status quo for ourselves against pressure from society, from friends, from our own desires. Or, thirdly, we are faced with really thinking through the issue for ourselves and separating that which we want to retain from that which we reject—and perhaps living with some ambiguity about such statements and our feelings about them. We may even find that there are some myths that we want to continue believing as they are, and others we may want to discard completely.

When we find ourselves questioning tradition, saying, "why is it this way?" we may also find ourselves questioning the previous generation or generations and their participation in the myths we are questioning. One subsequent conclusion may be that previous generations were "wrong" or that we ourselves have been "wrong" or we may fear that coming generations will judge us harshly. But the categorizing of past behaviors into "right" or "wrong" is seldom necessary or useful in changing our perspective. What is helpful is to try to determine what purpose was served by the development and continuation of a myth, and furthermore to see if our needs are best met by the continuation of these myths in our own lives. You may find yourself saying "yes," "no," or "partially," when we examine some of the myths and stereotypes to be dealt with in this chapter. You may also find that you may want to participate in the creation of new myths that will encourage diversity in possible life styles and in career choices.

Along with the changes in the career and work patterns of women in the last few decades there has been an increasing necessity for women to attempt to integrate their paid employment with their roles of wife and mother. Decisions must be made about how and if they do want to integrate the three roles of career and marriage and family. When women attempt to either integrate all three roles or to make choices among the three, they have numerous myths and stereotypes to come to terms with within themselves.

HOW MYTHS HINDER CHANGE

Love they neighbor as thyself.

Does this quote imply that we should love ourselves, be kind and considerate to ourselves? Wouldn't that be selfish? A myth that is deeply rooted in many of us is that we should not be selfish. How have women translated this into their belief system about themselves? Does it mean that we should only think about the needs of others, or does it imply that we should always be willing to work on a weekend, even though we had made other plans? Is it an expectation that we never refuse a request of our parents, friends, employers, neighbors, or co-workers, or that we shouldn't pursue what we might want if it conflicts with someone else? If we are not concerned with what we can do for others, then we are being selfish and we are sure that this is viewed as terrible not only by society and others but even by ourselves. Can this feeling of paying attention to our own needs and positive regard for ourselves be redefined as self-caring?

In humanistic and existential psychology we find support for the idea that you must love and care for yourself before you can love and care for others (Carl Rogers, Abraham Maslow, Rollo May). One psychologist, Eric Fromm, believes that self-love and selfishness are opposites. He contends that the selfish person does not care too much for himself but rather he is covering up for caring too little about himself. This lack of self-love results in personal unhappiness and anxiety, causing a person to grab "selfishly" for whatever he can get.

We affirm our own life, happiness, and growth when we have the ability to love productively, which for Fromm includes care, respect, responsibility, and knowledge. And the opposite is true: if we can only love others, we cannot truly love at all.

But even after being exposed to the notion that caring for oneself may not be a "selfish" and "small" thing to do, many women find it hard to believe that time spent in caring for themselves, being cognizant of their needs and attempting to satisfy some of them, will also result in caring more properly for others. In respecting one's own needs, the way is paved for more properly respecting the needs of others. And even when a woman is convinced that such behavior would be beneficial to others as well as to herself, she may find that she is unsure of herself until she is able to determine how to develop a new pattern of caring for her needs and new ways of allowing herself time for and attention to her own pursuits.

Our patterns are usually deeply ingrained and it takes time and repeated effort before new patterns are learned and old patterns are eliminated. Considerable energy must be expended in changing those patterns and at times we may find ourselves wanting to seek refuge in the old patterns. They are comfortable both to ourselves and to others. It may actually be easier to remain the "martyr," or to continue to do for others without evaluating the cost, than it would be to reflect upon our own desires and to plan for their attainment. Efforts to maintain the status quo usually result in change in our feelings or perceptions.

The reactions of Lois, when taking part in a self-growth group, are typical of the reactions to apparent selfishness. Another group participant was asked the question, "Who is the most important person in your life?" While the woman was thinking, Lois struggled with the same question. Her husband? Kids? Mother? Father? She just couldn't decide. Then she heard the other woman answer, "The most important person to me is myself." Lois was stunned. How selfish, she thought. But, the group leader and other members seemed very pleased with the woman's response. This woman had come up with an answer that was acceptable to that group because they felt that by learning to value and care for her own needs she would become a much more independent person with a more positive feeling about herself.

Answering that *she* was the most important person had not even occurred to Lois. The thought of giving that response made her feel guilty. She had been raised to believe that you should put others before yourself. It would not be an easy task to change this perception. What she could accept, perhaps, was considering herself *equal to* others. That would mean that her needs and preferences would be as important to her as those of others. This new way of looking at herself would present new options for change as well as challenges for problem solving, when her desires conflict with those of people around her. She began to see her new behavior as responsible instead of selfish.

This myth of "being selfish" may hinder women when they think about planning for working within their total life plan. If a married woman's husband does earn enough money to support the family then is it selfish for her to seek a career outside the home? Is it selfish for a single woman to choose an unmarried life style or for a young couple to choose a child-free life style? When a woman considers her own ideas and needs when making choices is she being selfish or is she being responsible? These are questions that have no "right" answer. Obviously, you must decide for yourself.

THE MYTH OF FAILURE

Man will always be making mistakes as long as he is striving for something.—Goethe

The myth that has evolved around failing infers that the consequences of failure are so distressing that it is better not to try at all. Yet John Gardner, an educator, writes: "We pay a heavy price for the fear of failure. It is a powerful obstacle to growth. It assures the progressive narrowing of the personality and prevents exploration and experimentation." He suggests that this fear can be immobilizing and therefore keep us from doing the very things that are necessary for promoting personal growth and eventually helping us be successful at making changes.

The impact of this myth is to make us believe we must be perfect. It is unacceptable for us to make a mistake or fail at something. Children who participate in organized sports learn that if you do poorly one time you must "shake it off and get back in there and play." "That's okay," is frequently heard after a missed ball. "You'll get it next time." These responses encourage a child to take risks and to put himself on the line. Mistakes and failures are seen as temporary, not permanent. Learning to do well becomes a process of striking out, learning from mistakes, practice and perseverance. However, other children with different experiences develop different attitudes about the possibility of failure. Until recently, proportionately few women reaped the benefits associated with team sports, especially that of learning how to accept that mistakes are part of the game. That is not to say that all men who played sports have learned that lesson well.

Why the differences in attitudes toward success and failure? Once again our past experiences prove to be important. Perhaps when chores were done at home the comments heard were, "Well you finally finished; you sure are slow." Or, "I see you made your bed; didn't it occur to you to dust?" Refrains such as, "Don't ever do anything to embarrass me," or "Don't do something unless you do it right," were continually heard. These are examples that build a feeling of inadequacy and an expectation of failure. The greater our fear of failing the fewer risks we are willing to take. Women who believe it would be awful if they failed often find it tremendously difficult to venture out in the world of work and to accept or seek promotions with greater responsibilities. These fears also inhibit the prospective career changer who may not be satisfied with her present situation, but feel safer than venturing into the unknown.

Even if we didn't learn to be afraid of failure at home, we had the opportunity to learn it at school or through our peer groups. We need to attack those phrases and feelings which well up inside us when we are about to embark on something new. We can ask ourselves if failure would be the only outcome. We can try to visualize other possible outcomes. We can anticipate learning from this situation so that even if our initial attempts are not right on target, the successive attempts are closer and closer to the goal.

Having looked at some inhibitive factors of myths about ourselves as persons, let us look at some myths about marriage that can retard growth in ourselves, in others, and in our career preferences.

THE MYTHS OF MARRIAGE

Believe me, females ought to seek to enliven the domestic circle by their acquirements; and while they admire talent in others, they ought not to be led away by the vain idea of being poets, painters, and musicians themselves. . . . The humble violet, shaded by its broad green leaves, is more secure from danger than the hollyhock, which woos the summer sun.
—Mrs. S.C. Hall, 1846

At first glance, we would hold that we have come a long way from this stance toward the position of women in the family circle. But at second glance, we might recognize that this has actually been our historical heritage as an American daughter. Whether or not you are married, take a moment to state some of your opinions about marriage. "It is the most intimate bond between two people." "It isn't all that it's cracked up to be." Both of those statements, plus numerous others, indicate our reactions to the myths or beliefs about marriage with which we have grown up. We find that the myths hold true for us or we are disappointed by not having them hold true for us. Or we may find that the reality for us is just not consistent with the myth we hold regarding marriage. Let us examine a few of them in more detail.

One myth that seems to be of recent origin is that we will have all our needs met by the marriage partner; we won't have need of other people or other types of satisfaction. Now, we may have many or even most of our needs met, but to expect that all needs will be met by the partner is a myth. It does serve its purpose well, to maintain a bond or relationship in which to raise children. The purpose is the survival of the species. In fact the perpetuation of this myth may in time be detrimental to the marriage bond. We may find that as a couple we are able to meet the needs of our partner to a great extent; but to expect that at *all* times and in *all* situations this will be the case will be to rely on the myth rather than on the personal commitment and efforts necessary to sustain an ongoing, growing relationship. And besides, regardless of hopes and plans, we cannot continuously nourish another person without receiving some nourishment from outside ourselves. After a nine-month period the infant can no longer gather sufficient nourishment from the mother. He/she must seek additional nourishment outside the womb. The gathering of food outside the womb does not necessarily reduce the bond or relationship between mother and child. In fact, a growth and enhancement of that bond is now possible.

We have found that this belief that all fulfillment will be found in the marriage partner is not true of only those women who are over thirty. Many young women in their early twenties harbor that secret belief. We do, however, find this belief more openly stated by women who enroll in personal development courses than by women who are working at a professional level in industry and business and education and who have not enrolled in such courses. Women who enroll in personal development or career exploration courses are feeling discontented with some aspect of their lives and want to determine positive, productive ways of dealing with this discontent. Though they may see a roomful of other women who are also enrolled, they often feel alone with their feelings, that only *they* are feeling discontented. They ask the question, over and over again, "Why am I more dissatisfied with being home and caring for my family than women seemed to be ten, thirty, fifty years ago?" (In one in which this question was asked by a woman in her late thirties, the woman sitting next to her said, "Thirty years ago I was doing my wash by hand, everything had to be ironed and the days were filled with keeping a house, even though I only had two children. But I'm here now, just as you are.") The question "Why am I dissatisfied?" is really a statement "I don't think I should feel any dissatisfaction. I love my husband, and children and home. Shouldn't that be sufficient for satisfaction?"

Many of the women thirty-five to forty years old who are employed and do enroll in personal development and career exploration courses seem to have already dealt with the question of the normality of feelings of "dissatisfaction" at various points in their lives. They are struggling with dissatisfaction like the others, but rather than questioning its existence, they are seeking ways of dealing with their discontent. Many women in business and industry are saying to themselves, "I have decided that at this point in time, having a career is a priority. Some things will fit into my life now, and other things will have to wait." Others feel good about earlier decisions, but now want to move on in new directions. ("I do not believe, however good and kind and wonderful my spouse is, that I will find complete fulfillment in him or my children or my career of unpaid nurturing." "I may never have a fantastic career, but I want one of my own.") And we have found that many of the women who are working in business and industry do not feel that they necessarily have been able to combine the three roles to their satisfaction. They have decided not to try to conquer all three roles, remaining content to handle two roles at any one time. However, they still fall prey to the belief that all three could and should be carried out at the peak of our proficiency.

Another myth of the marriage partnership that can hinder the possibility of a changing perspective is that the person we marry will always remain the same. And when in many cases that does not occur, we are disappointed or frustrated or at least we need time to adjust to the growth and change of that person. ("He's/she's not the person I married.") He or she is *and* isn't the same person. During the period of courtship, we usually want to put forward our best self for the other person. We are not consciously trying to deceive them, for we truly want to be our best self for them. And when we are "courting" we are not with them all day, every day, so we are usually able to save our best self for them. But when we are with another person constantly, we must and need to show them our whole self.

Many marriages accommodate to this reality, but there are some people who cannot accept this fact of life. Either we may try to keep the person behaving in the same way as they did before marriage, or our partner wants us to remain as we were at the time of marriage. The realities of living closely with another person, or perhaps having a family, or the career paths of at least one partner plus so many other factors, have significant impact upon us. We would find it hard to remain that same person even if we tried to. We expect physical changes to occur in both ourselves and in the marriage partner (though we seldom applaud their appearance), but somehow the psychological, emotional or intellectual changes sneak up on us. We do not all grow and change at the same rate or to the same degree. Even the same external factors do not affect each of us in the same way. "We didn't grow in the same directions" is often a statement underlying some marital breakups. And yet members of other marriages could make the same statement, but the partners have allowed the differences in growth for themselves and the other to be accommodated within their relationship. The difference seems to be in the expectations of the couples. Those couples who do not expect the partner to always remain the same, those who allow for growth and change, paradoxically, seem to remain closest.

Some may hope for change after marriage. ("After we're married he'll/she'll change." "I'll change him/her.") We know intellectually or we have seen the fallacy of this belief by observing other couples. Such a supposition is not a good basis upon which to start any relationship. But still many of us secretly hold that belief and never give up trying to change our spouse. We must caution against hoping that we can change the other person to meet our desires for their behavior. We can really only change our own behavior. The other may decide to change, but it is truly his/her decision to do so.

We are also cautioned by professionals and nonprofessionals alike that we should share a commonality of interests, values, and goals. Doing so is certainly an aid to the progression of the relationship. However, embedded in that advice is also the myth that if we do share values, goals, interests, attitudes, and the like, things will go smoothly. The case may be that those very things that initially attracted us to one another will also be the factors that cause eventual problems. ("We are both independent; that should be to our advantage.") Perhaps. But each wanting and needing independence may preclude some of the dependence that may be important to an ongoing relationship. "I like to be the protector and she needs to be protected," may be true at the time of marriage, but may change as she grows and develops in new directions. One partner may become overburdened with being the protector or the other may want to be less protected.

All of the above factors influence us when we are deciding about our career path, at whatever age we are doing so—eighteen, twenty-five, thirty-nine, fifty-six, or sixty-five, or at all of those ages.

THE MYTH OF AGE: THE RACE AGAINST THE CLOCK

"Never trust anyone over thirty." "Life begins at forty!" "*It* gets harder when you're older to _____ (fill in the blank)." "No one wants to hire someone over fifty who hasn't worked in years." "I can't keep up the pace I did last year." "What do you do to protect your skin once you've turned thirty?"

Do any of the above sound like something you might say today or remember yourself having sometime said? For the average woman, more so than for the average man, age is closely associated with changes in one's self-concept and one's role in society. The aging process possesses a far greater threat to an American woman's self-esteem than to that of an American man or to a European woman. American women still struggle to maintain the appearance of youth, even today, after almost two decades of messages from the women's movement that negate the importance of looks. Even when the age of the average

American is becoming higher each year, as a nation we are still preoccupied with youth. Even when we honestly feel that we are just reaching our peak as an individual, we still see the television ads bemoaning the finding of a gray hair and associating crabbiness and irritability with the discovery of wrinkles. We still flock to buy the products advertised as helping to "cheat age." We ask the question *Why?*

There are no simple answers, though there are a number of plausible theories. America is a young country: the media perpetuates this youth. We associate youth with vitality and life and creativity. It is difficult to grow up, assume the responsibilities of adults. These feelings about the supremacy of youth do exist, and it is important that we each take a closer look at our stereotypes and myths with regard to age. How do they help or hinder as we go about developing new life patterns? Whatever our concerns about age and how growing older helps or hinders us, it is certain that new career and work patterns are being developed by women. Becoming acquainted with our loudly spoken or quietly held beliefs about age can help us discover whether we are taking refuge in them and how these stereotypes about age may be limiting our personal development.

It would be unrealistic to claim that the world of work is as open to women over forty as to women who are in their twenties or thirties. Women in their early twenties sometimes experience an age bias, manifesting itself by having an aura of immaturity automatically associated with their youth. But by and large when we are under thirty, we do not bother to hide our age. As we near thirty, however, we do begin to feel the approaching of "age" upon us. Often suddenly, we begin to feel as though our youth is slipping away and we become involved with trying to retain the *look* of youth. In fact, when we concentrate on age itself, we spend much time telling ourselves that we are too young or too old to do something that does or does not appeal to us.

When women speak of being too old to do something, we are reminded of the movie made for television and aired in the early '70s, starring Jean Stapleton and Ernest Borgnine. Ms. Stapleton and a group of close women friends in the neighborhood decided to form a "consciousness-raising" group modeled on that of her youngest daughter's group at the local college. One of the women subsequently decided to return to school and a friend remarked that she would be fifty-five before she graduated from college. The first woman responded, quietly, "I'll be fifty-five *anyway*." The exchange is not profound; in fact the truth of the statement lends humor and perspective to the issue of age. Why must we be a certain age when we do things? Is there a specific age at which we should do and accomplish certain things? And if we are not of that age, is the possibility of that accomplishment forever lost to us? There are certain age restrictions on some occupations, but these restrictions are few and far between compared with the socially based norms that in the past dictated the appropriate activities for each age.

Age biases are becoming less widespread as the labor force has begun to recognize the advantages of maturity offered by the woman with some life experience. The possibility of rising to the top in a large corporation may be almost nonexistent for the woman returning to the marketplace after a long period out of the work force, but that would also be true of men; in fact very few people at all in a large corporation ever rise to the top. We are finding in some large corporations that women who have returned to the work force after spending some time out of it raising families are not necessarily anxious to rise quickly or to rapidly accrue additional responsibilities. They sometimes feel that they have had many responsibilities all of their adult lives, and now want jobs that expect a good day's work, but are left behind at the office. They are not shirking responsibilities if they are not anxious to supervise or manage others.

Other women are faced with age barriers to the type of jobs they would like; one option to that dilemma is to start their own businesses, do free-lance work, or enter a training program that will allow for ascending the ladder into management and supervisory positions.

THE HOUSEWIFE-TURNED-CAREER WOMAN

Newly created stereotypes surround the woman who has been working in her home, who may or may not have worked in the paid labor force many years ago, and would now like to enter the world of work. Often these stereotypes act as barriers to these "mature" women.

Many women in this position tend to devalue their skills and unpaid work experience, regardless of their achievements in homemaking, mothering, and in a myriad of volunteer jobs. Often lacking confidence in themselves, they are plagued with negative self-statements that reinforce defeating stereotypes. ("I'm too old; no one would want to hire me. Besides I don't have any experience.") With such prevailing thoughts, getting started can be slow and halfhearted.

Women rarely see a finished product for their work at home that can be evaluated or that endures. Meals cooked are eaten, a clean house is dirty the next day—often a child's triumphs are his own while his shortcomings are blamed on mother. She receives no monetary reward for her work and passing adulation. No wonder the woman who wishes to work outside her home finds little to recommend about herself. The thought of competing for jobs and promotions can be intimidating for a woman who is not sure of her abilities to start with and who has not had much experience in competition with others. She may question whether she can really manage a job *and* her responsibilities at home. And even if she could, she feels that it might be too late in life for her to try.

Prospective employers may also hold stereotypes that influence their acceptance of women seeking to reenter the work force. The homemaker may be seen as not being serious about her work. The belief is that she won't be dependable or invest herself in her work although studies suggest that she will be as dependable as fellow workers. She is also hampered by unflattering phrases such as, "reread," or "displaced homemakers" that have been used to depict women who want or need to seek employment outside the home.

Because elements of truth exist in stereotypes it is easy to accept them at face value, allowing an unchanging picture to dominate our thinking. Some of the difficulties that these stereotypes highlight reflect our perceptions of ourselves while others are a result of employers' perceptions of us; both must be faced and dealt with realistically.

PERSONAL STEREOTYPES

A quick way to zero in on our own stereotypes and to determine the ways in which they are limiting us is by completing the following sentences.

A woman's place is _____ .
A career woman is _____ .
A mother should _____ .
The husband is _____ .
A father should _____ .
Women and money are _____ .
The single woman _____ .
The best profession for a woman is _____ .
A man and a woman's world is _____ .
Children should have _____ .
Being feminine means _____ .
Being masculine means _____ .
The assertive woman is _____ .
My family expects _____ .
Working is _____ .
My friends think _____ .

There are other sentences you may wish to add, but these will give you a start.

How do you feel about the answers you have given? Are you satisfied with them? Would you like to change any of them?

The next step is to revise any of the statements with which you are displeased. State them as you would like to believe or feel. You might change the typical "A woman's place is in the home" to "A woman's place is anywhere she would like it to be."

The revised statements might be more consistent with how you would like to see yourself and the world. However, you might still harbor some doubts about the practicality or the reality of your now behaving in ways that are consistent with the thoughts expressed in the revised versions of your sentences. To trace down inhibitors that are preventing you from acting in accordance with the revised statements attach a *but* to the end of the revised statement and then fill in the blank in as many ways as you can.

A woman's place is anywhere she would like to be, but _____ . There are any number of possibilities that might follow the "but." You might feel that:

1. A woman's place is anywhere she would like it to be, but *not as a sportswriter in a men's locker room.* (Here we've gone for the extreme statement of where you may not want to be, not necessarily that no women should be there.)

2. A woman's place is anywhere she would like it to be, but *I don't know where I would like my place to be.* (You need to spend time considering your future options.)

3. A woman's place is anywhere she would like it to be, but *she should have her husband's approval.* (The word approval indicates that you feel that someone else should decide where you belong. In the situation where you wish to make your own decisions about the future, you would more likely discuss the options with your spouse and then come to a mutually agreeable decision.)

4. A woman's place is anywhere she would like it to be, but *I need to stay home with my young children.* (Fine, but don't ignore the future. You can use the present to prepare for the future.)

5. A woman's place is anywhere she would like it to be, but *I can't see myself as doing anything else.* (Do you want to do something else? If you do then get training in another area, or do some volunteer work in that setting so that you see yourself there, or find a group of supportive people who will encourage you to try other things.)

Continue to list as many reasons why you don't feel comfortable with your revised statements. Look at them realistically. See if they really hold up or if they are excuses for not changing, not doing other things you wish to do.

The fourth step is to list some possible changes or outcomes that might flow from acting in a manner consistent with your revised statements. If a woman's place is anywhere she would like it to be then _____ .

1. So is a man's.
2. I will have to think about and decide where I want "my place" to be.
3. I may have to get new training in order to go where I want.
4. I may have to overcome my own hesitancy and fears about changing.
5. My family might not like the choices I make.
6. I might like myself better.

The possibilities are endless.

The final step is to sort out the real restrictions from the imagined restrictions, to determine the changes you want to make in your perceptions about women in general and yourself in particular, and then chart a plan of action to accomplish those desired changes.

Self·Exploration: Your Guided Journey

❧

"Those who indulge *bulge*" is a sign that is prominently exhibited in a local gymnastic center for children. Obviously, too much sugar and starch could contribute to a bulge here and there, and to a less than perfect balance on the beam or the uneven parallel bars. But a would-be gymnast *should* indulge—in as many fruits and vegetables as she pleases and as much exercise as feels right; she would never add a pound or an inch.

It is time for *you* to indulge, to look inward, to begin listening to your gut and paying attention to your fantasies. Focusing on *you* in a thorough singleminded effort is essential to moving ahead. Censoring the time you spend on this self-indulgence will only limit your options and opportunities. We *want* you to bulge—not with inches and pounds, but with self-awareness, self-knowledge, and a heightened consciousness of where you are, what you have done in the past, and what you may plan to do in the future.

Who am I? An individual, with a past history unique to me, a present situation particular to me, and a future to be created that will be distinctly mine. Even after we gain comfort from knowing about the large number of similarities of feelings and experiences shared by women of diverse ages, educational, social, and economic backgrounds, we return to the implicit fact that no two of us are exactly alike. And even when sharing in the same process of self-exploration and -examination, no two of us come to the same conclusions about ourselves.

Each of us has developed a filter, or framework, unique to us, through which we see and judge the events of our lives. It is our means of organizing and selecting everyday happenings, in order to cope with the tremendous number of options that are continuously being presented to us or confronting us.

This mental framework, by which we judge events and live our life, is a little different for each of us. For some of us that framework would be described as our *values*. For others, it is defined as "attitudes" or "interests" or "learning styles" or "prejudices." (It is not just a matter of the same concept being called different names; each of these concepts indicates a subtle difference in how our framework—or views of the world—developed and how that framework is used by us to live our lives.) Each of us makes our choices based upon our own particular framework. And from each of these frameworks we see life a little differently; we have a slightly different set of words or phrases to describe the same situation, and these various words or phrases stimulate us to act or respond to life in a certain way. Some of us find it easier to contemplate our future goals when they are discussed within the context of exploring our "values." Others find it easier to talk about the future in terms of the development of our "interests."

Here we need to stop and ask ourselves: "What is our particular framework—or how do we see life?" Which words or phrases make the most sense to us when we are talking about planning for our future? Do we want to explore our "values?" Are we concerned about clarifying what our real "interests" are? Do we seek to find our future *"directions"*?

In *Individuality*, by Leona Tyler, George Kelly has described the importance of realizing that although we share many common experiences with other people, each of us has an individual way of viewing those experiences. We are encouraging you to use your own individual framework in viewing life's events, rather than trying to adopt the framework of someone else. It is when a person does not have a solid sense of self or when they are not pleased with who they are, that they succumb to assuming someone else's view of the world. For example, teenagers, who are in the process of discovering their identity, are easily influenced by the values, beliefs, and perceptions of their peers. Or they may choose to emulate a favorite teacher, rock star, or guru, and for the moment those ideas and beliefs become their own. It is by sifting through the various identities they assume that a unique one of their own emerges.

Kelly describes these individual frameworks as "transparent patterns" that we ourselves have created and then use to "fit over the realities of which the world is composed." These patterns for viewing the world may not be perfect. But trying to sort out our life without a pattern of our own to follow would be like a sailor trying to navigate by the stars but having no knowledge of how to find the North Star or without knowing the differences between winter and summer skies. The sailor would look up at the sky and see only a mass of stars. Through experience, this sailor might develop his own pattern for navigating by the stars, but if he is going to repeatedly find his way from the starting point to his destination, he will have to develop a "pattern" for doing so.

A number of women who have been involved in the exploratory classes we teach have mentioned that they have shared and even worked through the exercises with other women who were not enrolled in the class. In a recent class one woman mentioned that her mother called her as soon as she returned home from class each week to see what had been discussed and what exercises had been assigned. The mother went out and got a job just before the last session. At the same time she suggested to her daughter that she now felt that maybe she, herself, would like to enroll in a course similar to the one her daughter had taken. The daughter told her mother that she had already taken the course, through her. And in fact, she *had* done significant processing along with her daughter.

Two other women mentioned that they did some of the exercises with their children who were in their teens and early twenties. In none of the cases did the women set out to "instruct" their friends or family, but in all the cases, the women discovered that the acts of sharing and processing with people close to them, and with other women in their classes, helped them to try out and finally to develop new and uniquely individual ways to think about themselves, their past, their present, and most important, their future.

In this chapter we are encouraging you to take a hard look at who you are right now, what you think about yourself, how you view your past, and then to develop a plan for what you want to be in the future.

First we want to help you discover what your own *pattern* is for looking at the events of your life and the world around you. What is your particular filter for viewing your own life? Do you say, "Whatever happens is for the best"? Or, "Life is always a struggle"? Or, "I can't plan for the future, things never work out for me"? Once you have some idea of your own filter, then we will point out ways of evaluating your filter and its limits and how you can grow and expand from your current base or framework. Our mental screens and filters are not set for all time. But they are the base from which we can explore various other filters or ways of looking at ourselves and our lives. We might want to alter the attitude of "Whatever will be, will be," so that we now say, "I can influence whatever will be, by the things I do each day." The second filter gives us a greater sense of control over our future. And in reality, the actions of each day do influence the events of the following days. If I am always saying, "*Tomorrow* I'll take the course in computer programming," I will never be prepared for the job I say I want in that field.

When looking at our particular filters, we cannot ignore our current age, because the older we are the more complex are the patterns of experiences with which we deal. But age is not the deciding factor. The eighteen-year-old woman may find it difficult to envision herself doing the work of teaching or being an engineer, just as the woman in her late twenties perhaps cannot see herself having and nurturing children and *not* being in the labor force. The forty-five-year-old woman who has raised a family may find it impossible to see herself embarking on a new career. And it may be quite difficult for the woman who has worked outside the home all of her life to see herself engaged in leisure pursuits. Most of us allow ourselves to remain locked into one frame of reference until we are forced to seek movement away from it. Even though we must be aware of the restrictions that age, education, monetary status, and the like might impose, they are not as restricting as we might like to believe. The individuality and the variation in the people we meet attest to the fact that a woman's view of herself and her future are partially dependent upon the way in which she has selected and prioritized her past experiences.

Let's borrow some examples for the computer field to further explain how the past influences the future and how present changes can significantly change our future patterns of behavior.

Over our lifetime we have "programmed" certain patterns of interpretation into our own memory bank. Subsequent events stimulate that particular pattern and we give our own unique interpretations to that event. The phrase "good worker" calls up from our memory bank a particular image. That image will vary from person to person. One person might see a shiny gold star over the head of a "good worker." Another person might find that the phrase "good worker" is synonymous with feelings of boredom and lack of creativity. But again, like the field of computer programming, we are not destined to maintain that particular image forever. We can "program" new images into our memory bank. It is desirable to maintain an open system so that we are not operating only on the past. We want to program our memory bank to accept and integrate new information. Until we open our memory bank to a new way of processing information we are tied to our old concepts. And living with the old concepts may be why it is difficult for individuals, who supposedly have any number of career and leisure options open to them, to make a choice from among the possible options. Their old frames of reference do not allow them to see themselves as engaging in those "options." The possible activities that are suggested by a friend or a counselor are not consistent with the person's past patterns or do not fit their value system, beliefs about self, attitudes about appropriate behavior, their learning style, or their past interests.

And to further complicate the issue, within our own particular view of life there is variation in how we respond to situations. The current research in psychology only gives some objective validity to what we already know about ourselves. Even within our own pattern of responses to situations there is diversity.

Leona Tyler further emphasizes the uniqueness of individuals in their pattern of responses to situations. She proposes that most people do not have only one way of responding, even to the same situation. Most people have developed a "repertoire of possibilities or controlling structures" that are appropriate for different situations or for the same type of situation at a different time. Our habits, strategies, personal attitudes, and the values that govern our choices are put together in different ways. We do not always respond the same way to the same situation or person.

Put yourself in the situation of having worn a new suit for the first time. A close friend whose taste you admire tells you that "it doesn't seem right for you." What is your reaction? Most likely you'll be disappointed and reconsider your purchase. But if another person whose taste you don't admire or whom you don't care for personally tells you the same thing you might dismiss the comment as not important to you. Or what if you have just chaired a meeting or a fund-raising activity and you hear a number of disapproving comments from others who participated? What is your reaction? Do you listen to the group as a whole? Probably not. If you want to be reassured or encouraged about your part, you usually pick someone who will do just that. If you want to learn more about the specifics the people who objected might want changed, you would probably approach those people. Different situations, your responses to different people, your current needs or specific goals will prompt you to pick out different responses from your "repertoire" of possible behaviors.

Being aware of the fact that each of us has a different, individual frame of reference by which we engage in our processing of information, we have found it advantageous to approach the work of exploring the present and future from a number of perspectives. We believe that future goals can be formulated most effectively by evaluating learning styles, patterns of interests, values, abilities, and competencies and by encouraging fantasizing and dreaming about future possibilities. These approaches, presented later in this chapter and the next, will encourage and enable you to process new information through your own unique filter or filter patterning. Then, by approaching your processing from a number of reference points, you'll also acquire the ability to think in a more creative way about yourself and your choices from among the almost limitless possibilities that do exist.

Let us take a minute to look at the word "creative" as used in the phrase "creative choices" or the phrase "creative solutions." We do not mean "other" choices or solutions. We mean creative! Let's consider a comparison that was made between two groups of highly qualified, well-respected architects and was reported in *Individuality*. One group was identified as "creative" by their peers. The other group was considered to be effective, competent, and even outstanding, but not "creative." The significant differences between the two groups was not a matter of ability, but was in the areas of motivation, self-image and style. This finding was repeated in other studies of professional persons. The creative architects described themselves as "inventive, determined, independent, individualistic, enthusiastic, and industrious." The noncreative architects used adjectives such as "responsible, sincere, reliable, and tolerant." Creative persons more often engage in the type of problem solving called "divergent thinking." The creative person sees problems as having no single right answer; rather they see problems as having a number of possible solutions. This style of thinking is contrasted with "convergent" thinking, which implies that there is one right answer. Divergent thinking can be learned, and is helpful in creative problem solving and in future-planning endeavors. The "brainstorming" technique of problem solving, in which a large number of possibilities to a problem are generated with no censoring of thoughts, is an example of a divergent style of thinking. This process is particularly powerful for individuals and groups, once it is clear that no comments and no evaluations will be made on any stated ideas.

STAGES OF SELF-EXAMINATION

It is useful to know that in your process of self-examination you will go through various stages. We have found a moderate amount of self-pity to be a normal prelude to beginning the process of looking at yourself and to making new plans for your future. During the initial stage you may have feelings or make a number of statements about the ways in which you feel that your life is not as you would like it to be. You had hopes and dreams that were not fulfilled. You had expected more of yourself, now or when you were younger. You feel that your education was a waste because it was so long ago. Or you regret not having continued your education. You are disappointed that you have so submerged your needs to those of your husband or family that you have forgotten what they are. You might be disillusioned with your work or career choice or lack of either. You are afraid of the future, or intimidated by other "successful" women. You are insecure about their own abilities. You have undergone separation, death, or divorce. Above all, there is the need to get these things out in the open. You need to have aired these "pent-up" feelings before you get on with the process of building the future. And undoubtedly you are very much interested in planning for the future. You do not desire to dwell on the past, only to recognize and verbalize what it held.

After these initial statements of discontent, you are ready to begin the second stage with fresh vigor and enthusiasm. The time needed for this initial stage of self-pity varies from person to person. Some women do find it more difficult than others to develop a plan of action, for this plan of action will call for some amount of commitment. Some women find it difficult to make the leap from reevaluation of what they *have* and *want* to the point of commitment to the specific plan of action necessary to reach their goals. (Is this not the case for all of us?) We all have some hesitancy at the thought of venturing out into an uncertain future. But some of us have had more experience than others at taking the leap into the unknown. Some of us have met with enough success when taking risks that we are *less* hesitant to move on to a new situation.

Once we have tired of self-pity we begin the real process of exploration. But each of us must decide why we are hesitating. It is important to be aware of the "what" that is holding us back. Knowing that to hesitate *is* normal and experienced by most of us does encourage us to engage in an increasing number of risk-taking behaviors, so that we can make a manageable movement from the stage of exploration into the stage of implementation—the move from thinking and planning to creating and doing.

HOW WE LEARN

It is important to explore your feelings about learning and to take a close look at how these feelings impact the development of your life and work patterns. One woman, Cathy, who attended one of our classes, was an extremely capable secretary in a large corporation. She was approached by the manager of her department and asked if she would be interested in participating in their eighteen-month manager training program, which obviously would mean making a career change within the company. She would have a completely different job title and responsibilities, a significantly higher salary, and a chance for advancement, usually outside the expectations of future growth possibilities for secretaries. Surprised at being offered this opportunity, Cathy began to experience feelings of extreme trepidation, certain that other women would be more qualified than she and more capable of completing the training program. Her insecurity stemmed partially from her minimal college experience; she believed that a college degree was necessary for success as a manager. In her own words, she doubted if she was "smart enough" to accept this opportunity. She was afraid, as are many women offered promotions, that she would look stupid if she didn't ask enough questions. The only other woman that she was aware was also being offered this opportunity had a college degree. She later discovered that this woman's degree was in religion, and that she felt no more secure about potential success than Cathy did.

As Cathy explored further her state of near panic about this pending decision, she realized that her fears were largely a result of inadequate information—not knowing any other women managers, not knowing anyone who had completed the training program, not knowing what her responsibilities would be after the training, not knowing what a manager did in terms of day-to-day responsibilities, and not really knowing what was actually involved in the training. She was on the brink of making a major career decision without even the minimum amount of data necessary to make this decision. She conjured up in her mind images of rows of desks, thick textbooks, and exams with red ink slashed across the pages, all reminiscent of her worst experiences with learning and school. Clearly Cathy associated the learning that would transpire in the training program with her memories of formal classroom situations, and these negative associations came very close to preventing her from accepting a wonderful new challenge.

To explore your own feelings about learning, answer the question, "When was the last time you were involved in a situation that required a significant amount of learning?" Take a moment right now and think about that question. See if you can focus on a specific example or situation before reading on, in order to begin the process of getting in touch with your feelings about learning. Your responses may run the gamut from references to undergraduate school, night school, and classes at the "Y," to the answer that you have not been involved in any situation that required learning since you graduated from school (high school, college, graduate school, training programs). Most women, upon first hearing the question about learning, assume that we mean formal, academic learning situations. The fact is that a significantly large amount of learning takes place once we leave the confines of a traditional classroom situation. Consequently, your next question is, "When was the last time you were involved in a situation that required a significant amount of learning that did *not* take place in a classroom, and was *not* associated with formal education?"

Now, take another moment and try to come up with a response to this second question. What effect does this question have on your feelings about learning and education?

We always encourage women to examine their life experiences to determine how they learn, under what circumstances they learn best, with the most ease, and with the greatest degree of success and personal growth. The responses are most interesting, as competitiveness is eliminated and replaced by mutual interests and concerns. ("I learned how to make crepes and bread." "I learned how to adjust to a new city and find my way around." "I learned how to find a job without reading the want ads." "I learned how to integrate working with parenting and not experience tremendous guilt." "I learned how to cope with my husband's being out of work just when I got a promotion." "I learned how to remain sane when I had two little children under the age of three." "I learned how to handle comments at work by men who would rather relate to me as a sex object." "I learned to consider nontraditional jobs such as carpenter or plumber in spite of negative comments from my friends and family." "I learned how to read a map and planned a cross-country trip without my husband." "I learned how to hire people who would not become quickly dissatisfied with their jobs." "I learned how to set up a neighborhood child-care center." "I learned how to coordinate the Brownie car pool with the hockey car pool and avoid a migraine." "I learned how to type and began typing my children's elementary school newspaper." "I learned how to locate the resources I need without always having to resort to the yellow pages." "I learned how to live with my mother-in-law/mother/husband/child/children!")

Each of these examples of learning experiences conforms to Webster's definition that learning is: "to gain knowledge, comprehension, or mastery through experience or study . . . to become informed." There is nothing in Webster's about how we are supposed to gain knowledge or mastery, where this learning is supposed to take place, or that learning is necessarily work-related.

As you become more aware of the breadth and continuity of your learning experiences, you will more frequently ask the questions, "How do I *best* learn?" "What is my personal learning style?" "What environment is the most conducive to my learning?" The next step in determining your learning style is to think of four learning experiences either inside or outside a formally structured learning experience, and analyze them in terms of how you learned, what you learned, and the environment in which your best learning took place. We are encouraging you to look for patterns in your most positive learning experiences that will eventually be useful as you create your life/work plan. The following are suggestions meant to further facilitate the learning analysis process.

How Do You Best Learn?

Do you learn best through the written word? (What do you like to read? Books? Magazines? Billboards?)

Do you prefer diagrams or pictures to the written word? (Do you have heart failure at directions for knitting a sweater or putting together a swing set?)

Do you learn best by seeing and observing?

Would you prefer to listen and learn by hearing?

Do you like to learn by listening to lectures? Do you like to reinforce your learning by taking notes? (Does your mind wander in a lecture soon after the introduction?)

Do you learn best by doing and experiencing directly, rather than by reading or talking to others or being taught? (Would you prefer a demonstration of making pizza or would you rather read the recipe and learn by making the pizza yourself?)

What Is Your Personal Learning Style?

Do you learn best when you are alone? (Or do you hear every noise and become distracted?)

Do you like to learn with a partner? (Or are you worried that she'll be smarter and learn faster?)

Do you learn well in a group? Or do you find a number of other people detracts from the acquisition of knowledge?

Do you jump right in and start doing? (Or do you allow fears to hold you back?)

Do you think carefully and weigh the options? (Or are you more impatient, and go with the first alternative that is presented?)

Do you use your imagination and brainstorm many options? (Or do you stop with the first good idea?)

Do you approach your learning in a precise, organized style? (Do you have carefully marked folders or is everything in a drawer to be organized eventually?)

Do you banish your emotions from your learning state? (Do you try to remain calm when you have learned that your methods of repairing a leaking basement wall have thus far failed?)

Do you call on your emotions to help you learn? (Do you let your excitement lead you? Do you take advantage of ideas in the middle of the night, even though your notes in the morning turn out to be totally unrecognizable!)

Do you take risks in new learning situations? (Or do you let lack of experience with certain kinds of learning inhibit your attempts?)

Do you consult experts? (Or would you rather experiment and learn on your own? Do you experiment with making bread or do you wait for a class or demonstration? Do you try to learn a new sport on your own, or scout for lessons? Do you write articles for magazines or do you search for a class in free-lance writing?)

What Environment Do You Prefer?

Where has most of your learning taken place? (At home, at the library? Indoors? Outdoors? With other people? Alone? On the job?)

Do you like to be indoors or outdoors? (Can you learn in lovely weather or do you find that it diminishes your productivity and drive?)

Do you need space to learn? (Does the size and arrangement of your learning space matter to you?)

Does music help you learn? (Or is music totally distracting?)

Do you like a colorful environment in which to learn? (Or would you prefer a lack of color due to its potential for distraction?)

Do you like books at your fingertips?

Do you like other people around, or do you require silence?

Do you like other people around, but require them to be silent?

Do you like desks, pillows, arranged in rows or circles?

If you were to return to college/graduate school/training programs, which of the following would you choose, assuming the quality of education were comparable?

1. Lectures, small group discussions, seminars, papers, exams. (For many there is comfort in tradition, in structure, in predictability.)

2. Work/study programs with on-the-job training and classes at the work site and on campus. (The flexibility pleases some, causes others to feel pulled in too many directions, to wonder about what is expected of them.)

3. Lengthy small group seminar with a group facilitator, once weekly, with independent projects and study for the rest of the time. (The lack of structure would drive some people wild, and fits others' needs perfectly.)

The process of striking out in new directions is awesome to some, strikes fear in the hearts of others, and contributes to feelings of trepidation in almost everyone. Fear about our potential to learn can be inhibiting, can prevent new starts. Lack of confidence about our ability to learn can prevent us from attempting anything new, or from deciding to redirect our work life. Oftentimes traditional learning experiences may have prevented us from tapping our potential. We have been taught to believe that teachers will be able to recognize our aptitude and analyze our potential. Notable mistakes by teachers of Beethoven, Einstein, and Edison prove that not all teachers are quite as capable as that. Beethoven was described as hopeless as a composer; Einstein was dubbed mentally slow; and Thomas Edison was pronounced unteachable.

Unteachable perhaps, depending on the teacher, but certainly not unable to learn, to achieve, to develop, to grow to tremendous heights, given the proper learning conditions. The questions we should ask ourselves should no longer be: "Can I learn?" or, "Am I smart enough to learn that?" They should be: "How do I best learn?" "What other way should I try?" and, "What steps should I now take, considering my new awareness about my learning patterns, in order to achieve that goal?"

One woman analyzed her learning experience of moving to a new city when her husband accepted a new job, and learned a great deal about herself as a result of this learning analysis. Prior to examining her instinctive methods of approaching this experience, she assumed that every woman would approach transition to a new city in a similar, organized, methodical manner.

First Katie obtained a map of the entire city and adjacent counties, and studied the map in order to get her bearings. She had written to the local chamber of commerce, and received reams of material about the city and its educational and cultural opportunities. She ventured out from her rented apartment the first week to explore by car and foot the part of the city closest to where she lived. On subsequent days and weeks she explored other parts of the city until she knew the city better than many natives. Her newfound sense of security and belonging initially depended more on her geographical awareness than on meeting people or finding a job.

Katie enjoyed traversing her new hometown alone, without a thought of needing someone with her. She was not afraid of getting lost, which would have gotten in the way of her really getting to know the area. Her environment was the entire city, rather than books about the city, or speakers in classes designed to acquaint her with her new hunting ground. As Katie explored her other learning experiences, she began to see patterns in how she learned and in her personal learning style. These patterns became crucial keys to her life/work planning, to her changing perceptions of her strengths and capabilities.

Katie came to realize that she approached a new learning experience by jumping in and getting started, rather than by thinking too long about what might happen or where she might fail. She began to value her independence and her single-mindedness, qualities that were apparent in all of her learning analyses. She became aware that she loved operating in wide open spaces, disliked being sedentary, and thrived on being able to move from one work or leisure environment to another. These clues helped to guide Katie when she became more directly involved in life/work planning efforts. Flexibility and independence, together with leadership possibilities, needed to be built into her eventual career choice.

As women begin to analyze their learning experiences, they are more willing to "count" such experiences as being at least equally as valid as that learning which takes place in a classroom or formal structured situation. They often become aware of a subtle difference between these learning experiences. In traditional situations many of us were often required to memorize information and repeat it back, to learn to operate a machine and apply that knowledge directly, or to study data and know how to apply it. We were often expected to apply learning exactly as it was learned, or to adapt it to other similar situations. Women often choose to discuss learning situations, however, that require constant personal input, analysis, and change. Jean Baker Miller, M.D., in her book *Toward a New Psychology of Women*, discusses the complexity of the learning process that is required when women are involved in raising children. When parenting it is not always possible to directly apply learning from yesterday's to tomorrow's situation. What is effective with one child on one day often is not effective on a subsequent day. The parent is in a continuous state of reassessing what works best.

Many women have had extremely limited exposure to career options, having grown up mainly with awareness of traditional job choices for women. When you are questioning what career direction to take, you may decide to take some tests designed to measure both your interests and abilities. However, when analyzing the results of an interest inventory, you may discover that your interests still seem to be directed toward traditionally feminine occupations. You may then conclude that you are not really interested or qualified or smart enough for jobs that have not been traditionally open to women. However, it must be remembered that positive responses will often not occur in areas that are unfamiliar or that are stereotyped in your mind as inappropriate choices.

Many women also avoid chances for promotion or for new jobs. This may be because you are afraid of not knowing everything you need to know and of appearing stupid. Implicit in this thinking is the expectation that you are supposed to know almost everything in a new job at the outset. You may not assume that initially there will be time for learning, and that this time will be well spent in terms of eventual competence on the job. Many men who accept new jobs or promotions fully expect to have a learning period of a few weeks or months at the beginning of their job, a time when they are taking in more than they are putting out. They expect to ask questions, to study, to learn, to experiment, to make mistakes. They also expect that this learning period will reap benefits in terms of their competence, and in terms of their future career growth.

Look at John, who was an extremely successful sales representative for a company manufacturing computers when he was approached by another company that manufactured audiovisual equipment about making a job change. He decided to accept the new opportunity, confident that his sales skills were easily transferable to the new job, *once he learned* about audiovisual equipment. Though the company did not provide a training program, he negotiated for a four-week training program that he designed for himself. He spent the first two weeks in a television studio learning about the equipment that he would be selling, asking an enormous number of questions and admitting that he knew very little but was eager to learn. He spent the second two weeks with a successful salesman who agreed to let John accompany him on calls to clients in order to give him a feel for the clientele. After these four weeks of intensive studying and learning, John began to sell with a sense of confidence about both his products and himself.

Louise also made such a career change. She went into public relations with a bank, after having been an elementary school teacher for several years. She was subsequently recruited for a job in public relations for a local theater, a job which she accepted with a great deal of anticipation. Her new job was fascinating to her because of her love of the theater and her interest in amateur acting. But it was quite demanding, required significant learning in a variety of arenas, and bore little resemblance to her first job in public relations. Louise had learned, however, to give herself the gift of time . . . time to learn, to adjust to the new job, people, environs, and expectations. She no longer expected herself, as she had in her first job outside of education, to be able to jump right in and tackle a new job with finesse and expertise. She learned to be comfortable with not knowing everything necessary to the job, and with a process that allowed her to find out what she needed to learn.

Often women miss out on opportunities to enter nontraditional careers as a result of fear about how much there is to learn. A woman electrical mechanic, who was interviewed in a book called *Conversations*, by Terry Wetherby, talks about the need to learn to think mechanically. Lack of exposure and basic awareness do not mean that someone is unable to learn. They do mean, however, that learning will be basic at the start due to a lack of foundation in certain knowledge and skills. Another woman, interviewed in the same book, decided that she wanted to be a carpenter and prepared for the test required for entrance into the apprenticeship program. She bought books and studied the names of the tools and different kinds of screws so that she could pass the test and be admitted into the program. Her lack of background in carpentry necessitated this individual study. Many of the men who also applied for the program were sons of carpenters and had a basic familiarity with the equipment and how to use it. She became an extremely skilled carpenter after she completed the training program.

Richard Bolles, author of *What Color Is Your Parachute?* believes that enthusiasm is a crucial factor in getting a job offer, and in being successful in the career change process. A television vice-president interviewed in *Conversations* says that you should "jump with both feet into what seems exciting for you . . . the worst thing you can possibly do is program yourself into thinking it's difficult." It is important to pay close attention to the areas that excite you, and that charge your adrenaline, in order that you develop new directions in your life/work planning. *After* you thoroughly investigate these areas, sift out any lingering negative self-statements, and learn what you need to learn, then and *only* then will you be in a position to judge whether or not you are capable of learning what is necessary for you to become knowledgeable in the new area.

YOUR INTERESTS

Do you have the answer to the question, "What do you want to do next year, in five years, in ten years, for the rest of your life?" To begin to answer this question it is helpful to ask another, more specific, one: "What do you like to do?" Of course your interests are not the only parameter to consider; however we believe that life planning decisions based on an individual's interests will most likely result in more satisfying career decisions. Though this may seem obvious and simplistic, we have found that many people who report being unhappy in their work rarely gave strong consideration to what they would really like to do when they first became employed.

Emily, who had been a successful real estate agent for three years, enrolled in a career development course because she was unhappy with her work despite her successful work record. Because she had been determined to do well, Emily overcame her shyness and learned to use persuasive selling skills in her real estate work. She sacrificed weekend and evening time with her family in order to be available to her clients. Although she did not particularly enjoy her work she did feel a sense of satisfaction and strength in her ability to master the skills necessary in her job.

Emily's increased self-confidence resulted in her desire to search for a new career, one in which she could feel more interested and enthusiastic. When asked how she had entered the real estate field in the first place, she replied, "A neighbor of mine decided to take the course and didn't want to go alone, so she asked me to take it with her. I didn't know what I wanted to do and besides, I never thought I would pass the licensing exam." Many women have discovered that people close to them have influenced them in a similar way. This time Emily wanted her decision to be self-determined rather than allowing her life's path to follow a direction that may have been right for someone else, but not for her.

Begin an exploration of your interests by taking out a pen and paper and doing the following. List anything you have enthusiasm for or that you really enjoy doing. It need not be something that you do daily, weekly, or even yearly. One class participant, Emily, had thought so often about what she *had* to do or *should* be doing, that it was a treat to think about what she enjoyed doing. Her initial list looked like this:

Things I Like to Do
Reading
Baking

Sewing (mostly for my daughters)
Discovering new places to visit
Entertaining friends
Sight-seeing
Camping with my family
Sleeping late on weekends
Snow skiing
Taking long walks
Learning about the history of my city
Trying new restaurants
Quilt making (using old patterns I discover)
Drives in the country
Writing letters
Researching facts
Swimming
Visiting relatives and friends (at home and in other cities)
Planting a vegetable garden
Watching sunsets
Writing letters, short stories for my children, articles for a volunteer organization I belong to

The second step is to think more about each item you've listed and then to jot down further details about each interest. For example:

Reading—fiction, historical novels, books on crafts, tour guides, and travelogs

Sight-seeing—zoos, museums, monuments, presidents' homes (have visited ten already), historical sights, famous battlefields, national parks

Entertaining friends—being a good hostess, making my guests feel at home and welcome, planning things to do that are fun and different (I had a "five senses" party and asked each person to bring their favorite things to see, hear, smell, taste, and feel . . . the results were hilarious)

Writing—letters, keeping a diary of our travels, scrapbooks complete with descriptions and captions

By being more specific about the details associated with each interest, you will learn a great deal about yourself. Emily learned to identify her preferences and became aware of some common themes as they emerged. She began to identify herself as a person with great love and knowledge of history, a fascination with places, and an ease with people. She saw herself as someone who gets satisfaction from keying in on the many diverse aspects of an interest and synthesizing them into a whole, such as planning social events or trips and organizing scrapbooks.

The final phase of this exercise is a little more difficult and you might find it beneficial to do with a few friends. The task is to brainstorm all the possibilities you can imagine that would utilize several of your strongest interests or interest patterns and could conceivably relate directly to your eventual employability.

Emily did ask the group to brainstorm with her. With each suggestion from the group, Emily found herself saying, "I don't have enough education for that kind of job." Or, "Such opportunities do not exist at all." Or, "Surely I don't have enough experience to do that." It quickly became evident that her negative self-statements were inhibiting the flow necessary to generate new ideas. By putting those thoughts aside and struggling to adopt an "anything goes" attitude, Emily was able to generate an impressive list of options for her personal and career development that were directly or indirectly related to her interests. Her list included:

Become a tour guide for local group catering to conventions
Restore old houses
Write travel brochures
Become a travel agent
Work at visitor's bureau
Work at convention center
Become a goodwill ambassador
Work with historical society
Open a country inn
Create a party planning service
Join the Welcome Wagon
Plan special events for shopping center, museum
Offer service to help new families adjust to move to their city
(perhaps a service offered by a large company)

Become a museum curator
Write visitor's guide to city
Write articles about places of interest, restaurants
Develop column for entertainment for local paper or magazine
Plan banquets and meetings for local hotel
Develop service to entertain wives of businessmen

Appealing work settings, such as the historical society and the convention center, were listed, even though the group felt uninformed about the variety and kinds of work done in these places. A subsequent step would be to research that kind of information. Emily was nowhere near a final answer to her career decisions, but she certainly had some ideas about where to begin. She felt energized and excited about these new possibilities, since she had been utterly convinced that she had no alternatives. She was on the way to building a career that would incorporate her interests into it.

Another woman felt that she had no choice but to return to school for another degree. Plants and flowers particularly interested Cindy, but how this interest could help her generate needed income baffled her. She and her group brainstormed a list of jobs related to this area. They included:

Open a florist shop
Work in a florist shop making flower arrangements
Start a plant-party business (run on the same concept as Tupperware)
Become a plant decorator for private homes and offices
Work for a nursery, propagating and caring for plants
Work in a home and commercial landscaping business
Return to school for a degree in horticulture
Teach courses on plants at high school adult education classes
Grow plant cuttings and sell through sales advertised in local paper
Open fresh flower outlet in grocery stores
Temporarily volunteer at botanical gardens, receiving training that could directly apply to a paying job

This list provided the impetus to new ways of thinking and promoted an openness for Cindy to consider all kinds of ideas.

Her final decision was based on her interests but also included careful consideration of her abilities, financial situation, and life style preferences. She and another woman became partners, and with the emotional and financial support from their husbands, they started a unique flower business. They purchased fresh-cut flowers wholesale, bundled them and hired college students to sell them on busy street corners during evening rush hours and on weekends and holidays. It was a business that required minimum financial commitment, tapped her interest in flowers and utilized her skills in buying, managing, and following through on ideas. Her partner was an experienced bookkeeper who took care of that end of the business. They were able to run the business from their homes, a flexible arrangement that worked well since each had preschool children.

In time, their business grew, requiring the help of Cindy's husband on weekends and holidays. They expanded the business and purchased flower carts from which they sold fresh flowers at several large shopping complexes. Eventually the business literally "blossomed" and Cindy's husband gave up his job to join her full-time in the flower business. Subsequently, they bought out her partner and began to sell dried flower arrangements as well. And to think that the seed for this career path was planted in a short course on career exploration!

Another mechanism for exploring interests is to ask yourself, "How am I presently satisfying my interests, either in my work or in my leisure pursuits?" This may be an eye-opener, as you see how easy it is to let time slip by without doing those things you really enjoy. When answering this question, one woman wrote down that she loved active things like dancing, bike riding, team sports, and tennis. Perhaps "had loved" would have been more accurate because she realized it had been many years since she had done any of them! She had become a great spectator, attending and enjoying watching her children's activities. She had slipped into the habit of meeting these needs through her children and was clearly neglecting her own passions.

As a result, she has begun to ride her bike daily, an exercise proving to be good for the figure as well as the spirit. She joined a women's softball team, and was delighted when her family came out to root for her and watch her play. Class members are encouraged to think about many ways they could pursue their interests in their present or future through work, volunteer activities, leisure, or learning. Often, the process of uncovering repressed needs can have far-reaching results in determining future life/work patterns.

The ways we have talked about surveying interests so far have been subjective inventories, personal introspective journeys. There are several standardized tests that can help you gain additional information about your interests and can help you brainstorm alternatives. One that we sometimes find to be helpful is the Strong-Campbell Interests Inventory (SVII). This test is available at most school counseling offices, agencies, or from private counselors. The scales on this test are keyed to the responses of people who are successfully working in a variety of occupations. Scores on the SVII are an indication of how similar your likes and dislikes are to people working directly in specific fields.

For example, if your scores indicate that your interests are similar to the interests of physical therapists and dissimilar to those of artists, it is more likely that physical therapy or another related field would be a more satisfying occupation for you than a career in art. However, if your interests are similar to those of both physical therapists and artists, then you may find a job that combines aspects of both interest areas to be a better choice, perhaps art therapy or occupational therapy. It is important to remember that these scores are a reflection of interests and not abilities, so while you may enjoy music, you may not have a strong aptitude in this area. And it is particularly important to be familiar with the drawbacks of such inventories.

Many women only indicate interest in things they already feel comfortable doing, usually in the traditionally female areas. Although it is stressed that an interest inventory does not measure abilities to learn or to achieve, it is difficult to keep the results separated when studying test score charts.

One woman took an interest inventory in an effort to determine a career direction. Soon after having taken the test, and before the results had been reported, she was offered a job decorating windows in a local department store. The opportunity thrilled her, as she had a natural talent for color and design, though she had never worked in retailing before. Before accepting the job offer, she telephoned the instructor of her course to ask if interior designing had received a favorable score on her interest inventory. If it had not been favorable, she had actually planned to consider turning down the job.

In actuality, her scores on interior decorating were quite low on the interest inventory. Possibly, when she considered that field during the interest inventory, she had been thinking of decorating homes, ordering from catalogs, or spending a great deal of time in her car, none of which were to be part of the job at the department store. The test was accurate in assessing her reaction to her traditional stereotyped impressions of certain jobs, but could not assess her feelings and inclinations about related jobs in more specialized areas.

Using such inventories as the Strong-Campbell can be a helpful tool in learning more about yourself, but even their own manual explicitly states: "The SVII results will *not* tell you what career you should enter; in fact, *no* inventory or test can do that. Other planning and selection are outcomes of your own decisions and choices."

ABILITIES—STRENGTHS—SKILLS

In our work with women at various points along the continuum of life/work planning, we move from the stage of focusing on the multitude of interests most women have, to the stage of developing a specific delineation of the abilities, strengths, and skills that are apparent within each woman. An exercise that helps to emphasize these exciting skills in a nonthreatening manner is called "Ten Things I Do Well." Make a list of ten things you do well, being careful not to compare your capabilities with those of other women you know or imagine are more proficient than you are. The list can be drawn from any aspect of your life, including work, education, and leisure pursuits. It is particularly helpful to encourage the women to avoid excluding those things that *others* may not feel to be significant. Often this apprehension is unfounded, the women being genuinely impressed and supportive of each other.

One woman felt that making her husband's shirts (sewing) was nothing great. There was unanimous disagreement, as other women expressed their envy of that skill. Another woman wrote on her list that she listened well and was consequently sought out by friends for confidential help and advice. Somewhat embarrassed by this strength, she was unsure about whether it would "count" for the exercise, whether it was important enough. The root of her discomfort was that the skill had never been applied in a formal situation, and she also had heard listening described as a passive skill. Further analysis by the group emphasized the importance of her communication expertise, the total transferability of this to a multitude of work situations, and the redefinition of listening as being far more active than passive, requiring her total concentration and subsequent input.

The trick to the success of this exercise is two-fold. First, it is crucial not to censor the initial list. An executive secretary who was expert at organizing omitted that from her list because she wanted to change careers, to escape from this kind of work. A travel agent adept at handling telephone calls left this skill off her list because she had grown to hate the telephone. Besides, she assumed that the class would not value what she had written (the *real* reason). A former college English teacher who had developed a system for job hunting by analyzing the hiring process, left this area of proficiency off her list because she did not see its applicability to anything else. And because it was so instinctive she had difficulty standing back and seeing that it was an inherent ability of crucial importance. She eventually became a systems analyst in training at a large corporation without further "formal" education.

The second key to the success of this exercise, when done in a group, is to build self-esteem and to increase the ability to present oneself effectively to other people. The women, who are usually seated in a circle, state to the other women in the group one thing they do well. The person to whom they are speaking is encouraged to respond and ask any questions they wish. At first the feeling that they are bragging may inhibit their participation, but eventually the difference between bragging and valuing becomes obvious. The group leader responds supportively to the interchanges, encouraging awareness of eye contact, voice tone, and other nonverbal behaviors which may be unconsciously negating what is being said.

When you do not have a group of people with whom you can do this exercise, it is very helpful to stand in front of a mirror, in your most self-possessed manner, and state the thing you do best to your reflection. In fact since only your reflection is listening, go on and tell her about the other things you do well. And even better, have a tape recorder on when you talk to your reflection and then play back the tape. Repeat the process until you sound like a woman who is comfortable and sure about her abilities—a woman you would call assured, not arrogant nor a braggart.

For example, a woman may say, "The first thing on my list is that I can grow tomatoes," but she may accompany this with eyes on the floor and an uncomfortable giggle. Her nonverbal behavior is showing her discomfort with this sharing, and illustrates her questioning of the status of this ability in the eyes of the other participants. The facilitator might say, "Your voice tone is good, but I notice that your eyes are not directed at Susan." If this is stated with respect and support, the next interchange is less laden with ambivalent feelings. Though this is *not* a class in communications, specific feedback regarding patterns of communication is helpful. Though many women feel tremendous discomfort stating their skills and abilities to other people, this ability to present your skills with enthusiasm is necessary for successfully selling oneself for most jobs. Joyce was interviewing for an administrative position at a college, and made the statement that she was willing to learn, but that most of the procedures were new to her. The potential employer said in response, "You happen to be lucky. I am the best teacher around." Joyce was startled at such a statement, and instantly aware that she would never have had the "nerve" to say something so positive about herself.

For those of you not participating in a similar class, it is important to begin "rehearsing" saying positive things about yourself that, in fact, reflect the truth. You can begin by learning how to accept compliments without diminishing their effect. Whereas your normal response to a compliment about how well you organized the local political campaign might have been, "Oh, it was nothing" (when we all know it was *not* nothing!), your changed response can be, "Yes, organizing is one of my strengths, and I was really proud of how well it came off." When something you have worked on turns out especially well, make a point of calling a close friend and sharing your pride in your accomplishment. And pay attention to the words you choose to share your experience, replacing "humble" ones with more straightforward ones. Remember the teacher who said, "I am the best teacher around!"

What are skills? *Webster's* offers three definitions, including:

1. The ability to use one's knowledge effectively and readily in execution or performance
2. Dexterity or coordination especially in the execution of learned physical tasks.
3. A learned power of doing something competently: a developed aptitude or ability

Many people, when they hear the word "skill" think of expertise in the crafts—carpentry, crocheting, painting, or the basic skills needed in entry level jobs, such as typing, shorthand, ability to work various office machines. Many personnel directors, placement people, and potential employers also think in terms of these skills when thinking of lower level jobs. When they are looking for middle management people they are often unaware of the specific skills necessary to accurately match the person with the job. Richard Bolles explains, in *Parachute,* that many skills are necessary in every activity, task, or role that is a part of every job a person holds. Consequently, since every job is composed of any number of different activities and tasks, very specific skill requirements could be delineated for each job.

It behooves us, then, to further differentiate between the kinds of skills that each of us has already as an integral part of our repertoire. Richard Bolles and John Crystal, coauthors of *Where Do I Go From Here with My Life,* state that every person has hundreds of skills at which they are proficient. The three kinds of skills described include self-management skills, functional (or transferable) skills, and work-content skills. Awareness of the differences in the kinds of skills can help us more easily categorize the necessary components of different jobs we may consider. It becomes easier to get a handle on specific job choices. Our increasing facility with questions asked of people working in these fields can give us the insight that we need to make a confident decision.

Self-management skills include what we may have in the past called personality or character traits. Someone who is enthusiastic or patient or reliable or spontaneous may be aware that these are indeed aspects of her personality, not realizing how crucial the presence and/or absence of these traits/skills becomes in specific situations. Punctuality may not become important until one gets a job at a radio station where at 8:40 each morning there is a planning session that lasts only fifteen minutes and is of utmost importance to the agenda of the day. Having a good sense of humor may be irrelevant until one accepts a job dealing with customers' complaints. Being flexible is important in some jobs, whereas the tendency to be less flexible and extremely structured is more helpful in other situations. Using initiative may be necessary in jobs that encourage independence, but it may be a hindrance in a line position where there is less opportunity to operate independently. There is an implicit assumption that these traits/ skills are unchangeable, but this is not necessarily true. Someone with difficulty being assertive can learn to be more assertive with practice and guidance. Diplomacy can be learned with a good model as teacher, and poise and self-confidence can definitely grow and develop in nurturing situations.

Functional, or transferable, skills deal with information, people, and things. They involve action verbs (analyzing) in conjunction with information (analyzing the reports), people (analyzing their motives for doing such things), and things (analyzing the supply of a product in different parts of the country). These transferable skills (for a complete list see *Parachute*, pp. 206-224) are often the key to broadening career options, to determining new directions in life/work planning. Skill in communication is important in the family, in relationships, in businesses, in almost every potential work environment. Skills in writing can be used in publishing or reporting, and are transferable to a multitude of different environments that require the services of a writer, including museums, theaters, television stations, and training departments of companies. One woman wrote several books, and was subsequently offered a job to write and develop sales training programs. Another woman who taught English has also developed curriculum at a publishing company, done technical writing at a savings and loan, and is now considering a job writing training programs in a company that is in the process of expanding their training division. Being good at persuading and selling could be applied in any number of different tangible or intangible areas. Much additional information, specific content knowledge, would need to be learned and absorbed with each job change and added to the already existing transferable skill of selling.

Which brings us to the final category of skills—work-content skills, or those skills that deal with the learning and proficiency developed with certain subject matter or vocabulary. Witness training programs that teach this important specific knowledge. The potential carpenter usually needs to become an apprentice to learn the trade, as does a plumber or an electrician. Transferable skills are brought along to the new job together with the inclination and determination to learn what is necessary to do the job. The mastery of subject matter is obviously important. But lack of knowledge about a certain field, or of the intricacies of that field, need not preclude entry into it. Most people who start a new job find it necessary to master much additional knowledge even when the job is in their field. One man moved from vice-president of one company to president of another. The two companies were involved with totally different products, so there was a great deal to learn in the new job. But his transferable skills of organization, problem solving, and financial expertise provided the base he needed to operate effectively in the new job.

For a variety of reasons it is not always possible to adequately and accurately evaluate one's abilities. Sometimes an ability or skill may remain unknown because of lack of exposure to situations requiring the use of that skill. Perhaps fear of an entire area has prevented the exercising or learning of a particular skill. Many times potential skills remain dormant due to society's lack of support or varying expectations of women and work. Poor teaching or an unhappy learning experience, complicated by other factors, can lead us to draw inaccurate conclusions about our potential skills.

Often our perceptions of our abilities change drastically if we think about ourselves utilizing certain skills in an appealing work environment. Someone with a background in accounting may like certain aspects of the work, but dislike working in an accounting firm. This dissatisfaction with the work environment may lead to the conclusion that the accounting skills should be discarded. However, if this person could do accounting work in an environment that was exciting to her, such as working for a television station or working for a variety of small businesses, the skills may once again become more attractive.

Unfortunately, there are innumerable times when our misinformation or inadequate information about skills will obscure possible choices that could work for us. The overwhelming stereotype that prevails about being a certified public accountant (a C.P.A.) is that one needs to have extensive mathematical skills. One practicing accountant denied this vehemently, claiming that the prime skills are being able to analyze and to write good reports.

Another woman felt that if she could not write well, she was barred from the publishing field. However many good editors are much better at synthesizing, analyzing, and working with the writing of others than they are at writing. Specific awareness of the kinds of skills that one has can contribute to a much more accurate comprehension of the world of work, and eventually to a more realistic job choice. Being aware of the importance of skills along with developing a mind set in which we divide our experiences into the skills that are being utilized, can eventually help to expand options and opportunities in our life and work planning. After spending some time looking at our present skills, we are anxious to move on to the stage of clarifying our values, even though we probably would not call this stage value clarification if we were asked what our present concerns were.

VALUES

What are your values? Do you care? They do influence your decisions. To determine what your values are, do the following exercises. They may sound somewhat like party games, and are meant to have an element of fun. They will help you to be more specific about what your current values are (all values are not constant, some are situational).

> **1.** Answer the question, "Who am I?" Come up with at least twenty different answers. Don't bother to rank the answer from most to least important.
>
> **2.** If you were at an auction where values were for sale and you could buy the one you most wanted, which would you choose? Would friendship, freedom, beauty, love, health, or religious beliefs be one of your top choices?

3. Which side of this list do you feel more like?

a noun	or	a verb
high heels	or	sandals
steak	or	stew
lilies	or	buttercups
a stool	or	a reclining chair
a brisk walk	or	a warm bath
a crossword puzzle	or	a good TV program

There is not a right answer to any of these exercises, but they will help you to get a better picture of how you see yourself. These exercises can be a stimulus both for clarifying individual values and for clarifying how and if values fit into your frame of reference regarding potential choices. They bring to the conscious level of inquiry the elements that comprise your own value system.

A value system has been defined as a rank ordering of ideals, of values in terms of importance to the person doing the rank ordering. Gordon Allport defined value as a "belief upon which a man acts by preference." (Allport *certainly* meant the generic "man.") Values are also implied when suggesting one preference over another, or when describing what is desirable or preferred, or when stating one's anticipation of an outcome or preferred behavior. But according to Leona Tyler, "value" is commonly agreed upon as applying to a "firmly held belief that may govern preferences and choices of a fundamental, nontrivial kind."

Distinction has been made by researchers between instrumental and terminal values. The terminal values are end states of existence or end points such as security, peace, or freedom. Instrumental values are described as modes of conduct through which end states are attained, such as being honest, ambitious, or responsible.

Values are guides that determine action, attitudes, the way we present ourselves to others, evaluations, judgments, justifications, comparisons of self with others, and attempts to influence others. Values serve many functions. They help you to adjust to your life experiences. They provide knowledge about yourself. They help you to defend behavior that may be misunderstood by others. They give you goals toward which you can work. They can give a meaning or an order to your life. This attributes great weight to values; members of the social sciences have long been concerned with values. Anthropologists seek to determine the values of cultures they study. Sociologists use the concepts of values when analyzing a society. Psychologists are concerned with the ways individuals use values, as a key to their behavior. Keep in mind your answers to the initial clarification exercises as we help you define which values, both terminal and instrumental, are influencing your behavior.

"WHO AM I?"

How many ways are there to answer that question? (Exercise number one.) A multitude. We make that discovery each time we give that exercise. And the differences are not only in the specific answers given, but in the *way* in which the answers are given. The women are told not to put them in order of importance. They may be asked to do so later.

Some responses have been: "person," "wife," "woman," "mother," "daughter," "salesperson," "neighbor," "student," "athletic," "quiet," "shy," "outgoing," "lover of animals," "good listener," and so on. Some women are pleased with most of their answers; some are not pleased with many of their answers and wish they had different responses on their lists. It is important to realize that the answers given are the results of choices and preferences made at some earlier time. When these exercises are done in a group, the women are anxious to discuss their choices with the others in an environment where everyone knows that the goal is to assess where they have been, how they feel about themselves, and to move into a future with a strong, positive self-image.

An interesting trend over the last five years is that more and more women coming to the seminars are more often giving answers such as "person," "woman," and "individual" than previously. But we find that it becomes very clear to the woman and to the instructors whether or not the woman is pleased with the choices and preferences she has thus far made. Two women can respond "mother," "wife," and "nurse," in that order, and have very different feelings about the place of those answers within their value systems. One may feel proud and sure of her priorities, while another may feel that objectively she is mother, wife, nurse, but right now feel that these roles are not really high on her priority list. She may even be ambivalent as to how or with what she wants to replace these responses. Through the processing that takes place in the course it often becomes quite clear whether she does want to replace or reorder her list and in what way she plans to do so.

"Are you more like a noun or a verb?" (Exercise number two.) You might have chosen "verb" because you see yourself as free, independent, and adventurous, while another woman might make the same choice, but describe herself as "wishy-washy, flighty, dependent on other people." It is the action of stating the reason for the choice, not the choice itself, which clarifies the values held. The different patterns of experiences of two women may lead them to the same choice, one from an absence of, and one from a possession of independence. The question that can be posed to the woman "admiring" independence is, "What other values may be in conflict with your choosing to behave in a manner consistent with your choice of independence?" The way in which we act independently may vary for each of us. To one person it may mean taking a vacation alone, to another it may mean deciding which movie she wants to see when asked by someone else; to another it may mean making a choice that may not be popular among her peers. The decision to stay home and have a family or the decision to go to work while one has young children, both may be choices resulting from an exercising of independence. It is the processing of the information that is unique to each of us and brings us to unique personal decisions.

"Going, going, gone for six hundred dollars to the lady with a flower in her hand." If you were to choose one value above all others, which would it be? (Exercise number three.) If you had to give up all values except one, which would you choose to keep as being the most important to you? Would it be health, freedom, family, or something else? This exercise more than some of the others brings out the relationship of past experiences to present choices. Many women choose health as the one most important value. The "If you've got your health, you've got everything" commercial wins six out of ten times. And this choice is not necessarily made by the "older woman." The choice is often made by those who have either experienced poor health themselves, or have had a person close to them suffer from poor health. Yet not all who have had a serious accident or health problem choose health. One woman chose faith as being more important. She felt that faith could overcome everything. Another woman chose freedom, because she was currently experiencing a need for greater freedom and independence from her current situation. She saw her choice as open to change in the future, depending upon changing circumstances.

The approach used by most women in making the choice is the "bargain hunter's stance," which is "get the most you can for your money." Try to pick the value that in some way includes the other values you prize. The plan is to pick the value that seems most basic. ("If you have _____, then you might be able to get or do the others.") This exercise does help one to decide which are terminal values and which are instrumental values. "If you have your health, then you have the possibility of attaining happiness, or success. But if you are not healthy, then it is difficult to think of anything else," is how one woman explained her choice. With this exercise, as with those above, some women made different choices after hearing the rationale for another woman's choice.

SITUATIONAL VALUES

As we mentioned earlier, some value choices depend on the situation of the given time, and possibly upon responsibilities we currently have, but may not have needed to be considered at an earlier time or attended to in future decisions.

If you inherited a large amount of money, tax-free, what would you choose to do with it? Spend it? Save it? Invest it? Give it away? Rank your choices. Observe the relationship of one value to others within your own frame of reference. Do you have only yourself to consider, or must you provide for a parent or send children to college? Does security come first, followed by the freedom to spend? Do you feel that the possibility of a greater return on your investment outweighs the possible loss of the initial investment? Does that mean you are willing to take calculated risks? Personal preference may give way to other responsibilities.

If you were offered exactly the job you wanted in another town, would you take it and move your family? Turn it down? Or would you choose to commute? This and similar exercises can be found in Ruth Osborn's *Developing New Horizons*. What is your order of preference and what values would you place on your choices? Even the discussion of possible decisions gives you insight into how your decision relates to what you would "really" like to do. And again, the reality of your particular decision influences the hypothetical choices. We are finding that transfers that are related to the woman's job are increasing (although minimally), and not only among young, dual-career couples without children. And conversely, transfers related to the man's job are decreasing slightly. The possibility of diversity of such options is increasing, even if minimally.

WORK-RELATED VALUES

If you were able to choose those factors that are most important to you in a work-related setting, what would they be? Many careers and jobs are chosen on that very basis. Ask yourself the following questions: What do I want from a job? Interesting work? Would I take a lower salary in order to be involved in a job of great interest to me? How much of a decrease in salary would I take to get that interesting job? Where would I draw the line and look for a job with greater interest to me, but one in which the salary is still sufficient? And if I take a job less interesting to me, what other compensations do I want from it? Do I want to be in a job with lots of status among my peers? Do I want the job to offer me sufficient leisure time to meet family responsibilities? Do I need summers off? Do I want a job that is routine, with no worries or responsibilities once I leave for the day?

There are many questions to be asked that can be influenced as much by your values as by your interest in the job itself, and your attitude toward the place of work in your life. Another task in assessing your job-related values is to rate them on a scale of 1 to 10 and then to determine those that receive the highest rating and those that receive the lowest score.

You may find that some of your values are in conflict. Suppose the areas of greatest job interest prove to have little possibility of supplying the other things of value to you such as status, or the ability to begin in the job after minimal training, or job variety. You then must negotiate from among the list of your primary values to see which you feel you must maintain and which can be forfeited to some degree. You can decide which are situational, and may not be important at a later date, such as the immediate need for income or time for children. You may be aware that your need for self-esteem will be met if you go to work now, but there may be another impetus to your choosing to work at a later date.

Value patterns and interest patterns are structures for processing possibilities of action and of occupational selection. Also significant are one's patterns of rejections as well as one's pattern of preferences. Some interesting research by David Campbell, compiled over a fifty-year period of time, demonstrated that one's interests are often extremely stable components of individuality, changing very little in adults over long periods of time. This research lends some real value to the time you spend reaching into your past to assess what has influenced you, what your interests and goals have been, and to incorporate them into your future goals, and your life and work plans.

What's

Your Choice?

☙

It may be easy to decide you are ready to make choices, but quite difficult, in actuality, to do. It can be extremely helpful for you to gather all possible clues, in order to ease your process of choosing and help you to make decisions you either *want* or *need* to make. We have included a number of exercises and experiences that have proven useful to the many women we have worked with during the past several years. Try each of the following and see which are most helpful to you.

FANTASY: A PROBLEM-SOLVING MODEL

As mentioned before, one of the problems encountered when seeking change is the difficulty of getting out of your frame of reference and imagining yourselves doing something else, behaving in another way, or thinking differently about something. Most of us need a push in bridging the gap between what we see as possibilities and the almost limitless possibilities that do exist in the world. Divergent thinking is needed so that we can seek solutions to a problem rather than *one* solution to a problem.

One immensely successful way of increasing your frame of reference for your behavior possibilities is through the use of fantasy. As we recognize from our own childhood or from observing children involved in fantasizing, there are few boundaries to the imagination. When one is involved in a flight of fancy, minute details can be imagined and the most outrageous situations concocted. But as we grow into adulthood, it takes great determination on our part to retain our ability to fantasize, to prevent "reality" from taking too great a toll on our powers of imagination.

But all is not necessarily lost, even if your recent dreams have been limited to the practical and the necessary. Your powers of imagination can be recouped and revitalized in order to be of help to you. It is essential that you use them to move beyond your present frame of reference. You can use these powers to insure the continual setting and meeting of new challenges that will encourage your continued growth.

One challenge to your imagination is the exercise called "Twenty-eight Dreams." Try listing twenty-eight things you want to do or accomplish or that you have begun but not yet accomplished. Possible responses might include: fly in a two-seater plane, take piano lessons, learn to ski, finish a degree, begin a degree, get a job, have a professional pedicure.

For many women, this is a difficult assignment. Once they have written down the *major* things they want to do, such as go to Europe or go to work, they find that there are few other things they really want to list. After you have identified your major responsibilities, don't give up. Stick with the task and concentrate on all those small, seemingly inconsequential things that could easily be done, though you may rarely allow yourself to do them. Take a nap in the middle of the day. Call a friend long distance. Study a musical instrument. Allow your "ridiculous" as well as your "practical" hidden wishes to be acknowledged. Try not to let your dreams be limited because you imagine that age, monetary status, educational level, talent (or lack of it) are significant handicaps. Push on until your list numbers twenty-eight items. Force yourself to dream. The frequent brainstorming and sharing of these dreams either with one other person or in a group, will promote broader, more creative and honest thinking.

This exercise is particularly helpful to women who have been involved in family care for quite a few years. Such women have often encountered great difficulty when asked the question, "What do you want to do in the future?" or, "What do you like to do?" They have done and enjoyed a great many things. But most of their past activities have been husband- or child-centered.

Even if a woman enjoyed the activities, they were frequently initiated as a result of the children's or husband's preferences. She may have temporarily forgotten what she, as a separate person, likes to do. Or perhaps she finds that the things she liked before she was married and had children or that she enjoyed in the last ten years no longer hold the same interest for her. She needs to remind herself of her personal dreams and interests apart from her dreams and hopes for those close to her. And, as we have mentioned before, the age of a woman is not the major factor between being able to separate personal dreams and goals from family dreams and goals. The difference seems to center more on the woman's ability to recognize personal goals as positive and healthy rather than selfish and taking away from others. It centers on her being able to focus on herself when considering her future.

Many single women seem to have goals that are more work- and career-related. Often they can envision themselves moving up in their present job, or changing jobs or fields. Many dreams of single women still do include the possibility of marriage and family. But perhaps the biggest breakthrough in the past decade is that single women are beginning to define themselves in categories broader than "unmarried" or as having "such-and-such a job." They are setting personal goals that could accommodate marriage, but that would not necessitate it. However, many single women, interestingly enough, do some-times have some problems in fantasizing personal accomplish-ments and growth in leisure-related activities. Separated, widowed, and divorced women with children often clearly see the need to define personal goals, apart from child-centered goals, more clearly than do married women with children. And often when these women remarry, they retain the *need* to continue setting personal goals.

After completing your list of future dreams, divide it into two categories: the possible, and the truly impossible. We have found that women place very few of the items on the impossible list. And of that "impossible" list, some of the items are placed there because the women may feel that they do not want to exert the time, money, or energy necessary to reach that goal at this time in their life. For one woman, one such item was playing the flute with an orchestra. She eliminated this item because of the inordinate amount of work necessary to reach this goal. In the first place, she did not know how to play the flute (!) though she *was* musically inclined and played other instruments. She *could* envision the possibility of such an accomplishment. She could take flute lessons, and eventually join a community orchestra when she became adequately proficient. But other priorities in her life prevented her from considering it to be possible to work for this goal.

From the list of the "possibles," select one item that you can commit yourself to accomplishing or even just beginning during the next week. One woman selected "learning to crochet." During the week she bought the yarn and a book about crocheting, and asked a friend for help. Another woman had always wanted to take advantage of the department store demonstrations to have makeup professionally applied. She did it. A third woman, who had begun painting during a long illness, wanted to have a one-woman show of her work. She contacted a hospital that schedules such shows, and plans were set in motion. And a fourth woman who had never before treated herself to a real vacation away from the office, pulled out her dream of a Bermuda vacation and contacted a travel agency for information. Even just that contact was an important step, since this particular woman usually follows through after initial contacts of that type. As a result of this assignment you may begin to see yourself as a person taking some concrete steps toward accomplishing a goal or dream.

Included in the above exercise, when done in a group, is the use of the brainstorming technique of problem solving. The women are asked to select an item on their list, and to generate a multitude of ways in which they could accomplish that goal. Then as a group they are asked to do the same thing with another item. We all know that two heads can indeed be better than one when learning how to engage in divergent thinking. Try brainstorming with your friends and family and see how many solutions as a group you can generate for one problem. It is important not to *depend* upon other people to come up with solutions to your problems, but to learn how to seek help from others and then to make your own decisions regarding which solutions would be most appropriate to your unique situation. As mentioned before, in the brainstorming style of problem solving, all suggestions are considered. In fact, we encourage the proposal of outrageous suggestions. These seem to free the mental set and to set the tone for thinking broadly among the traditional as well as nontraditional solutions to problems and methods for accomplishing goals.

One woman wanted a degree in art that was available only from a college outside of her state. After generating alternative ways for her goal to be accomplished, she did put together a workable package. She was able to determine which courses would transfer from her local college and which courses she might take by correspondence or from individual instruction bases in her town. She was able to finish the remaining courses on that college campus during the summers. One summer, after discovering that the college rented dormitory space to families, the whole family went with her. She was able to plan numerous activities for the children in that locality as well as engage a mother's helper when one intensive short course was required. She did receive her degree, which was indeed a great thrill for her. And until that point, believe it or not, she would have described herself as an unimaginative woman. She would never have given herself the credit to come up with such a creative plan, much less to pursue it to completion. The key to her success was being able to fantasize multiple solutions to problems that she was confronted with while she pursued her goal.

Another beneficial task for you to try is this: Write a page or two on how you would spend a million dollars on *yourself.* Imagine that no one else will suffer from your spending this money entirely on yourself. Rather, others may actually benefit from this spending. This may sound like fun, but it may be difficult to stay with the specific task, to get to the point where you can even think about spending all that money on yourself! This fantasy will help you get in touch with your dreams and hidden fantasies. It can allow you to be quite specific about what you would do if all other responsibilities were accounted for. One woman shared her dream of starting her own horse farm and raising Arabian horses, since her first and longest-lasting interest has been with horses. Other plans included completing her education, traveling, doing philanthropic work, starting businesses, having groceries delivered, hiring a chauffeur, and last but not least, leasing an office for privacy, not just for work!

A more difficult task for you to work on now is:

Imagine yourself in a dream job. Describe a day or a week in this dream job in detail. Imagine yourself in a particular setting. Describe the setting. What does it look like?
What is the content of the work you are doing?
What kinds of decisions do you make?
Describe the people you work with.
How do you feel about yourself *inside* that setting?
How do other people relate to you?

This thinking can help you to crystallize the challenges you may decide to set for yourself, the information you may need, the people with whom you may decide to talk. You are the originator of this dream, *in* which and *for* which you can take total responsibility.

Now, take some time and begin to think about and plan what you hope to have accomplished:

In the next year.
In five years.
In ten years.
In fifteen years.

Next, divide your goals into the areas of:

Work-related activities (inside or outside the home).
Educational pursuits.
Leisure activities.
Other personal goals.

The goals and accomplishments of the first year would most probably directly relate and lead into the first five years, and so on.

Some women are hesitant to write down anything. It is as though writing ideas down means they have to commit themselves to those goals. They are hesitant to do that until they are "sure" that what they write is indeed right for them. Yet obviously such a fifteen-year plan is not an indelible road map. It is merely the initial charting of a potential journey. The first set of plans may principally involve learning how to distinguish between long-range and short-range goals, and perhaps to see how short-range goals can lead or make possible the accomplishment of longer-range goals. It is helpful to repeat this exercise frequently, as new plans and ideas emerge.

The use of fantasy can also be a good technique to handle the stress and tension that is often the by-product of steps you may be taking or contemplating in order to initiate changes in your life. You can begin by trying to identify the source of your stress as clearly as possible. It may be job-related, family-based, or centered around educational pursuits. Allow yourself to become aware of the physical symptoms that may accompany your discomfort. . . . headaches, stomach upset, insomnia. One use of fantasy is to enable you to imagine new and creative options for the handling of situations that are evoking stress. Another is to use fantasy to desensitize your reaction to the stressors in your life.

Find a place where you can be by yourself undisturbed for a period of time. Sit or lie down comfortably and relax your muscles. Imagine that a warm wave of relaxation is starting at your head and slowly drifting down your entire body. When you feel totally at peace, begin to imagine a situation that ordinarily causes you stress. As soon as you feel tension, stop your thoughts and give yourself a message to relax and go back to your peaceful state. With each successive fantasy, imagine yourself becoming progressively more relaxed in the stressful situations and envision yourself handling them with only a minimal amount of stress. Fantasize yourself handling the problem in as many ways as possible until you have become comfortable with one or two ways of dealing with the situation. As you begin to gain control of tension and stress, you will free energy that can be used in more positive ways.

In the last two decades more and more women have put themselves into stressful situations without learning how to deal with the stress in positive ways. Women who are in decision-making positions in the labor force are developing the same, often stress-related, diseases and physical reactions that men in those or similar situations have experienced. In fact, women have at times multiplied the amount of stress they must endure by expecting themselves to perform at maximum efficiency in all areas of their lives, both public and private. They are supposed to be the best worker, the best athlete, the best-dressed, literally the best at whatever they undertake. That is the ultimate fantasy. Perfection in everything. Now *that* is high stress.

THE "SUCCESS" INTERVIEW

One activity that we have found to be particularly helpful in career exploration is to select and interview a woman whom you consider to be successful. Doing this interview will help you tremendously in the process of becoming comfortable initiating contact with someone you may not know very well. A face-to-face interview with someone you previously considered "too successful" to want to speak with you will frequently result in an extremely enjoyable and rewarding experience. And the wonderful thing about this type of interview is that usually you need only come up with one or two questions; the other person will take it from there! Most people are quite willing to talk about themselves and to share their journey toward their own personal success. And participating in this interview may decrease the distance between you and "them," thus allowing you to acknowledge or develop goals you had not previously permitted yourself.

The person you choose may be someone you know, perhaps have briefly met, or only know about. When thinking about who to interview, define "successful" in a way that makes sense and seems valid to you. Write down or remember the positive statements that the person interviewed makes about herself, and watch for any patterns of behavior, thinking, decision-making, or responding to problems that may have been instrumental in her attaining success. Often a single phrase may be repeated in the course of the interview that may give insight into the reasons for her success.

You can use the following questions as a guide for your own questions:

1. What obstacles or problems did she have to overcome? (Yes, we are assuming there were some!)

2. Were there any role models that she was aware of on her road to success? Who inspired her, or presented options for her? (Parents, relatives, teachers, employers, others)

3. Did she have any mentors? Did she initiate a mentor relationship? (That is, were there people along the way who took a personal interest in her, provided guidance along the way?)

4. What choices did she have to make along the way? What alternatives did she consider?

5. What personal qualities that you admired emerged in the interview? (Did she put you at ease? Was she easy to talk with? Does she seem authentic? Was she enthusiastic?)

6. Do you still consider her a success? How does the reality differ from your impression?

7. Does she agree with you on the definition of a successful person? (Often those chosen to be interviewed are shocked that others perceive them as so successful.)

Earlier in the book, we explored some differences in perceptions about the word "success," suggesting the possibility of breaking down our image of success as an end product into subcomponents, each of which could be indicative of a smaller, but equally valid, success. ("Even though the class as a whole was nearly unmanageable, individual children made startling progress." "Even though the speech I gave was not as smooth as I had hoped, it triggered wonderful interaction among the audience." "Even though the profits were down for the month, communication has drastically improved and we are all set for the coming month." "Even though I was not as good at this job as I had hoped, I learned a great deal about the kind of work I want to do.") Through this interview we hope to decrease the distance you may feel between yourself and "those successful women." Participating in this interview is a helpful beginning to your career exploration and job-hunting processes. It will help you build self-confidence by narrowing the gap between you (what you know and are familiar and comfortable with) and "them" (what you are unfamiliar with).

The interviewing process is of crucial importance in determining where to work, the realities of the job market, and the possible job options. Interviewing becomes the key to combating the traditional, often humiliating and degrading, methods of job hunting through want ads and employment agencies. An initial interview that is based on a "mutual enthusiasm," one in which a person seeks out and interviews someone else with the same strong interest, is a beginning step to the job-hunt process.

The "mutual enthusiasm" interview is a nonthreatening one, one that will help you become more comfortable and confident in the career search and job-hunt processes. This is a perfect time to go speak with a photographer if you love taking pictures of children, or to a weaver if you have become interested in this art form. During this interview you can share your enthusiasm for a common love, and begin gathering important information about work options that may be possibilities for you. After experiencing the "success" interview and a few "mutual enthusiasm" interviews, it is considerably easier to begin contacting people who may have information to share with you about where you may decide to work. You will feel your intimidation begin to evaporate!

At a career development conference, one of the authors became acquainted with another conference participant after having spent the afternoon in a small town doing "mutual-enthusiasm" interviews. This man, Sam, had a deep love of sailing and traversed the town searching for another person equally as addicted. He was referred to the fire station from the sporting equipment store, and the fire station referred him to a doctor with an office full of patients. It turns out that the doctor spent all of his vacations sailing in the Caribbean, so the story goes, and would want to meet with Sam. When Sam asked the receptionist to buzz the doctor and tell him that he was visiting from out of town, was addicted to sailing, and wondered if he would want to spend a few minutes sharing a mutual enthusiasm, the receptionist looked at him as if he were crazy, as did the office full of patients! But she *did* buzz him, and the doctor *did* take a few minutes to talk with him. They concluded their repartée at dinner later that evening!

However encouraging the story of Sam's success on his first mutual-enthusiasm interview may be, many women find the "success" interview much less threatening. They see the prospect of a success interview as more possible to accomplish. They need to ask very few questions, and usually receive lengthy, enthusiastic responses from their interviewee. They feel more in control, and more comfortable with a specific agenda that they can follow if they wish. This sense of feeling in control is important to maintain throughout exploratory interviewing and even into actual hiring interviews. Having questions to ask, an agenda to follow, and an ease in the interviewing process are all important to the success of both the career explorer and the career changer.

There is an interesting origin to the existence of the success interview. One of the authors was talking with her grandfather, a wonderful man who had built a successful career in retailing. She wanted to know how he had become such a success and whether or not he had ever had any doubts about his potential success. There was over an hour response to those two questions, during which time her grandfather, with great enjoyment, detailed his earliest experiences as a traveling salesman, relating very specific memories of customers' reactions, particularly those who gave him constructive criticism. Even then, he interpreted their critical comments about his presentation as indications that they cared and wanted to help him. Instead of depressing him, they energized him and contributed to his eventual success. Throughout the recollection he repeated, "I always knew that I could do it," with variations such as, "It was only a matter of time until I owned my own store, as nice as those I am selling merchandise to." Those phrases demonstrated his tremendous self-confidence and optimism about his capabilities and his future success. He perceived few barriers to his success (just temporary setbacks) in spite of extremely hard times in the early years. His pleasure in remembering and sharing was the inspiration for the success interview.

Most people who are approached for an interview are as equally interested in sharing and require only a few initial questions to get started. The positive responses that are received are stimulating to the interviewer. Self-confidence is significantly increased with respect to the interviewing process. Subsequent telephone calls requesting twenty minutes of someone's time are easier to make after such positive interviewing experiences.

The initial response to our suggestion to do this success interview is usually hesitancy, partly due to discomfort with calling someone who is considered to be successful, and with the fear of imposing on someone else's time. When you stop to think of it though, wouldn't you be flattered if someone called you up and said, "I have a class that I am attending and I'm expected to interview someone whom I consider to be a success and I chose you. May I come and talk to you for a while to get some insight into your secrets for success?" The fact is that most people contacted are very receptive to the idea and willing to take the time to share their thoughts and experiences, even when they are only acquaintances, or perhaps even strangers.

The major barrier to your making that initial phone call may be that feeling that you are imposing on someone else. It can be overcome by asking yourself the question, "What is the worst thing that could happen, the worst response that I could receive?" This very question is helpful throughout the career exploration and job-hunt processes, whenever new contacts are necessary for generating new options. The worst response might be, "Don't be ridiculous. I have better things to do with my time." But this has *never* occurred in our experience. The most negative responses that we are aware of are: "Sorry, I would like to help you but I am too busy," or "Sorry, I do not have the time." And very few women have had anything but enthusiastic responses from the women they contact.

Interestingly enough, a number of the women chosen do not perceive themselves as successes, and may respond, "Who me? I am not a success; you should interview someone who is really a success, such as _____ ." If this does occur, then an appropriate response might be: "But you are a success in my estimation," and then be specific about why you are interested in speaking with them, and why you consider them to be successful.

To help you overcome any inertia you may be experiencing with this assignment, it may be helpful to share your intention to do a success interview with a friend or interested person. If you need help in generating alternatives, ask for ideas. Sharing ideas often helps to break down anxiety, and will present options that would otherwise have been left dormant.

One final help to decreasing the anxiety level preceding an interview request, both in groups and on a more individual basis, is to role-play the initial interview request as well as the interview itself. Often it is just the first sentence that needs to be conquered, just like the first sentence of a paper you need to write or a speech you plan to give.

The role-play can actually be authentic in a group, by having one woman in the group choose another that she admires and sees as a success. You, as an individual, can choose someone close to you that you are really interested in talking with, for your run-through. Pay attention, and ask for feedback on your nonverbal behavior that may influence and/or inhibit the success of the experience. Did you give the person time to think, without barraging her with questions? Are you looking her directly in the eye, even though you may be feeling slightly uncomfortable? Are you speaking shrilly, perhaps because of feeling nervous? Following the role-play it can be helpful to do a reverse role-play and allow yourself to experience what it feels like to be the person being interviewed.

One woman chose to interview her boss, a psychiatric social worker in group practice. (She was the receptionist and bookkeeper.) Another interviewed a neighbor who has six children and had returned to school. A third interviewed a cousin who had decided to run for local office. A divorced woman with a child who decided to apply to medical school at age twenty-nine was the choice of another woman. Sometimes the success interview is directly related to an area of interest. Such was the case with one woman interested in photography who called a local photographer who was a friend of a friend. The response of this photographer was wonderful, and the woman learned a great deal about the field that she was contemplating. She found the interview to be effortless and subsequently signed up for a course in photography in the fine arts department at a local college.

ASSERTIVE INFORMATION GATHERING

Jane, a college graduate with a degree in teaching, has been working for six years with a large company as a secretary and has received some training with computers. She would like to change jobs but is afraid, because she *knows* she could not change jobs and make as much money somewhere else. At least she *thinks* she knows. She made the decision to stay in her present job based on *one* phone call to a bank.

Beverly, a teacher before her two children were born, would like to prepare for a different career in preparation for when she is ready to reenter the job market. She has a strong interest in social work, but has decided she should not pursue that field because of what she perceives as a lack of available jobs. She has not made any phone calls, checked with placement services at schools of social work in her city, or talked either to social work agencies or employed social workers. She has made a career decision as a result of accepting assumptions that may or may not be based on fact.

Some women say they would like to return to school but

would need financial assistance. Often they refrain from pursuing this goal because of strong convictions that such money is unavailable. Other women contemplate entering new career fields for themselves but are not exactly sure what they need to do in order to evaluate their new career hopes and goals.

Frequently, significant decisions related to work and careers are based on inadequate information, both about ourselves and about our career options. Feelings of frustration and disillusionment often result. We encourage you to think of information and information-gathering as a source of power. Well-informed choices will reduce the amount of uncertainty you will feel while you are making important life/work planning decisions for yourself.

Up until this point in the book, your goal has been self-exploration. Your attention has been focused on defining learning styles, interests, abilities, and values. In moving from the stage of exploration to the stage of implementation, you will now need to search out answers to many specific questions and fill in any information gaps. Often class or seminar participants hope that the leader or instructor will be able to tell them what they should do and answer all their questions. You may have had a similar expectation of this book. However, it is unrealistic to expect one person or book to be knowledgeable, thorough, and current in all fields. You will need to make a commitment of your time and energy in order to seek out the information you require. It may be helpful for you to consider for a moment how you usually get information. From personal experience? From what others say? From experts? From reading reliable sources? Whichever way you choose, acquiring information usually requires the specific skills and behaviors of seeking, investigating, careful listening, evaluating, and experiencing.

We have found that exercises that expect specific action seem to be the most threatening for class members. In the activity "A Success Interview," each person has a chance to experiment with initiating a meeting and talking extensively with a successful woman. For many women this is the first step toward building the confidence and skills necessary for interviewing for a job.

The "Assertive Information Gathering" activities are another chance to build upon that base. However, many people *still* feel hesitant about these assignments. The fear of imposing on someone's time or being rebuffed persists. But avoidance of assertive information-gathering can be a way of insulating yourself from rejection or failure. *Never* taking an appropriate action, however, can also prevent you from achieving success, or at the very least from feeling good about yourself for having tried.

EXPLORING CAREER POSSIBILITIES

Make a list of questions you have concerning any aspect of a career choice you are now considering or are interested in learning more about. Circle one area you are willing to research thoroughly during the coming week. Write down specifically what you will *do* to gain this information.

Andrea was interested in giving art lectures at the city art museum. She knew the museum had a training program for volunteer lecturers, yet for years she had not inquired because of fear. She feared finding out that she did not have the qualifications. Or that they would say she was too old. Or of discovering that there were no openings. She feared that hearing these things would mean the end to her dream. Finally she made a commitment to herself and to her classmates by saying that she would at least call.

Kim's choice was to get more information about being a medical technologist. She said she would call different hospitals to find out if they employ medical technologists and what kind of training was required. She also decided she would ask for the names of people already working in the field and contact them to find out what it is really like to be a medical technologist, what the specifics and realities of the job actually were.

Teresa was going to make an appointment with someone at the convention center to find out the scope of the jobs available there.

June has always loved horses. She decided to telephone some stables to inquire about whether they hire people to groom and train horses.

Decide on an area you would like more information about, and make a commitment to doing an interview. Give yourself a time limit. Share your plan with a friend or cohort. Keep notes of the results. You have begun your personal search for information that will help you make good decisions for yourself.

In our classes and seminars, as each woman contracts with the group about what she will do, emotions begin to build. Some feel a sense of adventure. Others feel that they are finally moving forward toward finding some answers. Still others have the distinct feeling of, "What am I getting myself into?" And for some there is a sense of panic if no overriding interest emerges. Whatever your feelings, it may be helpful, once again, to do a role-play to help decrease any anxiety you may be experiencing.

Jane used the exercise to explore a work environment of particular interest to her. She had been curious about a large well-known outdoor summer theater and set out to interview the manager in order to gather information about working in such a setting. She returned to the group with a *job* offer in sales for that theater! She was thrilled as she reported to the group the surprising turn of events. She had made an appointment to talk with the director of personnel, who gave her a tour and talked about how the theater operated and about the functions of the staff. As they chatted, Jane felt very much at ease, primarily because she had initiated the interview, and was not job hunting. Her goal had been to become well informed. When the subject of the conversation turned to the sales and promotional aspects of the business, Jane was fascinated and asked many questions. By the end of the conversation, she was enthusiastically offering some of her own ideas. Although she was not expecting it, the director told her that a job related to her interests and skills was available, and asked her if she would be willing to take it on for six months, to start, with the option that it might turn out to be a year-round job at some point. Jane said she needed some time to consider the offer, but planned to accept. She was even pleased with the limited duration, for it would allow her to have valuable experience without a long-term commitment.

You may discover that you do not like a particular job or environment. You may return with great interest in an area, or information about requirements for specific jobs. You may acquire data about which schools offer appropriate degrees, the cost of various programs, and whether there is money available for returning women. All this data is essential for the formulation of your short- and long-term goals.

Information gathering can be tedious and frustrating. It may require ten phone calls to locate the one person with whom you need to talk. It often requires trips to the library or other resource centers, writing letters, sending for annual reports. Several information interviews are usually necessary. You may need to pore through school catalogs, talk to students who have already taken a particular course or are enrolled in a program of interest to you. Fortunately, this process of information gathering will carry over into many other areas of your lives, as you investigate what car to buy, which orthodontist to use, what stocks to invest in, which camp is safe and best suited for your children. Information gathering will give you the power to make informed decisions about all aspects of your life.

Individuals who thoroughly research an area of interest often feel a strong sense of accomplishment, an increase in self-confidence. This confidence results from feeling competent about information gathering experiences and from learning to make well-informed decisions. Indeed, information becomes a source of power. And a wonderful side effect is the increasing ease many women feel regarding subsequent, more formal job-related interviews.

DECISIONS, DECISIONS, DECISIONS

Often when women enter exploration classes, they feel hopeless because they do not feel that they will find any solution to their confusion. When they complete the seminar, they sometimes continue to feel confused, but now the confusion results because they seem to have generated too many choices. A great deal of information about yourself has been gathered. How can you utilize it constructively? A framework is helpful in evaluating all the data and drawing conclusions that will lead to a formulation of a life plan that is unique to each of your personal needs and life style preferences.

One framework, the SPOCS decision-making wheel, a method of problem solving developed by Sherri Muchnick, has been used to facilitate decision-making skills. The format is easily learned, and it can help you more effectively make choices that you feel to be right for you. Before looking at this model, it is important that you examine the current method you are using to solve problems.

Each of you already has a process you use to make decisions. Modes of decision making are partially habit responses, developed over time, that are precipitated automatically when there is a decision to be made. Obviously, no one decision-making model begins from scratch. However, your own processes of problem solving often take place so quickly that you may not be conscious of the steps you are going through that lead to your decisions. Identifying the elements of your decision-making process can help you to evaluate which components of the SPOCS model you wish to explore. In problem-solving classes we use the following exercise to facilitate awareness of decision-making techniques. As you read the experiences, see if you can determine the elements that are common to your own decision-making strategies.

The Lineup

The group is asked to focus on their decision-making processes by participating in the following activity: Their task is, without speaking, to form a line and decide where in the line they feel comfortable standing. If there are twelve or more people involved, two or more equal lines are needed. This is a nonverbal exercise and participants are asked to be aware of what they are thinking and how they are feeling as they make their decision. Instructions regarding where the head and rear of the line are located are given as well as permission and encouragement to try out different positions in the line if so desired.

The results of this exercise vary tremendously. Some group members go directly to one place in line and remain there, while members of other groups may feel free to experiment and move around. Often there is competition to be the first in line. There have been varying solutions to the conflict over who goes first. Two people (or more) may stand side by side at the head of the line, while others decide to form another line, and assume the position of leader there. Some feel there is no way to be first, and decide they are content to be second or third. Others may go to the rear of the line and attempt to turn the entire line around. Since this is a nonverbal activity, each person must analyze and solve the problem on her own. Since decision-making behavior is often a habit response, participants often find that their process of deciding (or in some cases not deciding) to be similar to what they do in real-life situations.

Once each person has made up her mind and found a place to stand, the people in line are asked to number off in sequence.

The exercise is concluded by having each woman state which number in line she was, and discuss the thoughts and feelings involved in making her decision. As each woman expresses her experience, the leader identifies which of the following components of the decision-making process they have been utilizing.

1. Goals—"My goal was to be number one." "I wanted to stand next to my friend." "I wanted to be where I could see and hear what was going on."

2. Needs—"I wanted to avoid conflict." "I wanted to be a leader." "I wanted to be able to follow and not be first."

3. Feelings—"I felt nervous moving in front of someone." "I was excited about putting myself first in line." "I felt satisfied that I made my own decision."

4. Information—"I didn't know what this line was for so I couldn't decide how important being first actually was to me."

5. Options—"I can stand next to a friend." "I can go back to my place if no one will let me in front of her." "I can try out several places and then decide where I'd like to be." "I can stand beside the first in line and also call myself number one."

6. Consequences—"If I move in front of someone she will be angry with me." "I will feel more comfortable at the end of the line where there is more room."

As a result of the Lineup, each participant is able to identify not only factors she typically uses in making decisions, but also those she usually does not consider.

Which factors do you usually consider? Which ones do you tend to ignore? How has this affected past decisions?

THE SPOCS DECISION-MAKING WHEEL

Each letter in SPOCS stands for a step in the decision-making process: Situation, Perceptions, Options, Consequences, and Selection. The model is designed as a wheel in order to reflect the belief that making effective decisions is often a circular process, one that may require going through the wheel several times until a good solution is found. After defining a problem, use each step of the wheel to help you develop solutions.

1. Situation
a. define the situation
b. identify goals

2. Perceptions
a. perception of your needs
b. perception of your feelings

3. Options
a. list as many possible solutions as you can
b. brainstorm
c. don't evaluate

4. Consequences
a. relate options to consequences
b. assess negative and positive outcomes of each option

5. Selection
a. select option which best achieves goal while considering your needs and feelings
b. try out option for specified period of time and reevaluate
c. get additional information that may be needed to make effective decision

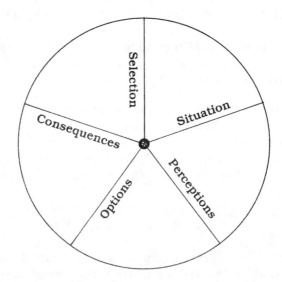

Below is an example of how one woman, Anne, used the model. For her, the problem centered around job dissatisfaction.

1. My situation
I am not happy with my job; it is boring and I have lost interest in it. My *goal* is job satisfaction.

2. My perceptions

My needs are: Self-esteem; Higher level of achievement; Security; Money; Better relations with co-workers; Recognition/Status; Feeling more effective; Desire not to be a quitter.

My feelings are: Rejection; Frustration; Anxiety; Fear; Ineffectiveness; Anger; Relief; Hope; Loyalty; Obligation.

3. My Options

Find another job; Talk to supervisor, state needs; Quit job; Restructure present job; Change careers; Get vocational counseling; Seek additional training; Grin and bear it; Ask for feedback or evaluation; Ask for transfer, promotion, or raise.

4. Consequences

Find another job. I could keep present job until I find another one. Maybe it's not the job, perhaps it is just me. I need more information about what is available in my field.

Talk to a supervisor, state needs. The supervisor may be cooperative and helpful; may give me some feedback that will change my perspective; or there may be nothing that can be done. Do I want to divulge my feelings?

(Anne continued until each option had been evaluated in terms of its positive and negative consequences.)

5. Selection

Anne chose to restructure the present job and stay with it for a specific period of time. This was done by initiating more cooperation and communication with her co-workers, by defining her priorities and by setting clear objectives. After an evaluation of what she had accomplished, Anne felt that she was developing her potential and abilities to use initiative and creativity. However, the job was still less than satisfying, because she received no recognition from management and there was no greater opportunity for advancement within her company. This new information was then fed back into the SPOCS wheel and considered when selecting a new option. It is important to emphasize that Anne did not fail. The *option* was unsuccessful in leading to job satisfaction, but Anne did reap many benefits from her experience.

Now try out a problem of your own on the following work sheet. Do not limit yourself early in the decision-making process by listing a possible solution as a goal. For example, if your problem is that you are not happy with your present job and you immediately list your goal as finding a new one, you have eliminated possibilities for changes that could bring satisfaction within your present job. These changes might include: reorganizing your job, rewriting the job description, requesting new responsibilities, asking for a raise, asking for a transfer to another department.

PROBLEM SOLVING WORK SHEET

Situation

Goal

Perceptions

1. My needs are:

2. My feelings are:

Options	Consequences

What additional information is needed?

Selection: The option(s) I will choose is (are) _____
I will try it (them) out for _____ and then reevaluate.

One of the most important factors in being able to make effective decisions is being able to brainstorm creatively, to be able to envision a multitude of options and to see problems from new perspectives. However unknowingly, many of us seem to be guilty of what has been called "tunnel vision." We have difficulty freeing our mental set to see outside the tunnel, our narrowly perceived world.

This tunnel vision is illustrated by Betty, a woman who enrolled in a one-day problem-solving workshop. The program was scheduled from 10:00 to 3:00, but Betty did not arrive until 12:30. When asked by the group leader why she had decided to attend only half the workshop she replied, "I couldn't help it. My son was home for spring break from college and he had a doctor's appointment this morning, so he needed the car." Though it may be hard to believe, the only options Betty was aware of were either to take the car and come to the workshop, or to give her son the car to go to his doctor's appointment and come to class when he got home. Since one of her primary needs with her son was for her not to rock the boat, she opted to be late to the decision-making workshop, a day which she had been eagerly anticipating.

When she arrived at class, Betty agreed to have the class use her situation as a simple problem to practice the SPOCS wheel they had been learning and to give her a chance to learn what she had missed. The group brainstormed options for her situation and came up with numerous possible solutions: call a cab; take a bus; have her son drive her to class, use the car all day and then pick her up; call the instructor or university to see if anyone else enrolled in the class lived near her; see if there was another workshop scheduled; ask her husband if he could get a ride to work that day so there would be two cars available; drive her son to the doctor and see if a friend could pick him up; give the son the responsibility of getting himself to the doctor, perhaps with a friend with whom he could spend the day.

Next, Betty evaluated the options in relation to their consequences, but she had to return to her needs and feelings before finding a solution that really seemed to fit. Since she had an overwhelming need to avoid conflicts, she would have felt guilty and uneasy all day if she had inconvenienced her husband or son. Considering this, there were still several options that could have been satisfactory. First of all, it just so happened there had been an overflow enrollment and there was another class scheduled for the following week. There were also several class members in her vicinity who said they would have been happy to give her a ride. Upon reflection, she also realized that her son probably would not have minded driving her if he could have had the car all day.

Our chapter would not be complete without the following story. When teaching a one-day problem-solving seminar, one of the authors had occasion to prove her skills. When she and her group arrived at the assigned classroom, the door was locked. It was Saturday, so the offices were closed and not even a custodian could be found. The group laughed at the irony of this being a problem-solving and decision-making course and challenged the instructor to find a solution. After quickly going through her options, she suggested trying the room with the same number only a floor above. Could there have been a mix-up? Believe it or not, the door of the room on the next floor was unlocked. Problem solved. The second problem had yet to surface.

Everyone had noticed the band instruments and the gaily uniformed kids in the lobby of the building when they had entered. No one had known exactly why the kids were there, but as soon as the class began, loud marching music could be heard coming from the lobby of the building. It was so loud, in fact, that no one could hear without actually shouting. There were a few chuckles, and all eyes turned to the instructor. She excused herself and went to tackle the problem. In her most assertive and practiced manner, she approached the conductor (a large, formidable-looking man) of this fifty-piece drum and bugle marching band. "Your kids sound just terrific," she began. "Thanks," he said, "We're practicing for a competition this afternoon." "Oh, I understand how important that must be to you, and I'd love to listen some more, but I have a problem. I'm the instructor of a course being held upstairs today and we can't hear each other speak. I really must ask you to find another place to practice." By the time she reached the classroom, incredibly enough, the halls were silent.

Those incidents would probably have been enough to insure her credibility, but she was to get another "opportunity" to test her skills. When the group took their lunch break, they all went to a restaurant near campus and several rode in the instructor's car. They returned to her car after a pleasant lunch and her car would not start. This time the laughs escalated to large guffaws.

But she blithely opened the hood of her car, unscrewed the carburetor, stuck a pencil in a little hole and turned on the ignition. To her surprise, it started immediately. She matter-of-factly replaced the top to the carburetor and got back in the car. To say the least, the group was convinced that she was qualified to lead the seminar in problem solving. She had earned her credibility.

Many women who finally attend a career-exploration or career-development course report that they have avoided their problems for a long time. Some psychologists feel that often people avoid problem solving because they cannot accurately identify the problem. According to Jacqui Shiff, MSW, some methods of avoiding problems include:

1. We can deny that the problem exists. ("I don't like my job, but I'll ignore my feelings.")

2. We can tell ourselves that our feelings are not important. ("Most people don't enjoy their jobs anyway.")

3. We can deny solutions to the problem. ("Even if I do dislike my job, there is nothing that can be done about it.")

4. We can tell ourselves that we are unable to solve the problem. ("Maybe someone else could, but I can't. I know Jo-Anne changed jobs and it worked for her, but that would never be possible for me.")

"I'm a procrastinator," is a comment that is heard in almost any discussion of decision making. Class members are asked to think about what prevents them from deciding, from seeking a solution, once a problem is recognized. The responses vary, but they often fall into the following categories.

1. The outcome is not guaranteed.

2. If I wait long enough, time and circumstances will decide for me.

3. Beliefs such as fear of failure, fear of the unknown, fear of disapproval, fear of someone's anger, all contribute to procrastination.

An important emphasis of this chapter is to help you establish control and influence in the shaping of your life/work plans. When you allow time, circumstances, or other people to decide for you, you lose power and control. Using creativity to generate options and gaining confidence in effective decision making and problem solving are extremely important in influencing your ability to direct and impact your future.

AN EVALUATION

The final step of your exploratory process is the evaluation of what you have learned about yourself. What are your specific plans for the next year, and long-range plans for the next ten years? Your personal evaluation can either be written in great detail, or be oriented toward a general response to the following questions. You may want to think through the answers to these questions over a period of weeks or months, or you may prefer to think them through at one sitting.

1. Who am I?

2. How does the above answer differ from the last time I asked myself the question?

3. How do I learn?

4. What are my patterns of interest? What do I take great satisfaction in doing?

5. What skills would I like to use in a job setting? In a volunteer setting? In a leisure setting?

6. If I decided to continue my education, what area would I pursue?

7. What limitations do I want to strengthen?

8. What are my priorities now, for myself?

9. Do I see my priorities changing in the future? In what way?

10. What are my dreams? Which ones would I like to see come true? Which are possible?

11. What are my fantasies—the little ones I never allow myself to enjoy in reality?

12. What is my definition of "success"? How has it changed during the course of this book?

13. How do I solve problems?

14. Could I improve my problem solving in any way?

15. What five things do I want to begin or accomplish within the coming year?

16. What five things would I like to have accomplished at the end of five years?

17. What five things do I see myself doing or having accomplished at the end of ten years?

As mentioned earlier, the responses to these questions may change with new experiences, so it is important to ask these same questions of ourselves periodically. A point that cannot be stressed too often is that as circumstances of our lives change, plans and decisions made at one time need to be reviewed, often altered or even totally transformed into new, more appropriate life/work plans.

Raising Your Antennae: Staying in Training

❧

A MIND SET

Staying in training is not something you do only when you are not working—or only when you are. Staying in training is a total mind set. It is a state of preparedness. It is a positive stance. It is seeing oneself as being goal directed, as being ready for whatever might occur. It is future-oriented. It is a way of keeping in tune with oneself, a way of periodically calling to mind one's strengths, reinforcing them, and strengthening one's weaknesses.

Depending on your situation, there are different ways to stay in training. We are aware of the value of keeping in training for the athlete, the musician, the dancer. So must the surgeon, the filmmaker, the computer programmer, the dentist, the teacher, and the accountant work hard to stay in training. To any person involved in the performance or execution of a skill, the time spent practicing between performances is as important as the performance itself. In fact, the performance might not be possible without the training. And to those people conscious of the demands of a performance, there is an acute awareness when they have not stayed in training. They are significantly more aware of their loss of skill than would be someone who has never tasted that level of expertise. Their knowledge of that lack, their feeling of being off-target, that subsequent self-doubt, can be more damaging to the performance than any actual loss of competence. The individual is aware of how they were, compared with how they might be, and this disappointment in self is often "felt" by the "audience."

This analogy applies to any skill that has been learned and practiced, but that has lain dormant, even for a relatively short time. Take the example of Diane, who got her master's degree in counseling. She practiced as a counselor for a year and a half and was recognized by her peers as quite competent. Then Diane had a child and took a year's leave of absence. During that time she and her husband decided that it would be important, career-wise, for her husband to have some European training in his academic area. Diane was anxious to experience European living and to try to find a job there. She was able to find a job as secretary. It was interesting work, but unrelated to her academic training. The experience of living in another culture and acclimating herself to that style of living, speaking, and thinking was challenging and all-encompassing. After only one year in Europe they returned to the United States and Diane sought a position as a counselor.

After securing a new job, she called upon her past experience in setting up a guidance program. But her difficulties surfaced at professional meetings. The terminology used and some of the issues discussed had become "foreign" to her training and work. Diane suddenly felt very removed from her own area of competence. She felt as though she were still living in a foreign country. Although she had previously been quite outspoken in her views and opinions, she now hesitated to make comments. Her feelings of self-doubt at these meetings inhibited her participation. She feared that her remarks would appear disjointed and unrelated to what was being discussed. It was only after talking to other professionals in her field that she was able to discover that indeed some issues had changed, but that it was primarily the terminology or jargon, not the content, that was unfamiliar to her.

Consequently, in her own work setting Diane was able to rely on what she was sure she knew and on the skills which she felt confident that she still possessed. She experienced a feeling similar to one a runner might feel in the first race after recovering from an injury. She felt as though she were running in slow motion while the other contestants were moving twice as fast.

As a result of this experience, Diane has always made certain that whatever else she was doing, she was always involved and keeping current with her counseling skills and with new developments and research in her field. She has kept abreast of the issues under discussion and the trends taking place. She wants to maintain her professional identity, at least to herself.

Staying in training is a phrase which also describes the mind set of seeing oneself as *constantly involved in learning.* As discussed earlier, all continued learning does not have to take place in your original area of training or interest. The very act of being involved in learning new things can keep you aware of your ability to assimilate and assess new information. The "new" information might take the form of a continuing education field trip offered by the local community college to the site of an archeological dig. Or it might involve learning the technique of productive gardening. Or it might be going to seminars offered in your field of training. Or it might be learning the skills necessary to be an effective den mother for a group of cub scouts. The key issue is that each step contains an element of challenge. This stance of being and staying in training urges us to see ourselves as having the energy at our command to move forward to new and goal-related challenges when we decide it is time.

ISSUES IN TRANSFERABILITY: THE COUNTRY BUNNY

A lovely children's book written in 1939 by Du Bose Heyward entitled *The Country Bunny and the Little Gold Shoes* can help us illustrate the important issues of staying in training and the transferability of skills. The story unfolds with the introduction of the main character, a young girl (Cottontail), who dreams of growing up and being chosen by the wise grandfather bunny to be one of the five wise, kind, and swift bunnies who have the honor and privilege of delivering Easter eggs on Easter eve. Though her femininity was cause for male bunnies to scoff at her ambitions, she tenaciously held on to her dream.

Now, as is sometimes the case, Cottontail suddenly found herself the mother of twenty-one bunnies, with sole responsibility for their upbringing. (Whether there was a marriage, separation, or divorce was never discussed, these complex issues being left to the reader to infer.) Naturally, Cottontail's motherhood was cause for great teasing, since none of the male bunnies could imagine *how* she could ever expect to become an Easter-egg-carrying bunny now! She herself began to have doubts.

So Cottontail's dream became submerged, though not entirely abandoned, as she proceeded to train each of her offspring to perform the tasks necessary for the smooth running of the household. Never for a moment did Cottontail assume that she alone was supposed to accomplish these arduous tasks. Her optimism and positive nature prevailed, as she lovingly taught her bunnies to sweep, cook, sew, clean, sing songs, and even paint pictures to help create an appealing environment. These skills were all learned diligently and happily by the twenty-one children, and they developed a sense of self-sufficiency and reliance in the process. When Cottontail faced a problem, that is, one of not enough jobs to go around, she created a very special job for that remaining bunny . . . Keeper of her Chair. He was anointed with the rare privilege of holding her chair when she sat down to eat. She was aware of the need for this job for the remaining bunny to be important rather than just an afterthought, in order to have him see and believe that he was an integral part of the family team.

The scene changes to the Palace of the Easter Eggs, where the bunnies are all congregated in anticipation of which of them the grandfather bunny will choose to replace the bunny who was becoming too slow to deliver Easter eggs on Easter eve. Cottontail once had had a dream of succeeding to this position, but now could no longer imagine herself being chosen, especially in comparison to the handsome white rabbits she assumed had had a lot of experience running and chasing. She was not particularly sad, just resigned to watching another lucky rabbit be chosen for this coveted post.

While Cottontail was standing ever so still with her twenty-one bunnies by her side, the grandfather bunny noticed her and kindly asked to speak with her. As he questioned her, he learned about how well she had trained her bunnies, was surprised to learn that they were always happy, and discovered that she was indeed wise and kind. He openly lamented that if only she were also swift, perhaps she could be considered for the job. But then, even if she had had the time to develop her swiftness, her family responsibilities would certainly prevent her from assuming the tasks of Easter-egg-carrying bunny, for he could not imagine how the family could carry on without her.

In response, Cottontail whispered to her bunnies to rapidly disperse, and confidently demonstrated her agility and swiftness by quickly gathering them back into line. Though she may not have had time for formal training, as did some of her competitors, through everyday experience she had developed the prowess to qualify her for the job. Then, aware that she had an edge, she began to introduce her bunnies two by two, explaining their functions in the management of her home and demonstrating their cooperativeness and self-sufficiency. Cottontail was promptly hired; that is, she was bestowed with the status and responsibilities of the job.

Throughout the remainder of the story it is clear that Cottontail's skills were indeed transferable, as she proceeds to accomplish the tasks of the job magnificently. That is not to say that she never had to struggle or that she had nothing to learn. But she was able to work through these struggles and attain a dream that her contemporary bunny society had succeeded in convincing her was not possible.

When Cottontail initially thought about the position of Easter-egg-carrying bunny, she only vaguely considered herself for it. She was well aware that the stringent requirements for the much-desired post were essentially the qualities of wisdom, kindness, and swiftness, and understood why these were the conditions of the job. In addition, Cottontail labored under the common stereotype that this wisdom, kindness, and swiftness needed to have been acquired through experience in a directly related field, say that of chasing after small rodents (developing speed) and working in a school for maladjusted bunnies (kindness and wisdom). If she had been invited to apply for the job by submitting a résumé, she may have presented herself in the following manner.

Résumé of Cottontail

> **Name:** Cottontail Bunny
> **Address:** The bunny village
> **Phone:** none

Objective: A responsible position as Easter-egg-carrying bunny for the grandfather bunny at the Palace of the Easter Eggs.

Work experience: Many years as mother of twenty-one young bunnies.

Areas of effectiveness:

Cleaner, mender, cook, sweeper. The home of Cottontail is always thoroughly cleaned and well maintained.

Song leader. The bunny children are taught many songs to help during work periods and cheer them.

Teacher. Each of the bunnies is taught a number of tasks and skills in the household.

Lover of young bunnies. Cottontail's true devotion to young bunnies qualifies her for this job.

If the grandfather bunny had received this résumé, he would have found it extremely difficult to understand how Cottontail was qualified for the job. The only area of effectiveness she suggested that he would have been able to correlate with the job was that of lover of young bunnies. However, he was not able to determine what she did, specifically, that gave her the right to declare herself a lover of young bunnies. It did look, perhaps, as if she may have been a hard taskmaster, requiring her young bunnies to do all the housework.

Now, those of us who have read the story know that Cottontail was eminently well-qualified for the job. Her young bunnies were happy and well-adjusted, thrilled with their sense of contribution to the family and the resultant feeling of independence. The grandfather bunny could not be expected to know how to extrapolate from her résumé the qualities that she has excluded. Her résumé does not reflect her skills, nor does it delineate her capabilities in transferable terms, in language that the grandfather bunny finds relevant. In fact, her résumé permits her potential employer to perceive her only as homemaker, with little idea of her true capabilities. It is important to remember that Cottontail did get the job, however, and as we read the tale we learn that she carried out its responsibilities even better than the four other carriers with which she worked.

Now, if there were a guidance bunny in the bunny village, Cottontail could have been helped with both her résumé and her mind set. She would have learned to present herself in transferable terms, rather than in the traditional terms that described homemaking duties. She would have learned to present her experience in a way that would allow the grandfather bunny to view her as the mother of twenty-one bunnies who has had the time and dedication to develop numerous areas of effectiveness, most of which would be applicable to the job of the Easter-egg-carrying bunny. Most important, though, Cottontail would come to honestly believe in the transferability of her skills, and in the process would regain self-confidence that she had lost in the interim years. When she was a young female bunny she believed she could do that job. And now she is even wiser, more patient, and more skilled in areas directly relevant to the job she is seeking.

Revised Résumé of Cottontail

Name: Cottontail Bunny
Address: The bunny village
Phone: none

Objective: A responsible position as Easter-egg-carrying bunny, for the grandfather bunny at the Palace of the Easter Eggs utilizing demonstrated skills in managing, organizing, individualizing, and needs assessing. Special interest in the development of communications skills, risk taking, and swiftness.

Work experience: Many years as head of household.

Areas of effectiveness:

Manager/Organizer. Organized twenty-one children into sub-groups, to teach skills necessary for running of home. Managed twenty-one children during their growing years, with minimal dissent among them. [Now don't criticize . . . we all know this is just fantasy!] Organized and managed time effectively, allowing time for the development of individual pursuits.

Individualizer/needs assessor. Responsive to the individual needs of the young bunnies. Developed jobs appropriate for each bunny, especially for one bunny who required additional reinforcement, job of Keeper of the Chair. Attended to details of running the home, while always remaining aware of the importance of the emotional climate.

Communicator. Encouraged communications among the bunnies. Developed songs to increase camaraderie. Emphasized cooperation in all interactions.

Swiftness. Developed speed and swiftness by virtue of running after and caring for twenty-one young bunnies. This rigorous daily exercise has contributed to a top bill of health, and an extremely low pulse rate. Daily jogging not necessary.

The grandfather bunny, alias employer, should be interested in interviewing Cottontail from this résumé. She *sounds* as though she believes in herself. "Well, maybe all that fancy jargon is just a cover-up, or a diversionary tactic," he may think, but his interest is piqued. And as we all saw, Cottontail is far from pretentious and would easily sell herself once given the chance.

When thinking about the job of Easter-egg-carrying bunny, the grandfather has in his mind the qualities of wisdom, kindness, and swiftness. From studying Cottontail's revised résumé, it seems clear that she has developed these qualities. She is wise, in that she has so competently organized her young bunnies, training them to be independent and self-sufficient. She has managed her time so that she is not the epitome of the hassled bunny that he has so often seen at the park. She must be kind, for she was aware of the needs of her one special bunny, creating for him the job of Keeper of the Chair. She seems to exude self-confidence without sounding conceited. She would probably be able to work well with the other four egg carriers because she has had such extensive experience in working with groups. And finally, Cottontail has stayed in training by chasing after her youngsters, and so her speed and agility can be counted on.

To carry this tongue-in-cheek example one step further, let us look at a want ad that the grandfather bunny may have placed in the *Bunny Gazette.*

Carrier

The primary Easter egg distributor, the Palace of Easter Eggs, is seeking to fill an entry level full-time position of Easter egg carrier. Potential candidate need not be degreed, but does need to have developed kindness, wisdom, and speed from five to seven years of extensive experience in directly related fields. Applicants without these qualifications need not apply.

If Cottontail were reading the *Bunny Gazette*, it is unlikely that she would have even read beyond the heading of this want ad. She does not perceive herself, in general, as a carrier. But she does have the capabilities to do the job that includes carrying as its base. If she *did* continue to read the want ad, she may be put off, again, by the declaration that the position is a full-time one. It *is* full-time; but full-time to Easter egg carriers is the entire night of Easter eve, once each year. Additionally, Cottontail may perceive herself as having the qualities of kindness and wisdom, but would never think of her years of mothering as directly related experience. And finally, she may think of herself as swift, but probably not realize just how swift she has grown by simply caring for her young brood. Yes, Cottontail would be intimidated by the ad, and the grandfather bunny would miss out on a valuable potential employee. The reality of the situation is that Cottontail's experience *is* directly related, but it is her responsibility to prove it, to demonstrate her capabilities to someone with little experience employing the mother of a multitude of young bunnies.

Career Changing

Thinking in terms of transferability of skills is crucial to the mind set of staying in training. It means anticipating how the present will or could be applied in the future. It means a readiness, an openness to alternatives that may present themselves. It implies a bias toward personal growth and change.

To be tuned in to transferability is to have a mind set, a preparedness, a continuous sense of the present intertwined with the future. Having one's antennae raised, and being aware of future application of present activities and priorities, is a safeguard against the loss of self-confidence that was exemplified by Cottontail. It is not being advocated that she would have been happier had she decided to pursue a career and not have any bunnies. Nor is it being advocated that she should have been working part-time while her young bunnies were small. It *is* being suggested, however, that Cottontail continue interacting with the "outside" world, talking to other bunnies who were working or doing volunteer work, and perhaps doing some exploring in areas that interest her. Also, she should be evaluating her work at home in transferable terms, rather than just work-content language. For example, her natural bent toward organizing and supervising would indeed be transferable to another setting. Though she may never intend to work in another setting, or at least not for many years, she will *feel* stronger, more powerful, more self-confident if she is mentally evaluating her acquired and developed skills.

When Amy, a successful psychiatric social worker, decided to stop working for a while to spend time raising her infant daughter, she seized on the opportunity to learn about and develop her aptitude in artistic arenas. She discovered that she had a natural talent for pottery making, and began to take classes and study this area more seriously. Eventually Amy decided to share a studio with several acquaintances who also needed the part-time use of a studio. Amy became quite proficient in her work. She began, tentatively at first, to sell her better creations and found, much to her surprise, that she quickly established a loyal following. Amy had never originally intended to become so seriously involved in making pottery, and so to safeguard her professional status she had maintained her membership in professional associations and continued to read journals and books that would help keep her attuned to the issues current in her field.

When her child was entering nursery school she found herself at a crossroads, with more than one option for work. Amy decided to create pottery full-time, for she had learned that she could earn as much money in this endeavor as she had made in social work, and she had grown to love this work. At this time in her life, she felt less inclined to thrust herself back into a field that was emotionally draining, and not particularly lucrative (since her experience had been in clinics that did not pay high salaries). Amy's raised antennae and her high level of self-confidence contributed to her growing success as a potter.

Jennifer, a high school chemistry teacher, had returned to full-time work after her children entered school. She adored her job, loved working with extremely bright students, and found herself at the top of the salary schedule due to her advanced degrees. At about this time, Jennifer's school system began to suffer from a loss of enrollment and Jennifer faced the reality of either obtaining tenure or being dropped in favor of a less experienced teacher who would cost the district less. According to Jennifer, no other district would hire her because of her salary requirements, and she might very well find herself looking for a different job.

Interestingly enough, this situation was not as threatening as it might have been. Jennifer had always wanted to be a doctor, but grew up at a time when girls who intended to have careers were expected to become teachers or nurses. She faced this potential employment squeeze with an optimism about other opportunities. She had been learning about new developments in health-care fields, and was particularly interested in the work of nurse practitioner in the Ob-Gyn specialty.

She had never allowed herself to become mentally or emotionally locked into her job teaching chemistry. She had continued to remain current with the development of related fields *and* to envision herself participating in them. She did not think of herself as only a teacher. She also thought of herself as potential nurse practitioner. She considered her expertise in chemistry to be a stepping-stone to future opportunities, not necessarily an end in itself. Though she loved her work, she had not allowed herself to remain complacent. And so if she lost her job she would not suddenly be struggling with a major loss of ego, but rather with an anticipation of her future.

Neither Amy nor Jennifer knew for certain where she would finally end up. Amy did not pursue work as a potter because she knew (or at least hoped) that through work as an artist she could generate income. And Jennifer was not neglecting her work as a chemistry teacher or investing any less energy in being an excellent teacher just because she was consistently integrating future work possibilities into her mind set. It does not follow that if one stays in training and thinks in terms of transferable skills that one will know specifically what future work will result. It *does* follow that having a perpetual state of "raised antennae" and an awareness of the transferability of one's skills, will result in an optimistic sense of possibilities, a stronger sense of self, an openness to change, and a tolerable degree of discomfort and anxiety when in the process of reentering the work force or changing careers.

Take the case of Donna, a high school English teacher who loved her work, had taught for twelve years, and was on maternity leave with her infant daughter. Incredibly, her years in the school system qualified her for a *four*-year maternity leave, with a guaranteed job upon returning. Donna wisely decided to explore options while on leave to consider alternative career paths for herself. She began to tutor adults on a limited basis and discovered that working with adults suited her better at this stage of her life. Gradually, a plan began to formulate in her mind. She learned, by maintaining contact both with her friends still in the field and those who had moved in new career directions, that there was a growing need in the business community for communications consultants.

Many businessmen and women who were extremely capable in their jobs found themselves in a position where it was necessary for them to write concise, coherent reports. Unfortunately, most of these people were business school graduates, many with M.B.A. degrees, and had not had a course in writing since high school. They found themselves spending an undue proportion of their time on the tasks of writing and were in great need of help in this area. Donna explored these new possibilities. She made an appointment with an acquaintance who was now doing this kind of work to find out if she would be qualified. She considered offering her services on a part-time basis to this consultant, and thereby experiencing firsthand how she felt about this new wrinkle in her career.

These people with raised antennae rarely find their sense of self only in their present job title. Kate, director of operations at a local bank, took great pride in her work and in her success at inspiring employees and promoting women within the organization. While she struggled to do her best job for her employer, she also studied her second love, photography, to the point of getting an advanced degree at a college specializing in alternative degree programs. Tucked down in her psyche, always within reach, Kate held on to the dream that somehow she would integrate her ability in accounting with her love of photography and her obsession with books. She was not sure *how* these interests, skills, and enthusiasms would merge, but she assumed a merger was possible, if not inevitable.

If she had allowed her dreams to be affected by society's expectations of her, she would never have eventually ended up in partnership in a bookstore. She supervised its operations and traveled extensively doing photographic documentaries. What was significant and impressive about Kate was her high level of self-confidence, her appetite for different experiences, and her ability to take risks. According to her, she had done an exceptional job while working in the bank, so that she could always return to that kind of work, and most likely at the same bank if she so desired. She had trained her employees so well that if someone stepped into her position, they would be completely capable of handling all details and problems.

Assuming Control

The fact that many skills are transferable from one work setting to another is not always common knowledge. Many people in that sometimes-threatening world of personnel people and potential employers still labor under the belief that experience must be in *directly* related fields. They may not be familiar with the differentiation between work-content skills and transferable skills. They may be uncomfortable with having to shoulder the responsibility of evaluating nontraditional work experience. Often these people do not have an in-depth comprehension of the responsibilities of specific jobs, and so are not in a position to evaluate transferable skills.

So it is just as you might have expected. The responsibility is yours. You must demonstrate the transferability of your skills, once you feel certain that you are representing your capabilities honestly and realistically.

Cottontail assumed this responsibility when presenting herself to the grandfather bunny. She took the bull by the horns, demonstrating her speed, agility, and success at generating independence and self-sufficiency within her behavior. She did not assume that he would know these things without being told. She did not react defensively to the assumption that she was probably not qualified. She did not become agitated by the belief that the grandfather bunny was prejudiced against girl rabbits, or mother rabbits. The grandfather bunny was *clearly* misinformed, but not malicious in excluding Cottontail from his theoretical set of qualified applicants. Cottontail trusted herself and her abilities, and proceeded to disprove the theory that she was not qualified or could not possibly be absent from her home to fulfill the rigorous requirements of the job.

Pat was competing with several women for a job in residential sales with a local real estate company of extremely high reputation. She had never worked in real estate, though she had recently acquired her broker's license. But she was so confident that she would be a terrific asset to the company that a combination of her enthusiasm and her description of her transferable skills landed her the job. She spoke about her expert sense of direction, her experience in other kinds of retail sales, her life style that could flexibly accommodate this job, her skills in communication and negotiation, and her consistently high energy level. She had a theory about selling houses. She felt that if she took the time to sit with a family in their home, listen to them describe their life style, their typical day, their special needs, she could more easily and quickly find them a home. She was comfortable talking with all kinds of people, was a good listener, and enjoyed analyzing needs and visualizing the kind of house that would fit these needs. Once employed, she became an almost immediate success, and the company was glad they had chosen her over other applicants who had had direct experience.

Cathy had been a teacher for a number of years. She enjoyed her work but felt ready to make a change. She went to an employment agency specializing in placing women in jobs and was subsequently hired to do recruiting for the company. Though she had no real concrete ideas about what kind of job she wanted, she had done an in-depth analysis of her own skills and abilities. She had transferred this investigation of self onto a résumé, and the interviewer was so impressed with her apparent understanding of skills analysis that she was hired to fill a growing gap in the company. She became invaluable in aiding women teachers who were changing careers to investigate options outside of education.

Sales is an area toward which many women are gravitating. Robert Shook, in his book *Greatest Sales Persons: What They Say About Selling* (Harper & Row, 1978), discusses the importance of salespeople exchanging ideas with people both in their particular field and in totally unrelated fields. The benefits would be multifold, for though the specific product may differ, there are a great many skills and ideas that are transferable from one sales setting to another. A computer salesperson can learn from a steel salesperson and an insurance salesperson can learn from an automobile salesperson. Ideas naturally will need to be adapted to fit each salesperson's needs. An interesting result of such interactions would be the increasing ease of changing from one field to another and the evolving awareness of the transferability of skills. There are many skills that would remain relatively unchanged, though the product, of course, would be drastically different.

Expanding Your Options

Talk of transferability of skills is all well and good, but of limited value without a continuous, growing awareness of viable options. It is important to first become aware of your transferable skills, and then to proceed to learn about work environments, jobs, and fields that interest you and in which you can utilize your transferable skills. A person who likes to write may be terrific at her craft, and be of tremendous value to any number of potential employers. Limited awareness of opportunities, however, may lead to her accepting a job in a publishing company about which she was not particularly excited, when she could have explored the possibilities of technical writing, advertising, developing sales training programs, working in the training department of a large company, writing for local television or radio stations, developing brochures for public relations departments, ad infinitum. Of utmost importance, then, is the process that follows the inventory of one's skills: that process of exploring, listening, learning, and evaluating the data about numerous jobs and fields in order to determine new directions. Assertive information gathering, as discussed earlier, becomes crucial in this aspect of raising your antennae.

A Treatise on Interviewing

We return to the subject of interviewing, because of its tremendous importance in the process of life/work planning, and because of the reluctance and insecurity of many women in this area. In one class on life/work planning, the women were asked to list five occupational areas that intrigued them, but about which they knew almost nothing. The composite list included dental hygienist, symphony conductor, engineer, news broadcaster, restaurant manager, writer, architect, pediatric nurse practitioner, lawyer, medical technologist, computer programmer, word processor, caterer, and many others. In order to find out what it is *really* like to be a medical technologist, it is most helpful to ask one. One could read about the kinds of work a medical technologist does or take classes. But to know how it feels to *be* a medical technologist is an entirely different matter. Many fields are constantly growing and changing. Even books that were once very helpful are often out of date. And more importantly, books cannot transmit the nonverbals, the enthusiasms, the facial expressions that direct contact *can* transmit. Books cannot respond to questions or explain a typical day as a plumber, or carpenter, a Xerox salesperson, or an auditor.

So what do we mean by interviewing, specifically? We mean talking to others, asking specific questions. We mean asking the questions that we fear may be too probing, too personal, in a way that is acceptable. (Not, "What is your salary?" but "Can you give me the salary range of people working in this kind of job?") We are encouraging you to ask the questions you may consider stupid. After all, you probably say to yourself, you are *supposed* to know! ("Does a lawyer have to go to court?" "Do most newscasters have terrific memories?" "What exactly do you do in a typical day?")

By interviewing we mean setting up a specific time to talk to someone, and admitting that you are seeking specific information. By interviewing people about their work you are admitting that, though you may know a lot about yourself, your skills, and abilities, you know very little about the particular field.

An added bonus resulting from these interviewing experiences is the opportunity to evaluate yourself and your expertise in interviewing. Are you talking too much or too fast? Have you learned that certain kinds of questions are more successful than others? Have you learned to eliminate questions that only require a yes or no answer when you are really seeking more information? Did you slip, and say something negative about a past employer? Were you frustrated with yourself because you did not seize on an opportunity to sell yourself, to ask a certain question, to ask someone for help? Did you sit facing the sun, too embarrassed to ask for the drapes to be closed? Did you need to use the bathroom throughout the entire interview, but neglect to excuse yourself, preferring to hurry through the conversation rather than speak up? Did you discover that you have difficulty looking someone straight in the eye?

Working through these small difficulties can have a major, positive impact on your ease and success at future interviewing when applying for jobs. *Then* the focus can be where it needs to be, the search for a fit—you and your skills, with the specific job for which you are really qualified. Accurate knowledge about further educational and training needs can be gained. Comfort with talking to other people is important in maintaining a state of preparedness, of readiness for discovering new personal horizons.

RAISING YOUR ANTENNAE ABOUT YOURSELF

So far this chapter has concerned itself with raising your antennae to externals, including new ideas, people, places to explore, fields to learn about, books to read and research, and methods of identifying transferable skills throughout all your experiences. It is also important to look at your responses to what has been said. It is time to look inward, to pay attention to feelings that may become obstacles to learning to raise your antennae. These potential barriers could work against the implementation of the "raised antennae" stage that we hope becomes permanent to your mind set.

"On Competition"

In the last few decades there has been some controversy about the place of competition in the development of children. Some people feel that competiton is a part of life and the earlier that children learn to handle it appropriately, the easier life will be for them. Other people feel that there has been too much emphasis on competition in our lives, and that it would be more beneficial to the children, and eventually to society, if there were less emphasis on competition. There are pros and cons on each side of the debate, as well as a middle ground.

But whether or not competition is healthy for children in the future, this question does not really deal with the fact that we have all grown up in a world filled with competition and we continue to react to that fact. Some of us thrive on competition and others of us tend to back away from it, not seeing it as a desirable part of our lives. We are suggesting that people learn to harness that existing energy of "competition," just as we learned to harness water and use it as a source for generating electricity.

Toward this end of harnessing our energy, one of the authors is reminded of an ongoing game that she had with a friend. They tried to top each other with a "least-known" fact. One challenge might be to come up with the middle name of the person who invented bubble gum. The outcome of the game was that each of the players was constantly in search of some point of trivia that was unknown to the other person. The relentless search led to the discovery of many interesting facts which, in turn, opened up avenues of interest in all kinds of fields, including science, music, literature, languages, history: areas which had been ignored previously by each of them. That "game" has since continued in the minds of the individuals who participated in it.

They do not see each other often, but when they have met, each has acknowledged that they are still interested in searching out the small, interesting facts that many people overlook. And these bits of information have opened many conversations and many doors for them. The name of some rather obscure piece of research undertaken by a physician in Australia could be just the point of entry that will lead to an interesting evening's discussion at a party. This whole activity is approached with interest as well as with humor. Many people just do not care about the Latin name of a wild flower growing in the Ozark Mountains, but seeking such little gems of information can keep our minds active while in their pursuit.

This example of harnessing energy can, of course, be applied to many endeavors. We can continue to be informed and active in many areas, whether or not we are formally associated with particular work settings, educational or leisure pursuits. What we are doing is keeping our minds active for the time at which we want to increase our formal activities.

Some people might refer to such an activity as "mental gymnastics," with a disparaging tone. But it is a well-known fact that a moderate amount of exercise is beneficial to keeping muscles toned. And toned muscles not only minimize injuries, they also have a total effect of generating a positive attitude toward life. We can take advantage of moderate competition. It can become an energizer which keeps us informed and ready for action when we decide to make changes in our lives or when, as a result of some event, it is necessary that we make changes. We do not, of course, have to play a trivia game and collect indiscriminate information. Rather, we can decide in what ways we would like to be competitive, to allow ourselves to become well-informed and more knowledgeable about our options.

Creative Envy

Both the word "envy" and the accompanying feelings have often had very negative connotations in our society. It *might* be acceptable to confess to having feelings of envy, but certainly not to act as a result of them. The expectation is that actions flowing from envious feelings would be unpleasant or negative. Envious feelings can, however, be positively and creatively utilized.

Reflect upon that last feeling of envy you had. Perhaps you were feeling envious about what someone else had acquired, or a job that she recently was offered and accepted. The next question to ask is, "What, specifically, does that person have that you wish you had too?" After you are able to sort out the answer to that question, a final, logical step to take is to determine if there is some way that you too could attain something similar to what she has that you also desire. This questioning can help you to cut across those feelings of "undifferentiated envy," and discover the root of the envy. Then it may be possible to establish a plan to try to satisfy that specific desire for yourself. Of course, after analyzing the situation, you may decide that you do not want to work as hard as would be necessary to achieve whatever you wish you had.

One woman in a personal development class gives us a good model for how she dealt with her own feelings of envy, when her husband went back to school to get an advanced degree. They were both interested in the same field and had both talked about returning to school to get the degree they needed in order to work effectively in that field. Suzanne had worked all of her adult life, taking only short maternity leaves to have their children. She considered their marriage to be on a fairly equal basis in terms of child care and household responsibilities. But when the subject of Jon's returning to school came up, she suggested that he get his degree first, and when he finished she would have her turn. Jon wondered if they couldn't both return to school at the same time. Suzanne felt that they could not afford it because they had just had a new baby. And since she was also working, she feared that she could not manage her children, job, household responsibilities and schoolwork at the same time.

On the surface all seemed logical and settled and Jon did

indeed go back to school. But Suzanne felt herself becoming angry when Jon came home and talked about his classes. Although they normally shared a great deal, she did not want to hear about his graduate school experiences. She was later able to clarify that she also wanted to be taking courses; she was envious of her husband's new challenges. So she decided that she could either spend the next four years becoming increasingly angry, or she could do something about it. She decided to apply for admission and began with a summer course in order to provide a testing ground to see if together they could manage. They had to eliminate most of their leisure activities, but they discovered that they were sharing a great deal and were offering each other mutual support, perhaps more than each would have been able to give to the other if they had decided to pursue their degrees at separate times.

Another woman in the group found it helpful to put those "envious feelings" into specific contexts. They asked each other, "When was the last time you felt envious?" They then helped each other to evaluate that last episode by asking, "What were you envious of?" "What do you wish you also had?" "Is there any way that you could have that thing you are envious of, that thing you also want for yourself?" "Are you willing to make the changes in your life that will allow you also to have what someone else has?"

One woman might be envious of another woman's figure. After evaluating what she must do to also be trim and better proportioned in terms of weight control and exercise, she may decide to work on gaining a better figure. Another woman may now be certain that she does *not* want to do what would be necessary because those changes would be life style changes that she is unwilling to make. But each woman has a better feeling about herself since she is able to see the potential of having a trim figure as a matter over which she *could* have at least partial control.

Eleanor envied a friend who had a wonderful job. When we asked her to delineate specifically what she envied about the other woman's job, she determined that she liked the idea of going to a lovely office in the morning, going to lunch with interesting people, dressing like a career woman, and accomplishing daily goals. She really did not envy the specific work done by the other woman. Eleanor's expertise was in secretarial areas, gained while working before her children were born. Then for the next question, "Is there any way you could attain any or all of those four specific aspects of her job you are envious of, and combine them with your areas of expertise?" she determined that she would enjoy, and was clearly qualified for, general secretarial work. She subsequently decided to look for a receptionist, secretarial, or administrative assistant job in a public relations department or firm. Eleanor realized that she might have to work her way up to a higher position, but was excited with the discovery of her new options, all which could potentially fulfill the specific desires she had. And so she had moved from the envious feelings, that could have been debilitating and draining, to discovering options that were right for her. As a beneficial side effect, Eleanor was no longer envious of her friend or her job, finding it delightful, once again, to spend time with her.

A beneficial use of your time may be to ask yourself about the last time you were envious. Who or what were you envious of? Specifically, *what* were you envious of? What concrete things or situations do you wish that you also had access to? Is there any way that you could acquire similar things or place yourself in similar situations? Are you willing to make the life style changes and compromises that may be necessary in order to attain the end result you desire?

Managing Your Time

This chapter has been focusing on raising your antennae . . . on extending your horizons . . . on analyzing and, perhaps, reordering your priorities . . . on using some of your time to enhance and enlarge the scope and pattern of your life/work plans. And all of these endeavors take time.

Time. When we are very young time seems endless, and as we grow it seems to diminish. As we age, we are more and more aware that life is time bound. Take a moment, now, to think through your personal feelings about time.

One of the biggest complaints heard from women contemplating a change in the format of their day at work or at home is, "How will I ever fit it all in?" We ask, "What is this 'it' that you want/need to fit into your day?" And with this question, we begin to look seriously at the role of time in our lives. We can learn to use time, or we can let time rule us. We may hear ourselves

saying, "It is time for _____," or "There will not be time to
_____ ." Often we feel as if time is some alien ruling force that
controls us, and consequently over which we have relatively
little control. For some of us, our lives are so full that we feel
exhausted and harassed with the efforts to get to everything. For
others, there is not enough to fill our time, and we find ourselves
looking for ways to fill it. Many of us may choose to believe that
we are not in control of how we spend our time, a belief that helps
to lighten the responsibility we may sense when we feel time
slipping away.

Take the phrase, "I have to," and see how many times you can
complete that statement. Your responses may include the
following. "I have to read the newspaper." "I have to market and
cook the meals." "I have to bring work home at night." "I have to
do some work on vacation." "I have to do the laundry." "I have to
call my mother every day." "I have to attend that meeting." Now
take your list and see how many of those statements could be
changed to, "I choose to." Now, what happens to your list?

Reactions to this exercise often include feelings of anger and
frustration. Statements are made such as, "If I do not do these
things they will never get done, so I really do not have a choice."
"I do not feel as if I have a choice, and it makes me angry when
you imply that I might not really have to do some of the things I
do." "My role as mother and wife necessitates my doing those
things." "As manager of the department, I do not have a choice. I
must do those things." "I *have* to entertain in this business."

However, if we were unable to do the cooking, shopping, and
washing because of an illness or handicap, most likely someone
else would do them. Usually we do the things we do because we
choose to do them. They are priorities to us. And we frequently
choose to do them in a specific way, in a specific manner that is
also important to us. For example, we may make homemade
bread or cookies because we value making them for our family.
Initially, the family does not require us to make homemade
things, or to spend our time in this way. But as we accustom the
family to these treats they may come to expect them, and we may
come to feel that our being good homemakers is dependent on
our continuing to function in this way. After all, our family's
health is at stake!

To use a mundane but actual example in illustrating the
point, we will use the story of the woman who uses cloth napkins

for her family, a decision that added to her laundry responsibilities. When she occasionally used paper napkins, her family objected, reinforcing the use of cloth napkins. She subsequently stated, "My family won't use paper napkins." But the fact is that this cycle started with her because *she* preferred cloth napkins for some reason, and her family learned to expect their use. Obviously her family could learn to accept paper napkins if cloth napkins ceased to be a priority for her and if she decided that extra time needed to launder all those napkins was a time waster in her life.

These specific examples are perhaps mundane ones, but then much of what we allow to occupy our time *is* mundane. The balance between the very important and the inconsequential is a healthy balance of time. The inconsequential can be a respite from more weighty matters. Essentially, this awareness is integral to the process of learning to manage our time, to set priorities, to balance matters of consequence with those of less importance. We can learn to take charge of the twenty-four hours of our day, and allot them to the tasks that we choose to have comprise our day. Obviously we can never have complete control over the events of our day. But we can learn to order our day in a way that allows space for those activities that flow from previous choices (marriage, family, job) and those we want to add because of current, expanding choices and future desires (going to work, back to school, volunteer work, special interests).

Controlling the time in your day may require learning how to delegate responsibility, and allowing others, after they have been carefully guided and taught, to share in the decision making. During the first session of a career awareness class Jessica stated that she felt very guilty being in class on that day because it was raining hard, and her husband had asked how her two daughters, aged seven and ten, would get home from school in the rain. Jessica felt torn. They did not live far from school, and she herself had walked home in the rain when she was a child. The girls had raincoats and umbrellas, but partly because of her husband's questions, she felt as though she were shirking her responsibilities.

While Jessica was taking the course, she was offered an early morning, part-time job in a bakery. She felt good about the opportunity and about having been asked; her family needed the extra income, so she decided to accept the job. She discovered, with pride, that her daughters could nicely, and quite independently, be counted on to make their own breakfast and leave for school at the right time. They were also quite willing to do some of the chores that Jessica had previously done, including caring for the plants, putting dishes in the dishwasher, putting the clothes away, fixing their own lunches. These changes required patience and persistence, for she knew that in order to delegate effectively, she would need to spend time in the beginning teaching her daughters the skills necessary to help out. She remarked time and time again throughout the course about the change in her perception of what she thought she had to do, and what responsibilities other family members could learn to assume. In fact, the positive outcome was that she made many changes away from her more traditional role of serving her family, which actually pleased them.

The family's Friday night routine, for example, had been to have tacos for supper. Jessica would fix the tacos in the kitchen and then carry them in to the family members, who were watching television in the family room. At times she remembered having some feelings of resentment while she waited on them. After she began working in the bakery, she decided that each person could fix his or her own tacos in the kitchen, and then they would each carry in their own plates. The change was enjoyed by the family, who perceived it to be a positive addition to the holiday atmosphere of Friday nights. Jessica, and many other women in the course, found these small, seemingly insignificant episodes to be indicative of large, more pervasive feelings that they had little control over how they spent their own time.

Many women not in the labor force have passed beyond that initial barrier and have uncovered or created large expanses of time for themselves. For them, the ordering of time sometimes becomes problematic. Some would like to feel a sense of accomplishment at the end of the day or week. Although they may enjoy their days, they often do not experience the sense of achievement they would like to feel. Their days may not be goal-directed enough. They may need more direction and specific goals in their lives. For them, having a "lot of time" is frustrating and they subsequently "waste" much of it. They may find that they have fallen prey to the saying that, "Work expands to fill its allotted time." Their job is to learn to have time expand to fit the necessary work.

Most women find that learning to plan reasonable schedules for themselves becomes a very freeing experience. Everyone is somewhat organized, but the important question to ask is, "Does this organization work for you?" An efficient method of organization will allow you to reap the most benefit from your time. Sometimes lack of organization makes it hard to become goal-directed. And often not having goals can encourage a lack of useful organization. Routines also encourage the elimination of unnecessary, although time-consuming, steps. We begin to ask ourselves the question, "Why is this appliance there when it would be more efficient to have it here?" Or we may decide to combine three steps into one, and thereby save time.

Following are some suggestions that have been helpful to women who are at home most of the day, to women who work full-time, and to women who divide their time between home and part-time work away from home, either paid or volunteer.

Organization

Make lists for home and work. Keep them all together, whether they are ideas, projects, appointments, or errands to be run. Set priorities for both the home and work responsibilities. Decide what can be accomplished each day. Break up larger, over-whelming projects into more manageable parts. If you need to write a report, organize it at one time, gather all the necessary information during another block of time, perhaps outline it at a third time slot, and finally write and revise it during a final time period. If you need to do some housecleaning, organize the operation into manageable pieces. Clean out one closet at a time rather than avoiding the task because it "takes all day."

One possible method of organization focuses on the varying amount of energy felt at different times of the day. If your mind is clear and alert in the morning, that may be the time to tackle the projects such as analyzing figures, writing a report, paying the bills, planning a school event. If your energy level is still good in the afternoon, but your mind less alert, you might plan activities that require energy, but are more routine. And when your energy level and mental powers are at a lower ebb, you could plan to do enjoyable leisure activities, or very routine but necessary tasks. If you are consciously aware of your energy levels, you can plan your time more effectively.

Next, set priorities among the items on your list for the day or week. Which important items must be accomplished during that day? Be reasonable and stick to having only a few items on the "required" list. In the organizing of your schedule or routine, be certain to set aside some time for yourself each week. Often time set aside just for you will revitalize and reenergize you. You will be able to frequently analyze the progression of your life planning. It will be more difficult for large time slots to slip by unnoticed, which could result from the continuing stress of responsibilities you have each day. Though this time for yourself may be more difficult to find, it is important to try to carve it out for yourself. Money spent on care for your children, if it can be squeezed from the budget, is justifiable, and will pay off in the long term. During the summer or after school you might plan to have a sitter come in so that you can go to the art museum alone, visit a friend, take a class, do an exploratory interview, research a new field, take up jogging, or do twice the amount of shopping that would be possible if you had the children with you!

Delegate Responsibility

Many of us find it difficult to delegate responsibilities to others. We may not know how we want to spend the time that is now available to us. So we might hold on to some of our responsibilities in self-protection. "Johnny cannot do this very well, so I will keep on doing it until he is able." Or, "The wash just does not get clean unless I do it." Or, "When I let someone else chair the committee, I always end up telling them everything to do anyway. It is easier to do it myself." Or, "I do not trust them to accurately assess the figures. I had better do them myself."

It may be true that for the moment it is easier to do what you have always done. But there might be other ways you would rather spend your time. In addition, a case can be built for your "responsibility" to your children, your employees, your fellow committee members to teach them your expertise. In doing so, you are also carrying out your responsibility to yourself for freeing up more time for other endeavors.

Delegate by teaching. You can give the people you work or live with rules of thumb to follow when making a decision, when handling a responsibility or problem. Then, when specific events or similar situations occur, they have learned to make decisions they can later submit to you for a final check. You can decide together upon the tasks which each should try to accomplish each day. You can facilitate learning about how to make decisions regarding which activity or responsibility takes priority when there is time to only accomplish one.

Plan for Emergencies

If you have told your children that they can offer to bring treats to parties throughout the year, keep the necessary ingredients on your shelf. Have birthday presents available that are appropriate to the age of each of your children so that accepting a last-minute invitation does not create problems and does not encroach on your time commitments. Do an inventory at the beginning or end of each week in order to assess what has been accomplished and still needs to be accomplished. All areas of responsibility, including projects at work, volunteer commitments, the state of the family's wardrobe, can come under this planned review and goal-setting activity.

Keep a large calendar handy for everyone's referral. At home list all appointments, deadlines, events for all the family, so that everyone can refer to it for information, and so that you can each have a sense of each other's time commitments. Do the same at work, so that those you work with and supervise have an accurate awareness of your time schedule.

Handle matters immediately whenever possible. Make decisions to answer incoming mail and telephone calls. Throw away unnecessary paper, return "response-requested" announcements immediately. Develop a system of filing incoming papers so that they can be quickly retrieved for information or action. It is important to develop a plan of decisive action that reduces the number of loose ends that can cause problems.

One important hint is to use your various roles of wife/mother/career woman/daughter/friend/athlete to balance one another. Allow the variety of roles to energize you, rather than divide you. If you are struggling at work or at school, enjoy the activities and affection at home. If your house seems to be falling apart and you lack the time to reorganize just now, allow yourself to take refuge in your accomplishments in other areas of your life.

Identify Time Wasters

Undoubtedly, by now you have begun to identify some of your personal time wasters, some of the ways in which you could expand and more effectively utilize your time. Following is a fictitious description of a day in the work life of Jane, a trainer in the department of training and development in a large corporation, with three other trainers reporting to her. Her responsibilities are varied, including training those under her, running groups, researching ideas, contacting outside consultants, surveying needs in the company, budgeting her department's needs, evaluating the success of the programs, and educating herself by attending conferences and workshops on a continuing basis.

When Jane arrived at work at 8:30 there were already two messages waiting for her. She was contemplating returning the calls when the phone rang again. She answered, redirecting the caller to another department. As she looked through her mail, she buzzed her secretary and asked to see the mail from the previous day, when she had been away from the office.

After that one of the trainers she supervised stopped in to ask her about a group they were supposed to run together later in the week. After working through the details on that group, Jane decided to finalize those plans and spent a few minutes arranging the books and articles that would feed into her plans for the coming workshop. She had spent about thirty minutes on that when she decided that she needed more information. She called her secretary in to compile a list of her resources, so she could suggest other possible references for the workshop. Just as she began to immerse herself in her work again she received a call from an outside consultant regarding the possibility of the consultant's being hired for a two-day workshop. Jane needed to check the budget to see if there were adequate funds for this consultant and promised to return the call in a little while. She then buzzed the director of the department and asked if there were any additional monies for consulting in an area relating to affirmative action, which was a a high-priority item on this year's plans. Her boss said "possibly," and to get back to him the following day since just then he was leaving for a meeting.

Jane then returned the phone call to the potential outside consultant and promised to call her the next day. Reports of the evaluation of a managerial training class were then brought in by her secretary, and she perused them while noting that she needed to leave for town to meet a friend for lunch. She spent twenty minutes driving to the appointed restaurant and spent about forty-five minutes at lunch.

When Jane returned, she tried to decide whether to finish her research or clear her desk and complete it later. Just then her boss knocked on her door and asked her if she had a minute. They spent the next hour discussing budget plans, and also plans for developing better rapport between the secretaries and other staff. Jane noted then that it was 3:00, time for an appointment with the head of a division that wanted her to develop some workshops for them. The meeting, which lasted almost two hours, was not as productive as it might have been. Jane realized that she had not given this woman adequate written information about her department and spent precious time explaining basic procedures of training.

She then returned to her office to pick up a set of guidelines for requesting a course or workshop, and set another appointment for the next day. By then, it was almost 6:00 P.M., and Jane leafed through her mail again, trying to decide what to answer and what could wait until the next day. She responded to one final call, which requested her presence at a planning meeting on Friday, at which she would be required to present needs for additional funding.

Finally, Jane decided to pack up the books and articles that she needed to finish her research, since she remembered that the sheets for duplication needed to be given to the copy center within the next couple of days.

Can you identify the time wasters in Jane's day?

Can you list steps or ways in which these time wasters could be controlled?

What could she have eliminated? Delegated? Preplanned better?

Take this time, now, to describe a day in your work life or home life or combination of both, and be as specific as possible. After having done that, begin to look for *your* time wasters, ways in which you could have delegated responsibilities or planned better for more efficient and effective use of your time.

Finally, make a list of ways you may want to alter the way you spend your time, and keep track of changes you actually make in your daily schedule. Perhaps you will come to have the feeling that time is no longer controlling you to as great a degree as previously.

Reflect again on how you currently see your time commitments. Who or what do you feel has a right to your time? Where would you like to spend more of your time than you are presently? Where or how do you feel that you are spending too much time? How would you complete the sentence, "It is a waste of my time for me to _____?" And what about the sentence, "I should take the time to _____"? When I ask a friend/spouse/child/business associate if they have a "minute," what do I really mean? What do I want? When someone else asks me that same question, how do I feel? What do I regard as my own rights regarding time? If I were seventy-five years old right now, what is the one thing/activity/involvement/achievement that I regret not having done?

The problem and the privilege of deciding how to allocate your time is always with you. What will you do with your time? How will you use it, allocate it, and fill it?

The Total Fabric

An important result of making a conscious effort to be "in training" is that you will see yourself as being goal directed and will see the daily activities and pursuits as being part of a total pattern, although at times seemingly unrelated to one another. You will become involved in weaving the fabric that is your life. The conscious effort to translate skills learned in one activity to other activities or job settings does not have to be an arduous task that takes time away from more desirable activities. You can approach it casually by asking yourself at the end of each day, "What new thing have I learned about myself, about the world around me?" "Even if mistakes occurred, what have I learned for the future?" "How has this mistake become part of the overall pattern of creating my own present and future?"

VALUABLE VOLUNTEERING

"I volunteered for ten years; now I want to get paid for my work." "Let someone else do it; I've done my share.'" The P.T.A. president welcomes a new group of room mothers, "I'm so glad you came today. With so many women working these days it's hard to find room mothers."

Is our volunteer force shrinking? One organization in

Atlanta pays people to address envelopes and saves their more interesting jobs to attract volunteers. Will volunteerism go out of existence? Statistics show that women provided many millions of volunteer work hours last year. It doesn't seem likely that volunteerism is in danger of extinction but it does appear that, like other institutions, it is affected by the pressures of a changing society. There is growing controversy surrounding the once taken-for-granted role of women as volunteers, and this raises many questions.

Feminists may ask, "Can women afford to volunteer?" Some feel women deserve to be paid for their work and that they are being unfairly exploited when they volunteer. The example is cited of the man who earns $15,000 a year for a particular job and the woman who earns $10,000 for a comparable one. Is the woman "volunteering" $5,000 worth of her time? However, other people may argue, "Can women afford *not* to volunteer?" Who will be scout leaders, room mothers, serve meals on wheels, and raise money for needed charities? You may wonder, how does our history as women predispose us? Our past conditioning strongly encourages us to see ourselves as voluntary servers of others, to do what is needed, regardless of personal cost. Our heritage as women supports our deep sense of altruism, and our experience as homemakers conditions us to not expect monetary reward for our labors.

Historically, women have had a firm commitment to improving conditions for their families, their communities, and others in need. Have these once-valued virtues, which fed our self-esteem, become a contributing factor to our own oppression? Must we give up these traits in order to become economically independent? Is money the only viable remuneration for work? This widespread questioning, as well as the increasing number of women joining the paid labor force, will inevitably bring changes to the world of volunteerism and to the way in which women participate in it.

Our purpose in this section is to heighten your awareness concerning your experiences as a volunteer and to help you explore new ways to plan your volunteer work so that it can provide both meaningful service and personal gain. We see purposeful volunteerism as a way for women to "stay in training" while they are not working in a paid job. For women who have left the labor force to be at home with children, women who are preparing for their first job, or women who are considering a career change may believe volunteer work to be an important aspect of their lives. Volunteer experiences can become a necessary ingredient in the life plan of a woman who wants to have generative work as a continuous pattern in her life.

Women volunteers have not emerged from a single mold. These workers have a multidimensional composition that may vary with age, marital status, or educational and economic backgrounds. The amount of time devoted to volunteering may differ, as may the degree of skills brought to the job. However, one predominant commonality exists: few women consciously approach their volunteer work as stepping-stones to attaining personal and career goals. More often, volunteering has connoted a selfless act, done primarily to render service to others. If their experiences did lead to a career, it was often an accident of good fortune and timing. Their movement was more often a backing into an area, rather than a stepping toward one. We are suggesting that women maximize their opportunities as volunteers and recognize that helping themselves as well as others are compatible goals.

One way women can do this is by establishing themselves as "professional volunteers." This term is being used increasingly to give recognition to the idea that volunteers are unpaid workers who are employed, trained, supervised, promoted, dismissed, and given references as are any paid employees. The challenge in the changing attitude is two-fold. First, the volunteer must begin to see herself as a competent worker who is developing and learning through her work, education, and experience. She can initiate efforts to behave professionally in order to induce others to view her as a professional. Secondly, through her efforts, or as a result of other influences, agencies must change their own attitudes and recognize trained volunteers. Some agencies and organizations have been forced to do this as the volunteer force shrinks and they find themselves competing for volunteers.

The greatest impetus for the change in perception of volunteers must come from the woman herself. It begins with a personal awareness that the work she is doing as a volunteer is important and worthy of acknowledgment. She must recognize that she is developing skills and expertise, and that her ideas and opinions can be a contribution to the organization in which she works. As her confidence in her own abilities increases she can learn to assert herself within her work situation.

Gail devoted many years to developing educational programs for adults within a community center. Much to her chagrin, she often found that plans that she had made and discussed with staff members were later changed without consulting her. She believed that she had earned the right to be taken seriously. One such example was the program she planned for couples, in which the opportunity to discuss issues on sexuality with some local professionals was planned. Since it was to be a discussion involving audience participation, she decided that she could create a more open and relaxed atmosphere by not having the guests on a platform above the people. She preferred to have everyone seated in a circle on the same level and discussed this arrangement with the professional staff person, receiving agreement.

On the night of the program she arrived early and to her dismay found the room set up with a platform and podium and chairs arranged in rows. She asserted herself and insisted on the room arrangement being changed. The professional staff member seemed surprised by her insistence, but finally agreed. From then on they had a better working relationship, one in which Gail felt that her ideas would be seriously considered. She felt more confident that when agreements were reached they would be honored.

As a result of her actions, Gail felt as if she was beginning to establish herself on a new level both in her own eyes and those of the agency. The next educational program that she planned was an all-day workshop on professional volunteerism which was attended by one hundred women from the community.

There is much that you can do to build your sense of professionalism by your approach to volunteer work. If you calculate that you have ten hours a week to volunteer, think about and plan how you will use that time. Five hours may be spent on the job while the other five hours can be devoted to educating yourself to do the job more proficiently. Suppose you are working in a senior citizen's center. Part of your time may be spent at the center while the rest might be allotted to include reading books in the field of sociology of aging, taking a course at a local college or agency, or going to the library to read relevant research and articles in the professional journals. The staff members who supervise you can be a wonderful resource. They may suggest books or courses and they may also know about training workshops that you can attend.

Andrea had been an elementary school teacher before her children were born. She realized that in order to be prepared to go back to teaching when her kids were older, it would be important for her to find a way to stay current in her field and to continue to improve her skills. She found several opportunities through her volunteer work. On several occasions she volunteered to substitute at her son's nursery school. One day the director mentioned a professional educator's workshop in which she might be interested. That was just the first of many she decided to attend. Each time she was exposed to new information and stimulating ideas. These meetings were one way that she maintained her own sense of being a professional educator although she was not actively employed. On another occasion she noticed the lack of creative writing experiences in her children's elementary school. She went to the principal and volunteered to develop and teach a creative writing course as part of a program for talented and gifted children that the school was in the process of instituting. In this way she provided service to her children's school, challenged herself to develop and implement a new program, and gained additional experience to add to her résumé.

And there are other actions that you can initiate to increase your professionalism. You may be surprised to know that as a volunteer there are many professional and business organizations you can join. Your membership in such organizations will be a factor in how you are perceived as a volunteer, and in your level of self-confidence.

Another worthwhile investment may be a subscription to a professional journal in your field of interest. Or perhaps you can create an environment at your place of work that communicates that you are a distinct part of the ongoing operation of that organization. Depending on what kind of work you are doing, this can mean a desk of your own, personalizing your work space (a picture of your family, posters, whatever may be appropriate), dressing in the same professional manner as the paid professionals where you are working. Whatever steps you take in this direction, you will inspire confidence in yourself, and others' confidence in you.

The next step toward bridging the gap between volunteer and paid work is to keep a written record to document your experience and to develop references that will be prepared to speak about your achievements. Bonnie is a woman who profited by using her extensive volunteer work history. Eventally she was given a year's college credit for her extensive volunteer experiences. As a result of her experiences, she became the program director for a federally subsidized living unit and community center for the elderly. Later she was approached by the owners of a privately owned professional nursing-care facility to be the executive director of a retirement apartment complex.

Bonnie credits her experience as a volunteer with a woman's organization as the vehicle through which she explored her interests, developed new skills, and made the contacts in the community that culminated in her getting the job offer. Initially she had joined this organization as a way of making friends when she had moved to this city. She became involved in numerous projects of interest to her, gradually holding each successive office, until she eventually worked her way up to the president of her chapter and then on to an officer's post on the citywide governing body. She directly credits her performance on volunteer assignments with her successful job performance.

Another position Bonnie held was program chairman of her chapter and council. In this capacity she became familiar with a multitude of resources within the community for educational and cultural programs that would be stimulating to her group. She met many interesting people in the community and became acquainted with places that would provide free quality programs, such as speakers bureaus, colleges, special interest groups, and cultural centers in the city. When she became the program director at the home for the elderly, she already had this knowledge to draw upon as well as the many contacts she had made.

Since she had worked side by side with the leaders of many volunteer organizations through the years, she knew where to go for help and discovered that they responded more readily than they might have to someone without volunteer experience. Part of her ability to coordinate a successful program was a result of the fact that she thoroughly understood the role of volunteers and their need to be recognized and treated as professionals.

There were other skills that Bonnie was able to transfer to her new work situation. She had held the office of treasurer and had been required to set up budgets and financial guidelines. She was able to apply this knowledge and experience in her new job. As a volunteer she had also been responsible for leadership training, and had become an effective group facilitator. These were abilities that were useful when she established self-governing groups in the retirement complex. Her volunteer work had allowed her to develop her skills in managing and supervising.

Bonnie's accomplishments and new abilities added to her confidence, but attaining a job required assertiveness as well. Through her volunteer work, she heard that the home for the elderly had received extensive funding, and that there were some paid positions to fill. Temporary economic necessity in her family prompted Bonnie to apply for the job of executive secretary to the board of directors. This was a temporary part-time job with flexible hours that fit her needs while her children were still young. This job provided a transition from volunteer to paid work and paved the way for Bonnie's developing career. She became involved with every phase of setting up this federally subsidized housing for the elderly. When funds became available through a federal grant to set up a senior citizen center in the same facility, Bonnie applied for the job of program director. Originally, the thought had been to fill this vacancy with a social worker; however Bonnie convinced them that although she did not have a college degree she had the expertise and experience necessary to do the job successfully.

She reports feeling like a "sponge" during this period, wanting to soak up all the information she could which dealt with aging, agency work, and social service. She was encouraged by the community center's staff members who made funds available to pay for courses and workshops, and adopted flexible hours for her so that she could include this education in her schedule. By this time Bonnie came to the conclusion that she needed further college education, in order to progress and feel proficient in her work. She decided to work on a degree in gerontology which was available at a local college. Even though the community center was paying for her education Bonnie felt strongly that her experience as a volunteer and her present job experience should be worth something in time and money. Consequently, she decided to apply for college credits for life experience and began to write up her years of volunteering in great detail. In forty typewritten pages she described each job and training experience. She included the duties she performed, what she had learned, and the results of her work. To do this she was greatly helped by her foresight in having saved training materials, notes, and calendars that contained records and dates of her activities. For her efforts Bonnie received thirty hours' worth of credits toward her degree.

Engaging in meaningful work has been a continuous stream throughout Bonnie's life. Her job as mother and homemaker, her volunteer work, her employment as a paid program director, attaining her college degree, and her current position as executive director of a private retirement living complex fed one into another. Bonnie's story is a clear example of the relevance of volunteer work to paid employment.

Many volunteer organizations have recognized the need for women to keep extensive records of their volunteer experiences. They see this as a way for women to increase their sense of pride and fulfillment in their work, and a way to gain credentials that can be applied to a future career. To facilitate the writing of a personal log, the National Council of Jewish Women has developed a manual called *The Personal Career Portfolio.* "This tool," they write, "will enable any member not only to chart her own progress, but also to validate her volunteer experiences for others. This *Personal Career Portfolio* can provide a graphic record of a member's individual growth, progress, and accomplishments through Council activities."

This manual contains an inventory of skills section that helps women assess and define the skills they have developed. It also contains specific forms: one for recording education and training in which they have participated, and the other to note job experience. On each form there is a space for the date and signature of the person supervising the training or work performed. This process enables women to recognize their own areas of expertise and to plan for the future by determining what new skills and on-the-job training they would like to acquire. The information gathered can also become the basis for a résumé to be written at a later time.

Sue is another woman who has successfully combined her desire to serve in a particular organization with her wish to personally grow and gain skills that would help qualify her to enter the paid labor force. She was aware that she had developed many transferable skills, and had received much positive response from her co-workers. She knew she was capable. But she was uncertain about how to translate what she had learned into language that would help others to see how competent she had become. As she analyzed her past work experiences, she began to isolate specific skills that could be applicable to any number of work settings. These skills could then be transferred to a résumé that would eventually help her sell herself into a position for which she was qualified.

First, Sue thought through her experience over the last ten years, during which she had been actively involved in volunteering. She had been president of a large volunteer organization devoted to rehabilitation through training that operates and maintains vocational training centers in thirty countries. The organization, locally, included some two hundred active members. Then she had assumed an even larger responsibility, that of vice-president of the regional organization, which was comprised of twelve hundred people. In addition she was actively involved in chairing several committees and projects along the way.

Next Sue analyzed her education and training. She had a B.A. in liberal arts received some fifteen years ago. Since then, she had participated in many training workshops, as well as leading several. Also, she had taken adult education courses in accounting, business management, and the art of supervising at the local community college.

Next Sue analyzed her specific achievements throughout those ten years, looking for patterns or clusters of skills that were repeated and in which she had become proficient. Her skills-analysis sheet looked like this:

ACCOMPLISHMENTS	SKILLS UTILIZED IN THE PROCESS
1. Motivated workers to produce to their maximum, in order to achieve our yearly profit forecast.	team building, training, supervising, managing, motivating
2. Developed short- and long-term goals and objectives.	planning, organizing

3. Designed and developed innovative programs that were successfully implemented.

delegating, organizing, planning, program designing

4. Identified the dollars, personnel, and material resources necessary to meet established objectives; handled the budget.

forecasting, analyzing, budgeting

5. Set priorities regarding objectives.

analyzing, evaluating

6. Organized programs into a logical sequence of units.

organizing, analyzing, managing time

7. Delegated responsibilities for various projects, their maintenance and continuation.

delegating, organizing, evaluating

8. Established methods of accountability to ascertain if responsibilities were being met.

evaluating, researching, analyzing, record keeping

9. Wrote appropriate reports.

writing, evaluating

10. Kept the books, prepared the budget, analyzed costs, purchased supplies.

purchasing, financial planning, cost analysis

11. Maintained liaison with the community.

public relations duties, public speaking, promoting, and advertising

12. Developed alternative plans for unexpected emergencies.

planning, analyzing, forecasting

13. Encouraged and built support and rapport among the workers.

listening, negotiating, communicating, coordinating, facilitating

14. Set up small business, learned every detail about its operations.

organizing, merchandizing, managing, coordinating

Sue became aware of the power of her experience. She also realized the need to further analyze her accomplishments. She needed to think in greater detail about the business she had organized and the responsibilities she had assumed. She began to see a pattern to her skills. Particular skills reappeared several times during her analysis of her achievements. Often repeated on the list were her abilities to organize, manage, supervise, analyze, budget, evaluate, communicate, and coordinate. Other skills were listed less often, but included areas in which Sue believed herself to be effective, such as public relations, advertising, writing, and effective time management. Finally she focused on those areas she was most interested in developing, such as expertise in merchandising and marketing.

Drawing from this information about herself, Sue began to search for specific courses she might take to further develop her expertise. She had become more directed. She was significantly more aware of the pattern of her interests and skills. She could now phrase a work objective that would accurately include her areas of expertise, although it would not necessarily be specific about the numerous potential work environments open to her. One possible objective would be the desire for a managerial position, utilizing demonstrated skills in planning, organizing, supervising, program development, and communication. Now Sue had the introductory segment of her résumé, and could accurately present herself on paper in a way that would minimize the chances of a potential employer thinking of her as "just a volunteer" without any experience.

Another way of planning the crossover to paid employment is through "volunteer apprenticeships." This term is currently being used to describe a person who agrees to work in a job without being paid, usually with the intention of receiving a salary after an initial training period or when essential job skills are acquired. Jody used this method effectively. She had a degree in physical therapy and worked for five years before stopping to have children. She decided to pursue other interests while her children were young. During the remodeling and decorating of her home, she rediscovered her talent for working with colors, fabrics, and design. She received encouragement for her creativity and selections from the decorator with whom she was working. This sparked her interest in further exploring the field of interior design.

She approached an interior design firm, and offered to work without pay in exchange for being permitted to learn the trade. Their initial response was quite negative, but through persistence Jody persuaded them to let her try. She set up a schedule in which she planned to come into their studio several half-days each week. This plan blended well with her routine at home. She learned quickly by being a keen observer and most of all by asking many questions. Within six months she was attending furniture shows in Chicago and New York and within a year the firm offered to put her on a salary rather than commission. During her apprenticeship Jody insisted on being introduced to clients as a designer; after all, no one would have confidence in her if she were referred to as an apprentice! Jody worked successfully as an interior designer for several years and is now reevaluating whether she wants to stay in this area, go back to physical therapy, or try something totally different. If she does decide to stay with interior design, she plans to return to school and take appropriate course work, particularly in drawing and drafting. She feels that she learned more from her on-the-job training than she could have from going back to school for a degree in design. In her case, it was a wise choice to defer further education until she could assess her responses to the work.

One woman volunteered to help her brother with some roofing work he was doing, and within two years wound up owning her own roofing company and six trucks. Another helped out her friend who was selling life insurance and used this informal apprenticeship as time to learn the business and develop her self-confidence. Eventually she began to sell insurance, and ultimately, several years later, she started her own company. The federal government has instituted similar programs for people who are economically disadvantaged. However, in many of these instances the participants are paid subsistence wages until they are qualified for paid employment. This area of volunteer apprenticeship deserves further consideration in the private business sector. There may be some creative arrangements that can be developed between women seeking to learn certain skills and gain work experience and local businesses who are continuously searching for competent, reliable employees.

Mary's Story

Mary epitomizes the way in which a woman can raise her antennae and stay in training, by always being on the alert for information that will lead her toward her goals. Like all of us, Mary has had her ups and downs, times when she felt very goal-oriented and times when she felt herself to be struggling with the identities of woman, wife, mother, daughter, volunteer, and more. Mary has not been formally employed since she had her first child. But she has consistently been involved in volunteer activities appropriate to the ages of her children and to her specific interests.

As her children grew, as she began to feel and respond to the vibrations of the women's movement, and as good friends returned to work, she began to search within herself and to assess what else she may want to do. This was a time of some discontent, a searching in a sea of opportunities and options. One of her long-range plans was to integrate her college major, home economics, with her organizational abilities and her continued interest in nutrition, and open a nutritious soup-and-sandwich "luncheon wagon" in the heart of a suburban business district. She thought through whether this would be a good decision for her. Her husband's position demanded that he travel a great deal, and she enjoyed being free to go with him when it could be arranged. Consequently, she really did not want to be tied down to a full-time job and a forty-hour week. Neither did she feel that such a job was necessary to her sense of accomplishment or sense of self at this point in her life. Significant, of course, was the fact that additional dollars were not needed in the family "money pot."

Since she was unable to find appropriate part-time work, Mary continued to participate in a variety of volunteer activities, to take exploratory courses, and to pursue other interests while her youngest child was growing up. When her husband was offered an excellent position with another company, they moved to a new, smaller city. It was at this point that Mary was ready to become more involved in volunteer work that was consistent with her skills, her education, and her emerging self-awareness.

As had always been her style, Mary began her planned research by asking many questions about the town, the governmental system, the educational system, and various large organizations in the community. She continued to take noncredit courses at the local community college in order to get to know people and to learn about her new town. She spent two years becoming acquainted with the various organizations, boards, and committees that are run or assisted by volunteers. She spent time actively participating in four organizations that appealed to her. By then, she was offered positions on the board of directors of two of the organizations. Ultimately, with the specific knowledge she gained about the various organizations, the self-awareness to know what she personally wanted to contribute, and personal expectations and goals carefully delineated, she decided to consolidate her commitments and accept a volunteer position that was consistent with her own goals and talents. In this position she would have the power to significantly impact the direction of the organization. She was particularly challenged because her new responsibilities would include supervising and training a large number of volunteers within the organization.

Mary has reached a comfortable plateau, doing what she would like with her work life, at present. She feels good about having approached her life/work planning in a way that broadened her awareness of options. She has not discarded her dream of opening a restaurant, but is allowing this dream to reside in an easily retrievable place, should she eventually decide to move away from volunteer work. And throughout the next few years, Mary intends to allow her perpetually raised antennae to sense new options, remind her of other dreams, and notice changes in herself, all of which may be tapped in her future.

Updating Your Attitudes Toward Money

❧

At first glance a chapter on money might seem out of place in the midst of a book on the emerging work patterns of women. But on second thought, most of us would say that such a topic is *very* appropriate. Money does affect our lives in numerous ways, whether or not we want it to. It is an underlying factor in many of our attitudes toward ourselves, our relationships with other people, and with our future goals.

For example, one woman's attitude toward herself was influenced by the comparison she made between herself and more financially successful women. Altough her job was low-paying, it met her needs and she enjoyed it. However, when she went to a professional women's meeting and interacted with women who held higher-paying, more prestigious jobs, she began to feel inferior.

Even our decisions of whether or not to work may be based upon our attitudes about money. For some women, their decision is based on how much money they will have left to contribute to the family money pot after having paid for new clothes, transportation, and baby-sitters. For them, the surplus money becomes the deciding factor regarding whether or not they work outside the home, and the issue of finding satisfaction through work is often relegated to the back seat. Other women may decide to accept jobs, whether they particularly like them or not, in order to maintain the feeling of power and independence they derive from earning their own money. One woman did not feel that she had the right to spend the family's money on an education for herself, although the couple *was* planning to finance the education of their children. This attitude makes a woman more cautious about spending money on herself, even when the investment would have a positive long-term effect on the entire family. Feeling dependent on someone else for money may increase other forms of dependence. The young woman of twenty-two may have a difficult time deciding to get an apartment and trying managing on her own, when she is living at home and her parents are supporting her.

The purpose of this chapter is to help us become more conscious of just how money does affect us, our present, and our future. And once we are aware, it is very difficult to then be unaware. We may choose not to act upon our knowledge, but then we have indeed made a conscious choice. With the ability to choose control or, at the very least, impact upon the direction of our life styles and upon our future as individuals, as women.

IMAGES OF WOMEN AND MONEY

What are some of our images relating to women and money? For the most part they depict women as being passive, frivolous, and rather incompetent with regard to money. The scenes we still visualize may be of money being doled out to women, women not being able to balance a checkbook, women mindlessly running up bills on their charge accounts, women being only in lower-paying jobs or women at their wits' end trying to stay within a budget. Another common image depicts women in the role of a martyr—doing without so she can buy something for another family member, stretching a small food budget, having a little "sugar bowl or teapot" fund to use for special needs of family members, always thinking of others and never of herself. Very few images depict women as able to control, manage or negotiate large or even small sums of money, even though women in recent years have been extremely successful as bankers and stockbrokers. In the world of business today women are managing, investing, and making decisions about large amounts of money very competently. Unfortunately, even these facts have not significantly altered the reality that, as a whole, women are not seen and responded to as being able to control money.

We might like to pretend that the women's movement of the last few decades has obliterated stereotypes of women as incompetent money managers, but that would be to ignore much of our deep-rooted societal influence. The myth exists that women who can successfully deal with money are the exception rather than the rule. Recent research does not support this belief that such women are the exception. Results have shown that, given the same opportunities and training, women as well as men can learn to manage finances with expertise. In a recent study at the University of Oklahoma, a group of women competed with a group of men in managing two equal investment packages. Seventy-two percent of the women, as compared with 33 percent of the men, turned in a better managed portfolio. But the very fact that this study and others like it take place indicates that as a society, we (men and women) are still struggling with the attitudes that women are, as a group, less capable of dealing with the total financial picture for themselves, for a family, or for a company. Even though intellectually we accept the possibility that no greater numbers of women than men fit the comic strip characterization of the muddleheaded individual with a perpetually overdrawn checking account, emotionally we may still operate within the confines of such stereotypes.

Our country's laws and economic system reflect society's influence in keeping women dependent on men and tied to a marital life style. It has only been a few short years since women could get charge cards in their own name without a fight, establish credit, or secure a loan to purchase a home or start a business (and it is still not that easy). An employed wife's income was not considered stable enough to be included when seeking a loan for a house. It was difficult for a woman to feel that she could be self-sufficient or choose a single life style. Though many women are single today, by choice or not, some of the laws and practices in our society have not kept pace with the changes in decisions to be single. For many women have traded a married life style for a single life (with or without children) and a financial struggle.

The advertising industry consciously appeals both to the stereotyped images and to the emerging image of the "professional working woman" in order to influence us on an emotional level. One ad selling a particular make of car emphasized the traditional view and consists of a series of interviews with people who have bought that car and are pleased. One interview is with a young single woman who is asked if she consulted "experts" to see if buying the car was a good expenditure. She replies yes, she had consulted her father and her brother because they knew about buying things for that amount of money. There is nothing inherently wrong with the process the woman used. She talked with people she considered to have more experience than she in such matters. A wise move. But what such ads do is to promote the image that women, independently, do not usually make decisions about large expenditures of money.

Nevertheless, our increasing awareness of women's ability to earn money, as well as changing laws and attitudes, are affecting women's feelings of independence, and offering us new options for living. This new awareness can give us the freedom to choose to maintain that image of the financially dependent woman, or to decide that we want to broaden our options and begin to see ourselves as financially aware and competent.

YOUR MONEY PHILOSOPHY

The topic of money is alluded to in many situations each week, but how many times in our lives have we been inclined to fully explore our feelings about money? During our adolescence and early adulthood many of us spent long hours talking or thinking about our feelings about ourselves, our friends, our family, the future, and life itself, but usually not about our feelings toward money or about making money, or about building a secure monetary base. Money was usually discussed in terms of what it could get us, whether we did or did not have it, or whether we would have to worry about it. And yet money, and/or the lack of it, has an impact upon us, for good or for ill.

We would like you to take the time to explore the topic of

money and to sort out your feelings, attitudes, beliefs, and thoughts about money in order to see if you want to maintain them as they are. How do they fit in with your future plans? Do you want to alter your attitudes and perceptions in some way?

What kinds of feelings are evoked when you hear the word "money"? Your reactions reflect your personal philosophy about money. Though you may not feel that you *have* a philosophy of money, you probably do. This philosophy is a belief system that has been shaped by many forces; the historical impact of money on your life, cultural traditions and customs, societal stereotypes, and your parents' mode of handling their finances all combine to contribute to your philosophy of money. Your present awareness about any issue is the product of your past knowledge and experiences. If your present goal is to gain a sense of control over your attitudes toward money, then it is necessary to begin by tracing the roots of these attitudes and beliefs.

What you learned as a child is influential in determining your current belief system about money. Much has been written on the power and lasting influence of behaviors modeled in families. And as an adult you may recognize that you are repeating and responding to behaviors and attitudes of your parents. You may even revert to repeating the same phrases you heard as a child. For example, if you had a parent who dreaded owing money, you may sense some vestiges of that fear in yourself. You may hear yourself repeating familiar sayings from your childhood, such as, "A penny saved is a penny earned," or, "Don't be a spendthrift." You may respond to your parents' "cash-only" method of keeping track of the finances by doing the opposite and overextending yourself on credit cards. Or you may find it impossible to utilize the luxury of credit cards when you should be able to take advantage of it. In either case your behavior may be related more to past learning than to an updated appraisal of how you consciously want to handle your finances today.

What child has not been impressed with the message that saving is important? That having money of one's own means making decisions about how to spend it. But in how many cases was it also impressed upon the child that spending can be exhilarating, that saving indefinitely without a goal in mind may not always be appropriate? It is important to explore what other messages were transmitted to you as a child, because your existing philosophy about money will possibly relate to and reflect that of your parents. How involved was your mother in the family finances? Was this your father's responsibility? Was money a subject that could be discussed? While certain aspects of the subject may have been open, such as negotiating for a higher allowance, or talking about how much something cost as a family before deciding to make a purchase, were other areas closed, such as how much a house cost, how much your father earned, how much should be saved, how much should be spent and for what?

How does what you learned about money in your family of origin affect how you feel about spending money now, as an adult? When a young child takes his carefully saved three dollars to the dime store, having been told that he saved it, and therefore he can spend it "however he wants," what actually happens? As he walks around looking at the trinkets, does his parent respond approvingly to some things and disapprovingly to others? Is he told that he cannot buy that toy car because he already has a dozen similar ones at home, and that he shouldn't buy felt-tip pens because he always forgets to put the top on and they dry up? Quite appropriately, certain restrictions based on safety considerations need to be made, even if no other rules are placed on the child's spending expedition. Often a parent may feel that he is giving free rein (within the limits set), but may respond oh so supportively to the purchase of one thing over another, or suggest that he look a little longer, before making up his mind (hoping, of course, that he discards the outrageously high-priced automatic bubble-blower). As a child, you undoubtedly absorbed the verbal and nonverbal messages about money that surrounded you during your growing years.

The more women we talked to about money the clearer it became that there is a connection between childhood experiences and their current reactions. In one personal development class, the women were asked to try to get in touch with some of the messages they received from their families about money, women and money, women and earning, and the appropriateness of talking about money. Most of the women were never included in a discussion of routine financial decisions, even into the teenage years. One woman stated that around the time of paying bills, her father always got rather grumpy and short-tempered. When she assumed these responsibilities in her marriage, she found that she also assumed those emotional responses to paying the bills. She got mildly depressed and had actual physiological reactions. The anxiety evoked by the situation was enormous. This anxiety, incidentally, was not based on inadequate funds, because as it turns out there was more than enough money to cover the bills. As this woman talked about her feelings with the group and shared the underlying sense of panic that she had felt as a child (always wondering if there was really enough money), her end-of-the-month accounting became more routine and less encumbered by emotional responses.

Learning to make decisions and becoming self-sufficient accompany an adolescent's passage into adulthood. In many cases women may have been protected by their parents, then are protected by a husband before ever experiencing the ability to take care of themselves. This may result in a feeling of dependence on another person for survival. Eliminating this feeling of dependence often opens up new dimensions in a relationship. Jacqueline Grennan Wexler, formerly president of Webster College in St. Louis, and of Hunter College in New York City, and now with a private consulting firm, was recently quoted as saying the following, with reference to her marriage: "I think the sheer reality that economically either one of us could walk out tomorrow and not starve is a very important condition of our freedom, of our being sure we want to stay together."

When did you learn how to budget or balance a checkbook? Who coached your decisions about what to buy or how much to spend? Have you ever purchased a car on your own or filled out an income tax form? Although decision-making involving money is only one of the factors involved in developing a feeling of independence, it can contribute to the impotent feeling of the woman who has passed into her childbearing years, yet in her own mind remains an adult-little girl. This may produce conflicting feelings for the woman who is caught between her own desire for self-reliance, a desire for partnership in marriage, and societal traditions that place money matters within the husband's realm of responsibility. Each of us must determine for herself if there is a correlation between our feelings of independence as adult women and our ability to earn and/or manage our financial portfolio.

MONEY AND SUCCESS

Considering a dictionary definition of a word is a logical place to begin an exploration of the history of a word, for definitions provide a window on what a culture or a society has agreed that a word shall mean. The *American Heritage Dictionary's* definition of money is a useful one with which to begin searching into your feelings about money. Money is defined as, "a commodity that is legally established as an *exchangeable equivalent of all other commodities* and used as a *measure of their comparative market value.*" Money has come to replace the barter system and to be an acceptable measure of the worth or value of some other commodity. The exchange of this legal tender evolved when our society became too complex to handle the simpler exchange between people, for example firewood or food for the services of a physician. (A form of exchange still exists between some professionals, such as between physicians, and is beginning to crop up again around the country. But the national government offers little support of such a barter system, because obviously, if such a system became widespread it would result in the loss of tax monies.) Once the system of exchange was simplified with the introduction of money as the legal medium of exchange, a philosophical shift also took place. This legal tender became a new measure of success, status, power, independence, and security, all of which significantly affect our personal philosophies about ourselves.

Do we see money as an indication of personal success and a lack of money as a mark of personal failure? Whether or not we agree philosophically, we live in a society that regards with awe those people who are wealthier than we are. And if we don't have much money, then we must have some other socially redeeming quality such as beng a dedicated teacher or a struggling artist or a humanitarian. But where do women fit into this scheme of things? According to a document presented at the 1980 United Nations conference on women held in Copenhagen, women account for half the world's population, put in two-thirds of the world's working hours, receive one-tenth of the world's income and one-hundredth of its property.

In most cultures, a woman's esteem has been traditionally linked to the success of her husband or her father. She shared in the esteem given her husband's or her father's financial success.

She might even have been significantly involved in the success of a family-owned business, working side by side with the men, but rarely was she singled out by society as successful in her own right, as were the male members of the concern. A woman's image has long been linked more with spending rather than with earning.

Just as we cannot pretend that stereotypes of women as incompetent money managers have ceased to exist, we cannot ignore the fact in the last decade there has been movement and change with regard to expectations of women. There is a subtle, and in some cases, a not so subtle shift away from placing a high measure of regard on service or nurturing activities of women. Previously many women were found in the service fields such as teaching and nursing, jobs everyone knew to be low in pay but were not held to be low in status. In these cases, the status of the position was more important than was the salary of the position. Low pay/low status jobs such as waitress or salesclerk were often seen as temporary (until marriage) or supplemental (for luxury items). Women who worked in factories, offices, stores, and beauty shops, whose income was a crucial determinant of the family's success at remaining afloat, were often looked at with great admiration, for their ability to survive in a man's work world. The woman whose degree of affluence permitted her the luxury of working only in the home had a different measure of her success. She was judged in terms of her homemaking and nurturing abilities, or in terms of her volunteer and civic involvement.

Along with the increasing possibilities for greater earning power among women, there is an emerging tendency to measure a woman's success by how much she earns. This has taken place as college-educated women enter traditionally male-dominated fields, such as engineering, medicine, and management—the professional who can command a high-level salary. Many women whose training may have been in teaching or counseling are choosing new titles such as trainer and consultant in an effort to portray a different status, to increase work options, and to reach a higher salary potential.

The unfortunate result of the "demoting" of teachers' status, particularly the elementary teacher, is the tremendous loss of conscientious, well-trained, concerned teachers for our children. Ten years ago, a woman was usually proud to say she was a teacher; today she may be hesitant to admit it. Though she may still love teaching, and may be gifted in working with children, this changing attitude of society often affects her negatively. It becomes important to consider the following questions. "Does she deserve to have a diminished status?" "Does the increased entry of other professional women into the labor force necessarily need to negatively affect her professional status?" and finally, "Does the traditional male model need to replace the traditionally female model, in terms of recognition and perception or measure of success?"

This monetary measure of success or worth or value is significant with regard to single women and to married women without children. In increasing numbers, single women enrolling in personal development classes are negating the value of their work in service-oriented jobs, blue- or pink-collar occupations, and entry-level positions in offices. Even though they may be happy and satisfied in their jobs, feeling challenged and productive, some single women are beginning to feel apologetic about holding such jobs. It is becoming very important for many of these women that they see themselves as being "professional." And even those women who are proud of their work, who experience great satisfaction from their jobs in traditionally female work settings, are becoming rapidly disenchanted with the low pay and lack of advancement possibilities. As more women are beginning to consider their work in a longer-term perspective (knowing they may spend twenty, thirty, or forty years in the labor force), they are becoming aware of the crucial need to plan for continued growth potential in their jobs and careers.

The married woman without children, as well as the single woman, is being judged more automatically as a career woman whose job takes top priority. The married woman *with* children, however, may at times not be taken seriously at all, regardless of the level of her job. The myth that her income is only necessary for luxuries continues to persist, even in the face of overwhelming evidence to the contrary. She is perceived as self-serving, because she "ignores the needs of her children"; or "too aggressive," because she has dared to enter a traditionally male field. She is often considered "the exception." And even though she is clearly a competent individual, the generalization is rarely drawn that other women who are doctors, lawyers, accountants, dentists, and pilots are also quite competent.

Frequently, successful women are perceived as having been "lucky," or as being in the right place at the right time, or as having an interested father or mentor, or accidentally attending a college that specialized in her area of expertise. This tendency to displace or ignore the credit she deserves for participating in the creation of her future is often the most frustrating of all assumptions, complicated further by the fact that women who have heard this line so often begin to accept it as truth.

One woman we know used a tremendous amount of initiative and creativity to create her own production company and develop a unique children's theater for a variety of groups. She derived enormous satisfaction from her work. Though she charged a low fee, partly because of limited monies available for such experimental ideas, she felt as if her talents and energies were being thoroughly utilized. Her contribution to her community was significant and important. Her needs to be creative, work with children, and be involved in theater were being adequately met. For the time being, she was exactly where she wanted to be.

Eventually, however, this woman began to feel somewhat uneasy about the inordinate number of hours she put into her work and its inverse relationship to her earning power. As she watched her friends and acquaintances moving into higher-paying jobs, she became aware of her emerging need to earn more money, to be recognized with more dollars for her work. She was not entirely comfortable with this awareness, having been socialized into believing that the work itself should be satisfaction enough. Not willing to sacrifice this enormously satisfying work in favor of something higher paying but unrelated, she decided to apply for a much larger grant, and requested double the salary she had been receiving. She had found a way to incorporate her emerging need for more dollars with her other needs that were already being satisfied through her work.

In the business world, performance appraisals have been traditionally defined as times to evaluate performances and give raises. Discussions of the quality of one's work were usually included at these times. There is now a definite attempt and emerging commitment to separate the issues of salary and performances by dealing with them at separate meetings; but it is difficult to make this system work. The importance of a salary increase and other fringe benefits are still the primary method we have of evaluating our performance. We can receive additional responsibilities, new job titles, reinforcement for creative ideas and doing a job well, but the praise will quickly wear thin for us unless there is a salary increase attached, even for those who do not really "need" additional dollars.

Even if there are really no additional monies available, as in a social welfare agency on government grant money, and even if we do not need the money (which does not apply to most of us), low pay and limited raises do make us reflect on our own perception of our success. And *if* we can "successfully" escape linking money and success in our mind, we still have the frustration of dealing with the feelings, often nonverbally expressed, of family, friends, and acquaintances of the people who do measure our success in terms of the increase in dollars we earn.

Such an attempt to separate performance from raises parallels that of a child who transfers into a nongraded primary school from a traditional elementary school. She now needs to become accustomed to extensive comments on her work, rather than getting a grade. She may continually ask her teacher, "What would I get on this *if* you would give me a grade?" This question may frustrate a teacher who has finally learned not to or has never had to assign a grade to a writing paper or a social studies project. And parents who may have always had their children in this nongraded school often still respond with feelings that reflect their own grade school experience, by asking what grade the child would be given if one were given. There is always the concern of parents who state that the world of education is a graded one, and that their child will suffer if they do not become accustomed to receiving grades for work. Perhaps the child who has grown up in an educational system that does not assign grades (of which there are a rare few), may stand a chance of separating in his mind dollars earned from how well a job was done. But there will continue to be those who "help" convince him that the true measure of his success resides in his monetary rewards.

One woman spent two years as a Sunday school principal developing curriculum, hiring and supervising teachers, and administering programs. When asked if she worked, she answered, "Yes, only part-time." Further questioning revealed a deep sense of pride in her job performance, as well as much individual growth resulting from her work. She devalued its significance, mostly because of an "embarrassingly low" salary for the amount of time and energy she had devoted. Did her embarrassment stem from her own need to be affirmed by salary increases, or from others' lack of recognition for her incredibly valuable services?

Or did her embarrassment relate to the lack of prestige that usually accompanies a "part-time" job? Whatever the source of her discomfort, the first step is for her to sort out her own feelings in regard to her job performance and monetary worth. She must feel convinced of her own competence and accordingly decide what salary expectations she has. She needs to acknowledge to herself the importance of the job she is doing in order for others to be positive and supportive.

If she decides that she deserves more money, she can move in this direction by negotiating for a raise. If no additional monies are available, she may choose to work for less than she feels she is worth because of the satisfaction she is getting. However, if she cannot feel good about herself continuing at that salary she may decide the experience she has gained in the last two years will pay off, will indeed have been a good investment, as she looks for a new job.

Another woman made a definite decision to leave a good-paying, full-time job in public relations to take a part-time job doing promotion for a theater group, which paid her only minimum wage. Why? First, she decided that she wanted more free time. Secondly, she was interested in the challenges of the promotion work. To her, success was doing a job she liked which allowed her free time for other interests. Although she was conscious of the low pay, and occasionally mentioned it, she felt very satisfied with her decision. It worked for her because she came to terms with the change in salary before she accepted the job.

And yet another woman decided to seek a promotion within her company, not because she did not like her work or feel that she had been unsuccessful in her job, but because she began to feel unsuccessful within the total organizational structure. Her low salary was well known since salaries there were public knowledge, and even though she was respected for her accomplishments, in that structure success was equated with regular salary increases and/or promotions. When it became clear that the salary increases would be very minimal for her current position, she decided to seek a position further up the ladder. She felt that the move was one consistent with her view, and the organization's view, of success.

Consider how societal messages that pair money with success affect your decision making in your present situation. Would you feel less successful if, in order to change careers, you had to start at a lower salary? If you had been successful in your job and were earning a good salary, would you feel equally successful if you stopped working? Do you regard a woman whose job is homemaker and mother to be less successful than a person who receives monetary remuneration for her work? If you are primarily a homemaker, how do you view your work? How do you think others view you? How do others' responses to you influence the kind of work you have chosen?

Each of us must evaluate for herself how important earning money, and the amount earned, is in determining our feelings of success, for the perception of people with whom we have relationships tends to be greatly affected by the opinion we have of ourselves. Consequently, when the Sunday school teacher begins to feel proud of her work, and views herself as valuable and successful, people around her will probably adopt the image she projects.

It is important to realize the necessity of redefining success as our needs change. During the stages of our life when our strongest need is to be productive in work, our success may indeed be determined by our earning capacity. In a stage in which rearing young children is dominant, our success may be more tied to our expertise at parenting. Similarly, when our need is to expand our horizons, our ability to take risks may be a new measure of our feelings of success. Even though our different roles may be concurrent (wife, mother, worker) the needs related to one role will very often take priority. What is significant is how successfully we meet these changing needs throughout our life.

You may go through different stages or phases in your attitude about the work you do and the salary you earn. When you first begin working in a job you have been training for or hoping for, you may be quite pleased to have the job, regardless of the salary. But the longer you have the job, and the more you look around at people who have similar jobs or do the same kind of job in a different setting, the more you may begin to feel dissatisfied with your salary as compared with theirs. This may be especially true if you believe that you handle your job much more competently than they do, or when you see your job as far more demanding than theirs.

It is extremely useful for all of us to periodically evaluate how we feel about money. Ask yourself the following questions on your personal journey into your feelings about this subject.

1. What were your feelings about your salary when you took your first job?

2. How did those close to you feel about the salary you received in your frst job?

3. How much would you be satisfied with earning now? Are you earning that? What do you hope to be earning in five years? What do you *think* you will need to be earning in five years?

4. What is the minimum amount of money you need to earn now, just to pay the bills? What steps can you take to reach those goals?

5. If you had an opportunity to do the same kind of work for more money, would you switch jobs? If so, why? If not, why not?

6. Are your feelings about the above questions very similar or very different from your parents' feelings about money? From your siblings'? From a spouse's? From what you would like them to be?

CHAPTER VIII

Managing

Your Money

After listening to many women discuss their ideas and preferences concerning money and its meaning in their lives, one fact becomes apparent. The spectrum of opinions relating to money and the options for handling it are endless. Obviously, no one way is the "right" way or viewpoint, but it is clearly important that throughout this chapter you examine your own ideas and beliefs and make *dealing with* money an integral part of your life. "Dealing with" means coming to terms with the role of money in your own life, gaining control over it, and developing ways of thinking about it which can allow you better control of your present and future. You want to see what money can do *for* you, not *to* you. Knowing about money, feeling comfortable talking about it, feeling confident that it is a subject that can be understood, and knowing where to go for guidance and information, are all keys to your security base, keys to having a greater sense of power and control over your life.

The importance of knowing about your finances has been heightened during the last decade and can only increase in the future due to changing marital and life style patterns. Increased longevity has led to the need for women to seriously consider long-term career planning. In fact, our work with various populations of women over the last several years has made it clear that it is absurd to talk about work patterns of women without dealing directly with the whole money issue and its influence upon our lives.

There are many books and articles about money, money and power, guides to financial independence, the joys of having and spending money, so it is unnecessary for us to repeat what can be gained from such useful guides and resources. We believe it to be imperative that we explore *if* and *how* our attitudes toward money affect our self-concepts and to determine what might prevent us from becoming as competent about money matters as we are in other aspects of our lives. It is necessary to pinpoint obstacles that may ultimately interfere with our readiness to examine the subject in depth, to become well informed, less anxious, less secretive and less intimidated about the subject of money. Our goal is to free ourselves from these obstacles, and move towards a greater comfort level in dealing with the subject of money.

LEARNING THE LANGUAGE

Many women are still uncomfortable with the vocabulary of the world of money. To "reconcile the bank account" at the month's end may sound formidable, certainly much more frightening than to "balance the books." To sort out the difference between whole life insurance and term insurance and sift through all the numbers on the chart (in fine print, yet) may at times appear to be purposely confusing. We may know that we have two (or is it three?) bank accounts, but not be thoroughly clear about where they are or how much we have saved. We tell ourselves, of course, that at any time we can easily find out where they are. Though we may want to do some investing in a small way, the broker we consult may seem to speak a different language, and when he/she begins to talk about the specifics of investing in stocks, we begin to tune out. We may have become so accustomed to letting others (husband, parents, lawyer, accountant) handle our finances, that we sign over participation to them. The important question to ask of ourselves is, "What do I expect myself to know about the money I/we earn, spend, save, and invest?" and furthermore, "How much do I expect myself to understand—and how much would I prefer to sign over to someone else to handle?"

In an effort to answer these questions, one woman enrolled in a day-long women-and-money conference that was offered by a local brokerage company as a basic introduction to investing and buying insurance. By the end of the morning, she was entirely frustrated and confused by the barrage of terms she did not understand, charts on which she could no longer focus, and people who did not seem to care if anyone understood anything they said.

At the luncheon break, she expressed her frustration to seven other women, anxious to find out whether she was alone in her bewilderment. Not one of the other women was upset. Astonished, this woman began to ask specific questions about her confusion, and it quickly became apparent that most of the other women were as confused as she was. The difference was that they had not *expected* to understand a certain proportion of the conference. They just assumed that much of the conference would be over their heads, and were "thankful" for whatever they "picked up." The word choice "picked up" was particularly significant, because it implies a lack of seriousness and commitment. In actuality their response was probably more of an indication of past conditioning regarding how hard it would be to understand. It explained their willingness to settle for less.

The question remains, "Why, in this day and age, do so many of us not take the time and energy to totally familiarize ourselves with our monetary status?" It may be partially because it involves an entirely new language that we must learn, and which at the outset may seem difficult. In addition, we may not have the support of others (for example, the people putting on the conference), though they may *say* they are committed to helping us learn the basics. After someone has explained something twice, using language with which we are unfamiliar, who has the nerve to say they still do not understand?

Many of us believe that we are not competent when it comes to matters of handling the family finances. In some marriages childhood messages discouraging discussions about money have been incorporated and it is not uncommon for the wife to have little knowledge of the family's financial picture, including how much they have invested, have in savings, or even have to spend. Widowed women from such families often say one of the hardest adjustments they had to make was to learn to manage finances. One woman ruefully discovered that she didn't even know how much insurance her husband carried or with what company he was insured. These details were simply never discussed for they both felt that money matters were not a woman's responsibility and/or within her realm of understanding. Similarly, the newly divorced woman who has been in a marriage where she was not knowledgeable about the skills involved in balancing a checkbook, filing income tax returns, or making decisions about major purchases, may find herself in quite a bind. Not only does she find herself having to cope with expected emotional and social stresses, but she has to cope with financial ones as well.

Those of you who are heads of households have no choice but to handle your own financial matters, and may not have the luxury of leaning on someone else. As more women acquire business training, they increase their sense of competence, and that insures a certain comfort level with their own financial planning. But many women do lack confidence in this area, become anxious when thinking about it, and often avoid learning what they know they need to know. This insecurity often stems from earlier messages about not being good in math. The fact is that for many years most women were not encouraged to take advanced mathematics courses. This lack of encouragement was a clear message about the unimportance of our learning math. And not encouraging women to continue in math conveyed an implicit message about whether we should learn it and whether we would, in actuality, be dealing with the financial planning of either a home or a business. Many of us had the feeling that if mathematics did not come easily (the way it seemed to for those math wizards in high school algebra) we need not bother to learn. There was little attempt to vary teaching methods or to develop new educational methods that would reach the temporarily confused student.

Even now, as more women are thinking about returning to undergraduate or graduate school, a frequently heard reason for not enrolling is, "I would, but I would have to take math!" In many cases, this fear of mathematics delays decisions about returning to work or to school. Math anxiety workshops have been developed to attack the problem where it often lies, in the emotions and learned patterns of behavior, rather than *necessarily* in a person's lack of ability. Many women, having moved beyond their fear and anxiety about math and statistics, develop methods to make learning easier to them. A study partner, to reinforce the day's learning, has proven to be very useful for many women. They may tackle assignments in smaller portions, try different times of the day, or admit confusion about a particular explanation and ask for an alternate explanation. One woman discovered that her main problem was that she assumed everyone else understood the presentation right from the beginning. Consequently, she already felt intimidated when she went back to study her notes. Much to her amazement, she discovered that many of the others in the class also did not understand a great deal of what was presented either. But they took careful notes so that they could later teach themselves the content of the lectures when they were calm and unpressured. All that time she had been telling herself that something was wrong with her because she needed extra time to learn the material.

There seems to be a relationship between our learning of mathematics and our comfort level in dealing with figures. Many books aim to teach us how to deal with money, how to invest, how to balance the books, often without acknowledging the fact that if we believe we can't, we might not try. We may try halfheartedly, but be easily rebuffed by "humorous" digs from spouses about our inability with numbers. Persons giving workshops similar to the women-and-money one given by the brokerage firm should not only state that they have a sincere desire for us to learn, but they should implement numerous methods to insure that this occurs. The conference should be followed up with evaluation that allows women to honestly assess their needs and the areas in which there is still confusion. The implicit message communicated needs to be, "We care that you really learn, understand, and become financially competent. We assume a large share of responsibility for making this happen, both by alternating our methods of teaching and by helping you attack the underlying messages that prevent you from feeling competent and confident in this area."

One woman was called by a female insurance agent who wanted to visit her home and present possibilities for investing in insurance. Though this woman did not intend to buy any insurance, she was committed to learning about financial matters, and she allowed the agent to make a presentation. She discovered that she was actually able to hear without anxiety what the insurance agent was saying. There was something in this female agent's *attitude* that communicated the following: "First, I want you to understand. I will talk slowly, but not condescendingly. I will stop when necessary, to clarify what I am saying and ask for feedback. Only then will I try to sell you insurance."

Naturally, not all female agents would have had the same approach or the same calm manner. But the woman listening felt very much at ease and felt no need to *appear* as if she were understanding. She was free to concentrate on whether she truly *did* understand. Obviously, the ultimate goal for this insurance agent was to sell life insurance, just like any other agent. But she appeared to be particularly aware of the necessity of acknowledging some women's discomfort with the entire area.

This experience was particularly significant to this woman because of what it contributed to her self-awareness. She realized how detrimental it had been in the past for her to appear as if she understood. Her confidence grew, as did her belief in her right to clear communication regarding potentially complex issues. In the future she intended to draw from what she had learned through this experience. She would not hesitate to request clarification as often as necessary without feeling self-critical because she may not understand or perhaps needs to ask a lot of questions.

After seven years of marriage, Ellen was working part-time, had one child in school, and decided that she wanted to begin paying the bills and reconciling the bank account, and assuming the responsibility of paying the taxes and insurance. For the first several months, when she had checked off each of the returned checks and attempted to reconcile the bank account, she had tremendous difficulty. Each time she went to her husband for help and he "lovingly" laughed at her incompetence, his undertone clearly suggesting that he had fully expected her not to be able to handle it. She recognized that she was partially responsible for his reaction, since she did approach him with laughter and jokes about her ineptness, albeit in self-defense.

She noticed her own joking and decided to change her attitude. She communicated a serious desire to master the task, and fought back her doubts about her ability with numbers. Her transition into full participation was probably delayed by her initial attitude. She could have stated outright that it was difficult for her, and that she needed his help and support. But that may have led to other difficulties, since her husband was being asked to relinquish some of his area of responsibility. He probably needed some time to adjust to her more assertive involvement in what had previously been his arena. But as he gained confidence in his wife's increased financial awareness, they began to plan their financial goals together. She shared in the joy as well as the burden of their financial planning.

There may be another underlying reason why some of us do not take the time to become well informed. The reason that we remain uninformed may be similar to the reason why some people avoid getting physical or dental checkups . . . the fear that something may be wrong, and that they will have no alternative but to deal with their need to lose weight, decrease their smoking, or undergo further tests in order to protect their health.

Likewise, many of us are afraid to take the responsibility to learn about our family financial picture. Perhaps we have superstitious feelings that we may lose our husband or that we are courting disaster. Or less extreme, that we fear we may not understand, that we will be too confused, or that others may laugh at us.

Following is a list of areas that are critical for you to understand, along with a list of suggestions on where to find information.

1. Areas to explore

Insurance

Personal budgeting

Wills, trusts, estates

Investments (stocks, bonds, property)

Checking and savings accounts

Credits and loans

2. Where to find information

Seminars given by banks, insurance companies, brokerage firms

Continuing education programs through local colleges

Books in libraries, written for the lay person

Popular periodicals and magazines that deal with money issues

The business section of the local paper

Discussions with friends

Free information given out by government, banks, brokerage firms, consumer affairs agencies

SPENDING

How do you feel when you write a check? Does it feel any different to write a large check, or charge a large purchase, than it does to write a small one? Is it easier for you to buy groceries twice a week, and spend less each time, or limit the shopping to once a week, or even bimonthly, because it is a more efficient use of your time? Have you, personally, bought anything large—a car, insurance, stocks, a stereo system, a television, a piano? Many single women have discovered that making such purchases is not particularly difficult; they are not encumbered by patterns of spending that may have evolved in marriages where the decisions are either made by the husband, or jointly, with the husband's opinions often weighting the decision in his direction.

One woman in her twenties, recently divorced and the mother of a young child, became quite successful in real estate. She was proud of her work, earned sufficient income to support them, and had enough money to consider spending on more than just the necessities. A significant step for her was the purchase of a piano, her first major purchase on her own. Later, when asked about her next large purchase, she stated that it would be life insurance. She saw this purchase as necessary, but difficult to make. She said it felt like a terribly "grown-up, responsible" decision to make, and that she now felt ready to do what she should have done "before buying the piano."

Comfort in spending and managing money evolves as we become used to dealing with money. Yet individual idiosyncrasies about the spending of money remain; while some of us give ourselves permission to spend money for something, others may feel guilty about doing so. Spending money on a large fine from the library may feel okay because "it is still less than it would have cost to buy the book!" However, spending money on dinners out two or three times a week is a justifiable extravagance to one man. He loves the chance to talk at dinner without having to think about cooking or cleaning up. For one woman, it is an unacceptable way to spend money. She would rather spend it on new records that she can repeatedly enjoy; to her a tangible result is necessary to justify spending.

Buying things on sale may be utterly crucial to one woman who may feel cheated if she buys something at retail price when she could have waited until a sale. Another would prefer to spend her money wisely, but may feel more strongly that she would rather have an item *when* she wants it than to wait for a sale. She would prefer to shop at sales first, but purchase the item anyhow if she is unable to find it on sale. It is simply a matter of priorities, being aware of them, and becoming comfortable in making decisions about spending that feel right.

Many of us continue to play the game of justifying to ourselves the money we spend. We may think it feels okay to buy that new stereo, because we drove on our trip last year instead of flying. Or we may say to ourselves, "I think I will buy these artichokes for tonight, because I ate at Mother's house last night, and did not spend anything on dinner." Often these mental gymnastics we use to justify the way we spend money are harmless, and perhaps they even help us to become more comfortable with spending money.

Too often, though, we are content to accept the judgments others make about our ability to handle money. When their ideas are different from ours, we may fall into the trap of thinking they are right and we are wrong. It may be more helpful for us to think, "Their priorities or preferences are different from mine, but not necessarily better."

We can gain greater power over our use of money when we acknowledge the games we are playing to "justify" some expenditures in terms of priority spending. You may decide that, generally speaking, you would rather buy a more expensive item, such as a blouse that you like very much and will wear often, rather than settling for another item because it is less expensive. In fact, the number of times you will wear the expensive blouse or use the preferred item brings the cost-per-use into line with your budget, and becomes a planned, carefully thought-through expenditure.

The habit of "justifying" expenditures is the process of looking at the total picture and making realistic straightforward budgeting decisions. What we are doing is legitimizing the "justifying" game by valuing the thought process that has taken place while considering the facts and making a decision that is indeed based on your budget.

What are your "justifying" games? Take a look and see if they are actual budgeting styles. Or are they only meant to help you decide that you can afford to buy an item or that you "deserve" an item. If the last statement is true, perhaps you can bring it out into the open by admitting that you want that blouse, or record, or trip, or to eat out, and will budget your money to allow that expenditure. It is quite possible to take control over the games or tricks you use with yourself, and bring your choices and actions out of the realm of "magical equations" and turn them into the realm of "mathematical computations."

"ARE YOU CRAZY? WE CAN'T AFFORD THAT!"

And so we come to the unequivocal need for each of us to work through and get in touch with how we value spending our money. Becoming comfortable with our own personal spending values is a crucial first step to dealing with those close to us who may have distinctly different convictions about spending. Chances are, those close to us will not hesitate to voice a dissenting view on how certain monies should be spent, judging our decisions to be based on poor or good values, irrational or clever thinking, a momentary loss of consciousness or a tremendous degree of foresight! At this point, their *valid* points can be heard, and taken into consideration, and clear communication can ensue. There may be times, given varying priorities, when it is not possible to justify spending to the satisfaction of others close to us.

"Are you crazy? We can't afford that!" is a frequently used exclamation in homes of every economic level. No matter how much money is in the savings account, someone could probably find a valid justification, within their frame of reference, for why *not* to make a particular purchase. And so begins many a marital disagreement about how to spend the money that is brought into the family bank account.

Neither does the single individual without children escape the judgments of others—family, friends, or co-workers. Parents frequently continue to monitor spending habits of their adult children, and many "friends" feel free to voice their opinions about another's purchases or expenditures, either directly or indirectly, with a "How can you afford that?" or "Do you really think that is worth that much money?" or "You sure take a lot of trips!"

One woman in a personal development class believed that

she was justified in spending any amount of money, within reason, on books. Julie fully expected to have a bill each month from her two favorite bookstores, but denied herself the privilege of a housekeeper to lighten her load at the ironing board. Her husband, Ted, on the other hand, resented her spending money on books—but felt no hesitancy about going to a movie each week. He felt completely justified in spending money on his leisure time in this way. Julie's feelings about spending money on books stemmed from her childhood messages about the importance of reading, memories of her family reading together after dinner, not having a television set in the home until she was a teenager, and bimonthly trips to the library from the age of six with her entire family. Ted did not have the same warm memories associated with reading—he grew up in a larger city, participated in movies and theater more, and spent more time seeking outside entertainment.

Another couple found themselves disagreeing over how to spend their rather lucrative income, also because of differences in values stemming from their childhood messages about spending money. Jean was brought up in a family that lived sparingly on a daily basis, but traveled extensively from the time she was quite small. Her father was a college professor, and they spent each summer camping in different countries, meeting the people, learning new languages, absorbing new cultures. Though she had few expensive clothes, she never wanted them, and she grew up with a wanderer's blood, a love of travel, and a desire to meet new people. She wanted to spend their extra money on travel. Her husband, George, had never traveled outside the United States. He grew up in a lower-income white-collar family, with dreams of owning a nice car, perhaps a boat, and certainly a house. He would feel like he had struck it very big if he could own a summer home, a speedboat, and maybe even a sailboat. As a result of the drastic differences in their backgrounds, both Jean and George had totally different beliefs about how money *should* be spent, and about how they wanted to spend their hard-earned money.

Neither Jean nor George is clearly right or wrong about how their money should be spent. They need to make a commitment to understand the reasons behind each other's spending desires, to respect their respective needs, and to come to a workable compromise that at least partially meets both of their needs. Jean's needs to meet different people could perhaps be met by becoming involved in an organization that entertains foreign visitors to the city. And George would perhaps be satisfied if, instead of owning a boat himself, they could share ownership with several other couples, thus freeing up some money for a trip now and then. Often spending decisions appear, initially, as if they are an either/or situation, with one person being the "winner," or the "right" one, and one being the "loser," or the "wrong" one. The goal is to find creative solutions that both can agree to, and that allow both to "win."

It has been helpful in some situations, when spending priorities are significantly different, for each person in a relationship to have some money of his/her own, money that does not need to be accounted for, justified, or ever discussed. Assuming there are adequate dollars for this solution, Julie, in the example above, could buy a few books a month without facing Ted's tirades, and he would have the same freedom in spending money on what Julie may describe as "frivolous."

COMMUNICATING ABOUT MONEY

Communicating openly and honestly about money is still difficult for many of us. And yet, *not* communicating can often seriously endanger relationships. One couple stopped inviting another couple to dinner when they could no longer afford to serve steaks and wine. They were embarrassed by their loss of income, and jeopardized their close friendship because of discomfort in talking about financial problems. Open communication about spending money can facilitate the making of good decisions, decisions that are comfortable to all involved.

Several women decided to jointly give a close friend a bon voyage party, and proceeded to discuss the details. One of these women had a much smaller amount of money allocated for the occasion than the others, and this became the source of subsequent arguments that hovered around, but never squarely dealt with, the real issues. To openly state how much money they were each willing to spend seemed crass; yet neglecting to state an amount at the outset contributed to inaccurate assumptions about how much money there was to be spent in total. Discord and embarrassment could have been avoided if the issue of money to be spent had been dealt with up front, in a matter-of-fact, nonemotional atmosphere.

The more clearly we communicate about money and the spending of it, the better we can manage it. In the example of the couple who could no longer afford to serve steak and wine, if the amount of money available had been dealt with, they might very well have decided to have potluck dinners, and combine resources. And if the women planning the party knew exactly how much they had to spend between them, they could get down to the business of making good decisions about how to spend that money.

Friendships can be jeopardized because of misunderstandings about money. Lucille lent her close friend twenty dollars to pay some bills, while Eleanor waited for a commission check that was due to arrive any day. When several weeks passed and Eleanor made no attempt to repay her debt, Lucille began to feel resentful and angry. She was embarrassed to ask about the money, and began to avoid Eleanor in order to prevent her angry feelings from showing. Rather than confront her friend openly, Lucille began to complain to others about her friend's lack of responsibility. When others convinced her to confront her friend and ask for the money, she finally mustered the strength to do so. Much to her surprise, Eleanor had totally forgotten, was very embarrassed and apologetic, and paid her immediately. More open and direct communication would have ended the incident and prevented the subsequent strain on their relationship.

In what areas have we learned it's okay to discuss money? For some of us it is easier to share information about ourselves and our monetary transactions when they depict us in a favorable light. Perhaps it is when we've gotten a raise or a new job with a higher salary, or perhaps it is when we have gotten a terrific bargain or were able to get satisfaction after having returned a defective item. Also, we usually don't mind talking about the amount of money we spent when we received poor service because we know others have had similar experiences. It may also be easy to relate success stories when they involve those people whom we see as extensions of ourselves. That person's triumph has a "halo" effect on us. Merely by association we share in some of the glow of their success. We were smart enough to have them for a friend, for a spouse, or as a parent and consequently we feel we can participate in their success.

We may also find it easier to share information about times when we were unfairly beaten out of some money which was our due. ("They began a new scholarship policy at work, right after I finished my courses!" "I got stuck with a car that was a real lemon!") We can all identify with these more negative incidents, because we have all had similar experiences. It may also be acceptable to discuss our low salaries, when it is commonly known that salaries in our line of work do not reflect our true value. These examples are not depicting us as unsuccessful people, but as victims. They are situations that are seen as being beyond our control. But we usually want to feel that we are successful at controlling our lives, especially with regard to money.

It may be harder for us to discuss money in areas where we feel we *should* have control, but do not. The times when we cannot afford to go to a restaurant or on a vacation; the times when we may want certain clothes, or an expensive car. If our friends can afford these expenditures, it may be much harder to talk about money. And if we feel uncomfortable discussing money, frequently our friends will too.

What happens when you are out to dinner with friends, and they order an expensive bottle of wine to accompany their dinner? Do you, when it comes time to split the check, mention the wine? Or do you just split the cost of the dinner, even if you are feeling that they should have absorbed the wine cost themselves? If you do feel that, why don't you bring it up—after all, they *are* your friends. Obviously, it is not so simple. Perhaps you truly do not mind splitting the check down the middle. But perhaps it wasn't just a bottle of wine, but two pieces of cheesecake for dessert also. Or perhaps they ordered chateaubriand for two, and your dinner is significantly different in price from theirs. Does it feel okay to bring up the subject of money for open discussion, or are you concerned that you will appear cheap? There, we've said it. None of us wants to look cheap or stingy, especially among friends. In a large number of cases it is expected that the other person would be shocked or offended at such "nit-picking."

But that is just the point: is it truly nit-picking, or is it merely a fair way to approach paying for the dinner? With that extra few dollars you have saved, you could go to a movie. Or if the money is not really an issue, then perhaps you begin to resent them on principle for not having offered to shoulder their own share. One couple we know thoroughly enjoyed another couple's company during long, leisurely, intimate dinner table discussions. But the second couple always ordered drinks before dinner and wine with dinner, sending the cost of the dinner sky high. Unfortunately, the first couple's solution to the problem was to curtail going out since they could not bring themselves to discuss the issue openly, even though they had participated in discussions of many personal topics over the years.

One woman went on a car trip with two friends. When they returned, the woman who drove requested reimbursement for a third of the gasoline from each, as well as a charge she computed on the wear and tear of the car. Reactions to this incident were mixed, though no discussion of the money involved ensued. One of the passengers felt that charge for the gasoline was certainly expected, but was surprised at being charged for car depreciation. Her friend (the driver) had approached the entire endeavor as a business interchange among friends, fully expecting to share all car-related expenses. Both the situation of friends at dinner and that of friends sharing traveling expenses should have been open for discussion and reactions, and perhaps negotiation, without being fraught with worry about looking cheap, or concern over possibly losing friends.

Another woman had made a decision to go to college in her hometown, because then she could live at home and it would cost less for her parents. There were other siblings, and they had all gone away to college. This woman felt that her family could not afford for her to also go away to college, but she never broached the subject with her parents. She made an important life decision, as a direct result of her perception of the availability of money, without discussing it. When questioned about why she did this without definite information, she stated that she was certain there must have been money problems since her father seemed very worried at the time of her decision making. In retrospect, his worries could have been for a variety of other reasons, and in reality going away to college would have been possible.

A common feeling among parents is one of desiring to protect their children from worrying unnecessarily. This is often used as a justification for not informing and including the child in discussions about money. Unfortunately, protection leaves much room for inaccurate interpretation of circumstances, as happened with the woman in the previous example. The rules of courtesy and propriety and privacy help to perpetuate the feeling that money is a somewhat taboo subject. Children do not know how much money it costs to purchase things, to rent a house, to go to camp, to buy a pair of glasses. Similarly, many of us do not know how much money our closest friends make, and consider it an intrusion to ask. This is partially due to the fact that the amount earned has in many cases become synonymous with degree of success achieved. Your salary has become symbolic of your worth as a person, as well as the amount you are paid to do a specific job. Being excluded from interaction about money while growing up may have contributed to your feeling insecure in talking about it as adults.

Guidelines For Talking About Money

If you are going to really benefit from learning to talk with other people about money and money matters, there are some guidelines you can follow.

1. If you are in the midst of discussing a potential purchase, stick to the pros and cons of the current purchase; do not bring in the past at this time.

2. Make it a habit to periodically sit down and discuss some of the following points with those you feel you need to, with a spouse if you are married, or with a parent or friend if you are single.

a. What are my "values" concerning money? How do I like to spend it? On what kind of things? Household items? Personal items? Leisure? Education?

b. How do I want to pay for my purchases? Cash? Charge?

c. Do I want some discretionary income for which I am not accountable?

d. Who should pay the bills, write the checks, and balance the account?

e. What kind of a budget do we want to set for: Household? Savings? Education? Major purchases? Leisure?

3. When you are sitting down to discuss money, use the rules of clear communication:

a. Give direct messages or statements about how you *feel*, what you would *like*, and how you *think* about the earning, spending, and saving of money. ("I would like some discretionary income." Or, "I feel more secure when I know we have $5,000 in savings, so I would like to make certain that we do so.")

b. Listen to what the other person says, and if you are not sure what he means, ask him. ("So you are saying that if buying the boat means that we will have to go below $5,000 savings you would rather take out a small loan to finance the boat, or wait until we have saved the additional money.")

c. Stick to the point of the discussion, eliminating irrelevant information, or emotion-laden statements. ("You spent money two years ago on that stupid machine that didn't work." "Your mother didn't handle money well, and you are just like her!")

d. Negotiate, negotiate, negotiate. Make sure that both of you are winners. ("If you agree to cut back there, I will agree to cut back here, and we can spend the money on a trip." Or, "I will agree to ask your advice on major purchases, and I would like you to let me handle my budgeting my own way even if you feel that your way is most efficient.")

MANAGING MONEY AS A COUPLE

If the families of a newly married couple had different methods of managing money, problems may arise when the couple tries to work out a common system for their new family, especially if the matter is not fully discussed (often couples make decisions by assuming rather than talking things out). For one such couple it was the husband's father who paid the bills in his family and the wife's mother who paid the bills in hers. The resulting difficulties were unexpected. You would imagine that each partner would feel that he or she should pay the bills, but not so. This couple had an added complication. They were also affected by what has come to be known as birth-order theory. (Simply stated as applying to this couple, the oldest child in a family tends to identify with the father and the second child tends to identify with the mother.) The wife of this couple was the eldest child and, like her father, didn't want to manage the finances. The husband was a second child and, like his mother, also preferred not to take that responsibility. If each assumed that the other should take on the bookkeeping responsibilities, imagine what havoc this could play not only with their finances but also with their relationship.

In this case the societal stereotype prevailed. The husband felt successful in being able to pay the bills and so assumed the greater responsibility for writing the checks, although they have also used a rotating system with each doing them for a six-month period. Each partner in a marital relationship comes to the marriage with his or her own preconceived ideas about how money should be handled. Understanding each other's perceptions, needs, and preferences concerning money paves the way toward evolving a mutually satisfactory arrangement for managing money.

When Jack and Martha married, they both assumed Jack would be the breadwinner in the family, and she would be its caretaker. This division of labor worked well until it became increasingly clear that they could not budget with only one income to accomplish even their short-term goals. Additionally, they dreamed of buying a home, sending their children to college, taking trips. Braces for their children's teeth, dancing school, new clothes, an increased rate of homeowners' insurance, the ever-increasing cost of food, all began to tear away at their previous safe plan for their future. In response, Martha decided to get a job outside the home to help pay for essentials, and save for a down payment on a very modest home.

Although both felt an immediate decrease in tension about money, the change in roles was not easy for either of them to accept. Jack's identity as a provider was challenged in his mind. ("Is there something lacking in me that I cannot earn as much money as my family needs without the 'help' of my wife?") And Martha worried about her role as wife and mother. ("What about the children—they need me here after school.") On the other hand, Jack relaxed as the financial pressure became more evenly shared, and he slept better than he had in months. And Martha began to discover how much she could accomplish by managing her time more effectively and reorganizing her priorities. Once it became apparent that the bills would be paid, both Jack and Martha could begin to explore the benefits resulting from their shared roles as providers and nurturers. Eventually, they were able to work through their feelings of defensiveness that resulted from departing from traditional roles. They learned to view themselves as co-providers and co-nurturers in the family.

They no longer worried about paying for food and clothing, and other needs began to take precedence. Martha realized the need to boost and protect Jack's ego. Jack became aware of her need for emotional support, for encouragement in her job. Both became conscious of the need to compromise, to assume different responsibilities at home. The conversion from a one-paycheck to a two-paycheck family eliminated one set of problems, and created another set for them to work through.

Whose Money Is It?

The issue of money between husband and wife can be extremely complicated, especially in the face of the differing messages each has retained about money from childhood and received from society. It is further complicated by patterns that may have been set early in the marriage. The situation is further confused by the issue of what each person—the husband and the wife—consider "work" and what this entitles each to in terms of power over the pocketbook. In one class of women exploring their feelings about money, the following situations were described:

Wife working part-time, contributing a small portion to the family income, and has main responsibility for raising two small children. One joint checking account, two savings accounts, and multiple investments in both their names, as well as the house in joint ownership.

Wife working full-time in the home, raising two young children in school all day, active in community affairs, no paycheck. One checking account in joint ownership, one savings account, numerous investments she did not know about in detail.

Husband and wife working full-time, the husband days, and the wife from 6:00 to 12:00 midnight. Separate checking accounts, separate savings accounts, and separate investments. Consult each other before investing large sums of money.

Wife, mother of two small children, finishing a graduate degree. Her own checking account was fed by half of her husband's paycheck—after the bills had been paid. Investment decisions made by wife.

The above are a few examples of the broad number of

possibilities from which couples can choose to distribute involvement and power over the family finances. What seemed crucial in each of these cases was how the husband felt about the wife's work, and how she felt about her own work. What seemed less important was whether she worked in the home, in the salaried labor force, or some combination thereof. The wife in the second example, who works full-time in the home, was asked if she felt that she should be contributing dollars to the family income. She answered, "But I do!" and then proceeded to describe how, in *both* her mind and in her husband's mind, her work was clearly earning them money. She listed cook, chauffeur, adviser, counselor, housekeeper, tutor, baby-sitter, as but a few of the jobs she did that would indeed cost dollars if she were to work outside the home and needed to be replaced. Now, we all know that most women working in the home do not fit our stereotyped image of drinking coffee and watching daytime soap operas. But not every woman can *feel* so unequivocally definite about her equal contribution to the family income without a paycheck to deposit each month. And not only did she honestly feel this about her work, but she is secure in her husband's support of the system they have worked out together.

In contrast, we have the example of the woman with small children, finishing her graduate degree in biochemistry. She is an example of a woman with significant future earning potential outside the home. However, she feels guilty, uncomfortable, and somewhat powerless because she is not contributing dollars right now. Her husband has none of these feelings; they are totally her own. He continually affirms her importance by encouraging separate bank accounts. This does not, however, give her the internal security expressed by the woman working in the home, in spite of her value in the work force being much more clearly defined.

So whose money is it? If he earns it, does he have ultimate discretion over it? Does it feel like "his" or is it "ours"? Is it okay, or perhaps even necessary, for each of us to have some of our own money in our own bank accounts, to have exclusive control over some of the money? Can each of us, coming to a marriage with different feelings about money, reconcile our differences and work out a system that gives both of us some power over the purse strings? And at change points in the marriage, when we have grown and perhaps feel differently about money, can we respond by renegotiating the handling of the family finances?

With the emergence of two-income families there is also the emergence of a number of new issues surrounding the total family income. Does the person who earned the most money have the discretion to decide how it is spent? Is there a shift in the traditional balance of independence and dependence between husband and wife? How does the fact of dual earning power affect the division of labor in a household? The answers would differ from household to household. They vary with age, with length of marriage, and with educational background. They also vary over time. As we have said before, no one way is the right way, but having consciously considered the situation as it exists for you, the options you have, even the tentativeness of the decisions which you do make, will increase the possibilities that you will control the issue of money in your life rather than be controlled by it.

Your Needs and *Beyond*

❧

Having analyzed your unconscious feelings about money—your stereotypes, impressions, and messages to yourself about it and its importance in your life—gives you some room now to reassess and redefine the role it is already playing in your life. What is a realistic appraisal of your needs regarding money, and how will awareness of your needs affect your living and working styles?

WHAT ARE YOUR NEEDS?

The most commonly understood meaning of the word "need" is "must have," for whatever reason we deem important. Clearly, our most basic need is for food and shelter. The psychologist Abraham Maslow, in his theory about the hierarchy of human needs, places our physical needs at the base of his Pyramid of Needs, indicating that these are the foundation without which other needs are unimportant. If we are hungry, or ill-clothed and cold, we are unconcerned with becoming financially aware or with becoming more powerful. We must have money to pay for a place to live, food, clothing, and other things we consider essential. Though money cannot insure personal happiness or peace of mind, lack of adequate money can prevent such happiness. Money is often the determining factor in controlling our style of life; it dictates the neighborhood we live in, the educational opportunities open to us, and the potential scope of the family's recreational and leisure activities. Lack of enough money to adequately meet our needs—and if we have a family, their needs—produces financial pressures that affect our relationships with other people. This is a situation most of us have experienced at one time or another, either as a child or as a parent. The pressure to earn enough just to combat the frightening rate of inflation is responsible for many of our work-related decisions and for the decisions of enormous numbers of women to seek work outside the home. These increasing numbers of women are much less concerned about their "needs" for job satisfaction than about putting food on the table and assuring themselves that their children will have new shoes and coats each year.

But there are tremendous variations in what different people feel they *must* have, depending on their ever-evolving personal definition of "need." A parent says to his teenager, "How much do you need for your weekend trip?" The parent may mean, "How much money must you have to cover the essentials—hotel, meals, and gas?" Or he may mean, "How much money do you need to cover every expense of the trip, including entertainment and spending money?" A vice-president of a company may ask the director of operations, "How much discretion do you need in order to purchase whatever supplies are necessary to develop this plan?" He may mean, "What is the absolute bottom-line, base amount that you will need to conclude this project?" He is aware of the need for the company to be quite prudent in spending, considering the last quarter's earnings and lower profit margin. But the operations director may interpret the question as, "How much money must I be given discretion over in order to use my initiative to make independent decisions about spending, and in order to increase our profits?" He defines "need" differently because of his own "need" to operate independently, to have discretionary power over spending, and to prove his potential to the company. If he "needs" to account for every penny above a base amount, he might feel less control, possibly some resentment, and certainly less powerful.

A woman completed her master's degree in urban planning, and began job hunting, while simultaneously searching for adequate child care for her two preschoolers. Her husband said, "But we don't 'need' your income. Why do you 'need' to go to work?" He meant, "I am making sufficient dollars to support us in the style to which we are accustomed, and your dollars will not significantly change or improve our life style." But she may feel that she does "need" to work—because she needs to increase her sense of self-esteem, and to contribute dollars to the family income regardless of whether they will directly impact their style of life. And more important, her contribution could indeed become necessary in six months, when her income allows her husband to reject a transfer and look for another job, or when together they plan for the purchase of a home, a decision that never could have been made with only her husband's income.

And finally, a husband may say to his wife, "Honey, I know you want to work, but if you do, you will not only place us into a much higher tax bracket, but the added expense of child care, transportation, gasoline, clothes, and lunch money, will in effect cancel any benefit to us." He is defining "benefit" to be "additional dollars above and beyond his paycheck." She may define "benefit" as "emotional in nature, a growing sense of self, an emerging self-confidence, a greater sense of independence and security both in and outside of the home."

Brian was fully aware of Kate's frustration at giving up her job as writer for a local paper in order to devote her time to raising their young child. When she voiced her need to resume working, at least part-time, he had numerous objections, most of which centered around the fact that any money she earned would be spent on child-care needs. Underneath these objections, Brian's self-esteem was threatened, as he wondered what he was doing wrong that would cause his wife to be unhappy at home, caring for their child. In reality, Kate's desire to work outside the home had very little to do with him, and she would not dream of expecting him to meet all of her needs. Once she communicated the reasons for wanting to return to work in spite of the lack of significant monetary gain, and once he could hear and understand her needs without confusing her needs with his failure, they could work out a solution that felt good to both of them.

Often there is a relationship between the maintenance of one's self-esteem and expenditures of certain monies. Phil was well aware that Jennifer planned to return to the paid labor force once it was feasible and the children were in school. Even so, when the time came, his self-esteem was temporarily threatened. He learned to allow himself to share the burden of supporting the family, while Jennifer learned to allow him to share more actively in child-care responsibilities. He compensated for his temporary loss of self-esteem by indulging himself in membership to a health club and treating the family to fast food restaurants more often. Jennifer's self-esteem grew as she began to make contributions to the family money pot. And Phil realized that his self-esteem was not contingent on her decision to work.

For My Soul

Certain expenditures may be required to maintain one's self-esteem, in spite of a limitation of funds. Spending the money on an appropriate dress or suit for a job interview could greatly influence one's performance, simply by virtue of making one feel attractive and self-assured. Consider the advice of a mother to her newly divorced daughter with two young children. The young woman was now responsible for earning and managing the family income. Her former husband's financial difficulties had left her shaken and reluctant to spend money on anything but necessities. The mother supported the daughter's austere budget, but cautioned her to continue to indulge in one luxury. "Even if you yourself have to go without some lunches, make sure you get a good haircut. When you look in the mirror, you have to see someone who is cared for, at least cared for by yourself." Though she had a far more restricted budget now, she still possessed the discretionary power to decide how her money would be spent.

As we more closely analyze the attitudes and feelings we have about spending money, and the decisions we have made regarding discretion over spending this money, the relationship between our money pot and our sense of independence becomes more closely scrutinized. We ask ourselves the questions: "For *me*, what exactly is the relationship between money and independence?" "Is it necessary for me and for my sense of independence to have an amount of money over which I have complete discretion?" "Should I have an amount of money of my own that is not allocated for any particular purpose, which I can dispose of in any way I see fit, without accounting to or asking permission of anyone else?"

Those women who are single may not have experienced the same feelings of having their income or spending open to the scrutiny of another person, but they do have specific feelings about what their needs are with regard to money. It is most useful for all of us, whether single or married, to step back periodically and look at how we as individuals see our money needs.

> Do I need a certain amount of money each month that I can spend "for my soul"?
>
> Do I need to know that I have a nest egg to fall back on in emergencies?
>
> Do I like keeping track of how I spend my money?
>
> Do I like to keep to an austere budget?
>
> Do I like to pay cash or charge my purchases?
>
> Do I feel that I must always look for bargains?
>
> Do I feel that my time is valuable and I would rather spend money on some services rather than do them myself?
>
> Do I like to ferret out free activities?
>
> Do I like to plan for and save for large expenditures?
>
> Do I like to spend money on family and/or friends?
>
> How do I now spend my money?

Even though we may live in a close personal and financial relationship with another person, we must also see ourselves as individuals with personal needs, with our own money "attitudes."

As these questions are further explored, often resentments that have been beneath the surface begin to show themselves. ("I hate to ask permission every time I want to buy something." "Why do I feel I have to explain to my parents when I take a trip?" "I wanted to use our tax refund to carpet the house but *he* decided it was time for a new car." "Just *once*, I'd like to buy my husband a present with my *own* money." "I would really feel guilty using *our* money to go back to school.") Many women discover the freeing feeling they begin to experience with their own allotted money, whether it was directly earned by them in a job, or indirectly earned by working in the home and placed in their own bank account.

Which brings us to the question of how to define "having money." To some it may mean personally earned monthly income; to others it means having equal access and responsibility for income earned by one's spouse; to still others it means having the potential for significant earnings, or a specific training that is an entry into the work force. Perhaps "having money" and "feeling independent" have nothing to do with who earns it or where it came from. Maybe having money means equal access to it, or comfort in dealing with it on a day-to-day basis. And perhaps "having money" means one thing at one point in life, and another a few years later.

Janet, an involved mother and Brownie leader at her daughter's elementary school, shared with us her feelings about money and independence. A few years ago she had been the divorced, single head of a household and mother of a small daughter, and was in need of a steady income. At first, Janet chose a secretarial job, but felt little satisfaction and a deep sense of frustration from being gone long hours from her young daughter. Next she decided to work evenings as a waitress so that she had more daytime hours with her daughter. After a while she wanted and needed to make more money. She talked her way into a lucrative bartending position at a hotel which, incidentally, would not even talk with her initially because of her being a woman. (And one with no direct experience in bartending, yet!) Janet's determination and self-confidence helped her secure a trial period at the job, and she has been there ever since. She remarried a few years later, but states unequivocally that she will never quit working, for she loves the feeling of independence that working outside the home gives her.

She feels fulfilled from the combination of being mother/wife/bartender. She feels independent as a result of generating her own monetary contribution to the family money pot. From our experience, there seems to be a difference in attitude toward financial security among single women stemming both from whether or not they have previously been married, and whether or not that marriage was a positive or negative financial experience. Previously married women seem to be more hesitant to completely give up their financial independence. There remains the memory of the need to be self-supporting, and the uncertainty about whether that situation could reoccur.

Jackie began exploring her feelings about money and independence in a semester-long career development planning class. At the start of the class she did not perceive herself as independent since she worked in the home, had no discretion over the family income, and was dependent on her husband for decisions and permission about how monies would be spent. But in every other respect, she was considerably more independent than any other woman in the class. She did all the traditionally "male" tasks around the home—from carpentry to lawn care, from landscaping to plumbing. In addition, she traveled extensively with her children, mapping out their trip, pitching camp, budgeting money. Still, any decision about how much money was to be allocated for the trip was made by her husband. She was not at all clear that she deserved to have discretion in the financial arena because she was not directly earning it herself. When Jackie began to redefine her contributions, mentally giving them monetary values, resentments about the situation began to surface. In reality she was so independent that her husband felt threatened, and by maintaining control over the bank account, he successfully prevented her from becoming too powerful. He was able to do so partly because of her messages to herself about the role of the husband and wife regarding family financial matters. Though she was uniquely different from many women with regard to division of labor at home, she was traditional in the sense that she saw the husband as having the right to exercise authority over money matters. Fortunately there was a workable solution for this couple. They participated in joint counseling, and learned to discuss all financial matters thoroughly and to make decisions jointly about amounts necessary for vacations and other similar expenses. They decided to place these monies in another bank account over which Jackie had discretionary power. Jackie's husband was able to get through his initial resistance, and came to see her involvement as a positive step for their marriage.

As we begin to explore the topic in greater depth, it becomes apparent that our individual needs regarding money vary. Our feelings about money are related to a variety of factors: our physical needs, our level of self-esteem, our financial awareness and competence, our comfort level in spending, and the degree of our need for a sense of power, independence, and success. Coming to terms with the complexity of our needs in each of these areas will give us greater control over our short- and long-term plans. Then we can begin to invest in ourselves and our future with some clarity about where we have been, where we are now, what we need, and where we want to go. The tenet "money is the root of all evil," might be replaced with "knowledge about money is the base from which we can properly establish careful future life plans." Our need to become knowledgeable and financially aware must be emphasized in order for us to make intelligent, well-informed, appropriate decisions regarding our work choices and our work future. Without such awareness, it is hard to make appropriate decisions about what our future direction, what area we may want to study, whether or not we may want another degree or further training, or in what work environment we ultimately choose to place ourselves.

Traditionally, many women were educated in specific areas such as teaching, nursing, or business, and perceived this training as backup financial support for the earnings of the main breadwinner of the family. Now in many families the woman is either the principal breadwinner, or at least "co-breadwinner." At long last, women are being encouraged to consider their interests and aptitudes, when deciding on a career choice or a career change. Awareness of present and future monetary needs, combined with information about earnings' potential in various fields, will help direct a woman toward a life plan that will work for her. She might still prefer a traditionally female job, but with greater knowledge of any financial limitations that may bring.

Women at all points on the continuum of life planning, whether going to work for the first time, reentering the labor force, planning to stop work for a while, or planning to continue working in the home, should be encouraged to personally explore the realities of earnings' potential in jobs that may be of interest to them. They should conduct an ongoing survey of their financial needs and of specific jobs that could help them meet those needs. Some women may feel that it is crude to include a discussion of what they might earn in the same conversation with what they would like to do; nevertheless a greater sense of power and control will result. It is clearly the combination of these factors, both self-awareness about interests and an accurate appraisal of what we need and can earn, that will liberate us to make the right choices for ourselves and help us build in a process for anticipating our future needs.

We need to protect ourselves from the dilemma many women find themselves in today; a teacher may be fulfilled by her work and either satisfied or reconciled to the fact that she will never earn more than a certain amount of money in this job. If she is thoroughly aware of the advantages and limitations of teaching, in terms of earning power, *before* entering the field, she will be in better financial control. If she loves teaching, but thinks that the future may bring increasing financial commitments, she can plan concrete ways in which she might advance in her field to a better-paying position, or transfer her skills to unrelated areas of endeavor, which might pay higher salaries. In other words, she does not necessarily make the decision to leave a field in which she is highly trained and successful. But she would benefit from continually assessing and reevaluating her financial needs and her work options.

Other traditionally female fields of work—such as nursing, secretary, beautician—continue to hold appeal for many women. If they like their work, take pride in it, and can financially afford to work in fields that are usually low paying, then they have made decisions that work for them. But with the rate of inflation what it is, they too should plan for change, look ahead to where they may want to be in five years. This long-term planning can protect them from being locked into a one-job pattern that may work for them during one period in their life and not during another.

The nurse can look for ways to augment her income if she needs to, by teaching a course or two, doing private nursing on weekends, inquiring about scholarships for more specialized nursing that would be better paying. The secretary may be satisfied with her job, and much respected by her colleagues as well as her employer, but may be taking a business course at night, or subscribing to business journals in order to increase her negotiating power when she asks for a promotion or for more responsibility and a raise.

Jill, a woman in her early twenties, chose to teach preschool, fully aware of the lack of financial growth possibilities. She has, in the back of her mind, the plan to open up a preschool of her own, and to write children's books. She is realistic in her assessment that one job, over a long period of time, may become old and lose its sense of satisfaction. In popular jargon, she may become "burned out." Jill feels that she can afford to do this chosen work now, with her limited financial needs, but thinks of herself in terms of a continuing plan—reassessing both her satisfaction from her work and her comfort level with the amount of money she is earning. Her very awareness of the possible limitations is freeing, and puts her at the helm, in control from the very start.

"HOW MUCH ARE YOU WORTH?"

Most of us would cringe at being asked the question, "How much are you worth?" In 1972, the Chase Manhattan Bank stated that women working in the home that year should be estimated at having made contributions to the family money pot worth $13,391.56. In 1980, talk shows were mentioning figures closer to $35,000! In other words, to duplicate the jobs done by the woman in the home would require out-of-pocket expenses equivalent to those figures.

There is overwhelming support for eliminating myths about any lack of worth of the mother working in the home. But unfortunately, the woman at home must still struggle within herself, when wondering what her actual dollar potential would be if she should want or need to enter the salaried work force. And the fact remains that, unaided by more marketable, directly translatable skills, she may have considerable difficulty finding a job.

The looming questions facing her are: "What dollar value could I command in that marketplace the world of work?" "How would I go about finding out?" Knowing her skills, strengths, and potentials in the labor market, and consequently how much she could earn, is definitely a key to her sense of power and a protection against fear of poverty and debt. But most women feel panicked when asked to place a value on their worth in the job market, partly because of not knowing how to transfer their skills to unknown work environments; also, they are often unfamiliar with other people's earnings. Often people in one field may know what potential may be there, but have no idea about possible earnings if they decide to change fields. And we have been so successfully taught *not* to ask, that we close ourselves into a corner and make it almost impossible to set realistic goals for ourselves. Many women do not know that public companies publish earnings of key executives in the proxy material sent to shareholders yearly, an easy source of salary data at upper management levels. To test our perceptions about what people earn, we should begin asking the question, "Can you tell me the range of salary potential for someone who might enter this field?" Phrased in that way it is not a direct question about any one person's earnings, and it will not threaten the people being asked.

One woman, a former teacher who had stayed home several years to raise children, returned to school for a degree in counseling, and found herself in a seminar for mid-life career changers for additional training. At one point in the workshop each person was asked to state how much he/she wanted to earn with the next job choice, and how much he/she deserved to earn. In other words, how much was he/she worth? This woman stated that she wanted to do career development counseling in the training department of a company, and estimated a yearly salary of $15,000. She had no basis for making this statement, other than the teaching salary she had made seven years earlier, which was not really comparable to the present-day business market. She was encouraged to do some serious exploration and questioning about earning potential, and to integrate into her thinking the amount of inflation that had occurred since she had previously worked. She found it almost impossible to believe that she could command a considerably higher salary than she had stated.

Many of us underestimate the amount of money we should be paid; we feel intimidated, uncomfortable, and reluctant to negotiate for more. If we are told, as is common in books about how to find a job, to negotiate for a higher salary, many of us listen and silently discard the idea for ourselves. We would be lucky to get a job, we feel, much less negotiate for it! Perhaps it is true that we would truly be lucky; that should not prevent us from accurately assessing what we should be paid, and attempting to negotiate what would be fair both to us and to our potential employer.

AND ON TO INVESTING . . . IN YOURSELF

When considering the question of how much we are worth, undoubtedly the question of whether and when to invest in ourselves becomes important. As many of us are taking a longer-term look at our careers, we are beginning to feel that investing in ourselves is crucial. It might be an investment in our future, might take the form of joining a health club, or a professional organization. It might be a decision to return to college or graduate school, to take out a loan for a business, or just to buy a new coat in order to make the right impression.

Many of us are beginning to sense the importance of investing in ourselves and our future. Though we may not always have support, we forge ahead, taking a risk that we may not have taken a year ago. One woman in her thirties, working as an elementary school art teacher, decided to invest in a weekend career-changing seminar, which helped her reassess her skills and learn to market them in a new way. She was able to make a transition into advertising fairly effortlessly, as a direct result of knowledge and confidence gained from her weekend experience. She had been quite reluctant to spend what to her was a large amount of money for that weekend. It seemed a large risk, particularly when her funds were rather low. But her learning about the job market and about the process of integrating herself into it was priceless, and well worth the investment. She acquired a newfound ease in thinking about the whole subject of career changing.

This idea of spending money on ourselves is very difficult for some of us, partly because we may not be accustomed to putting money where there is no immediate payoff. Many of us experience no difficulty buying gifts for others, but money used to invest in ourselves is hard to spend.

More and more women are making the decision to remain single, and simultaneously, not to put off some major investments until they are married. More and more single women are making long-range plans about their financial futures. It is no longer only reserved for the big wage earner to plan to buy a house, to invest in property or to invest in the stock market. Single women today are now desiring and sometimes requiring themselves to have a much broader knowledge of the intricacies of money management and long-range investment packages.

Susan, a woman in her mid-twenties, decided to change jobs, not having yet found much satisfaction from her work. She mulled over the possibilities facing her—she could use her writing talent to work in an advertising agency, but she feared that she would have to begin at a tedious, entry level job. Susan decided to take the plunge she had been avoiding for some time, and begin a singing telegram business in her town. She contacted a woman who had been operating a similar business in another city for less than two years, and learned a great deal about the details of setting up such a business. Once she had determined what initial investment would be required, she needed only to take the first step. Inside of a few months she was extremely successful, and satisfied customers generated new business as the praise about her work traveled. Her initial cash outlay was minimal, and included consulting fees, an answering machine, printing costs, and costumes. When questioned about how she felt about buying an answering machine, or paying for consultants to visit her town to help in the beginning stages, she stated that she *knew* she could earn back at least what it cost her initially to set up the business in her home. Susan was not concerned with how much she would earn, how fast, or for how long. She perceived the cash spent up front as easily earned back, without allowing herself to be plagued about such questions as, "What will happen if nobody likes my idea?" Or, "What if I cannot think of creative songs to write?"

When asked about her short- and long-term earnings goals, Susan stated that she wanted to continue to be fulfilled in her work, and to earn enough to buy the things she wanted. Her needs were simple, her material desires minimal. At this point, in her mid-twenties, she was not preoccupied with saving money, other than planning a few months ahead.

When Susan was asked about her long-term financial planning, she revealed a heretofore undiscussed, and not yet clearly worked through plan to terminate or gradually phase herself out of this business, and possibly work her way into a responsible position in an advertising agency. She perceived this three- to five-year stint as both a financial investment (if successful, she could undoubtedly sell out for a substantial profit), and as an investment in herself. She had created for herself a chance to develop her skills and expertise, to realize her potential, and to learn about her capabilities and her limits. Though long-term financial planning was difficult for her, she easily handled questions about her long-term career planning. She was not certain where she would end up, but she *was* certain that she wanted a chance to discover deep satisfaction in her work, and that she was thrilled at earning a good income.

We can observe stages in Susan's comfort with and decisions about investment, both regarding her monetary needs and her investment of time and energy in her business. Initial dollar investment was easy for her. She had the self-confidence that her idea would work and that she could recoup these dollars, and subsequent decisions flowed from this initial confidence. Her initial outlay of money was a real statement of self-confidence, and an indication that she believed the potential struggle to be worth her effort. She did not hesitate to admit that she needed the help of consultants who helped her cut corners and avoid pitfalls. She was also fully aware of the importance of advice and guidance from a good lawyer and accountant. Reinvesting her earnings in the business and wisely taking advantage of free publicity possibilities led her to consider expanding the scope of her business. She began hiring more employees to sing the telegrams on a free-lance basis, fully aware that her talents should best be used to write and manage the business. She was considering adding employees to her payroll, in order to free herself up to creatively expand the business.

One consultant went through an interesting transition regarding her fees to individual clients. When she first began doing extensive consulting she felt somewhat apologetic about her hourly fee for consultation, or her much larger fee for a weekend seminar. Her feelings were rooted in her lack of self-confidence about her work, her discomfort with placing a dollar value on her time, and a reluctance to charge these fees to people who couldn't afford it. As she began to see the concrete success of her efforts she felt less apologetic about her fees and more convinced of the value of her time and expertise. The major change in her feelings about fees occurred when she heard herself actually *selling* someone on the idea of taking advantage of her services. She had come to feel that the monetary investment they were required to make was insignificant in comparison to the potential rewards. She now felt that their money would be *better spent* on her workshop or consultation than on many other necessary purchases. She felt drastically different about the crucial need for people to invest in their future by utilizing her services—and was convinced that the payoff would more than compensate for the initial investment.

We may find ourselves still wanting to believe the often quoted line of the late singer Sophie Tucker, who said: "From birth to eighteen a girl needs good parents. From eighteen to thirty-five, she needs good looks. From thirty-five to fifty-five she needs a good personality. From fifty-five on she needs good cash." But the last few decades have made it clear that not only is that "girl" a woman once she enters her twenties, but her good parents, looks, and personality cannot be counted on as a base for her financial security. Though they may contribute to her sense of self-esteem, their existence will rarely guarantee additions to or the ability to deal with the money pot. Hopefully, this girl-turned-woman will decide to participate in continuous life and work planning between the ages of eighteen and fifty-five, and will consequently have access to the "good cash" that can help her build the life she desires.

Reading
the Road Signs

On your journey into your future you will pass many road signs that can either aid you or hinder you as you take the route to your goal. During the development of the route to your career or future, there will also be many points at which you will want some reassurance that you have not gotten off the track. We are going to point out some road signs or markers that can ease your struggle and facilitate the success of your endeavors. When you are traveling along any new route, it is inevitable that your periodically reevaluate your progress and either continue on your original path or rechart your course.

However you do decide to travel, undoubtedly there will be some crucial road signs along the way. Attending carefully to these markers will contribute significantly to the ease and success of your journey into your future.

RESUME FULL SPEED

You have moved beyond all hazards of the road. Your flat tire is fixed, your gas tank full, and you can comfortably pick up speed. You have decided to return to work, hopeful of a permanent part-time job with pro-rated benefits. You have arranged child care that satisfies you, and have communicated clearly to your husband that you will need help with household duties. You have purchased two outfits that have the necessary "business" look, and had the car fixed so that it can be counted on not to break down in the near future. Now is the time to learn to be your *own* catalyst, to take responsibility for your future.

Other people can help, but it is up to you to locate those other people. Learn to challenge yourself. Take the responsibility of linking yourself up with groups that may already exist, or initiate a support system of your own. Some "networks" of women in business and professions already exist, and many are in the incipient stages. These groups can be a helpful way to make contacts, get reliable information, and to generate necessary support in developing more options for yourself. Many groups welcome members who may not be working for pay, or who are committed to volunteering, or who are planning to return to school in the future. As a matter of fact, it is because of the heterogeneity of such groups that you may be challenged to design your own future and not follow a set path. Through communication, programming, and planned exchange of information and ideas, a network can help to support and encourage women in all their endeavors.

Once women have realized that only a small percentage of job openings are ever advertised, they understand their need to have a multitude of contacts. At a recent dinner meeting of a local network of women who were interested in promoting women in business and the professions, a woman mentioned that she had just received a phone call about a job as director of marketing. The job was open because the present marketing director was moving out of town. It was a private local company and the owner did not plan to advertise it other than by word of mouth. Within four days the position was filled.

Another woman at the same meeting mentioned that her division was being expanded, and management was looking for women to enter their management training program. Still a third woman at this meeting learned about some funds that were just recently made available for women who were heads of households and who needed child-care and financial help in order to enter college.

Interaction with other women at varying points along the continuum of your life/work plan can lead you to endless possibilities for personal and professional growth and development. Flexible career options can be shared. Financial planning, investing, purchasing real estate, choosing banks, establishing credit, and obtaining a loan are all areas that could be learned about and explored together. The fears and realities of executive stress could be explored. If you are planning to reenter the labor force you could begin to get a realistic sense of existing opportunities through contact with women in all kinds of work. Once the group resources are identified, there is enormous potential for individuals to seek out the person that could help them to find a lawyer, decide which M.B.A. program has the best reputation in the local business community, share ideas on child-care alternatives, learn how the brokerage business works, discover opportunities for women in the computer field, assess how to decide on a location for a particular business, share ideas for new products and services. And importantly, many of these individual contacts could help generate business and income for the members of the organization. There is a much higher comfort level doing business with someone you know and trust than in operating solely from a referral.

In gearing up to move ahead at full speed, take the time to assess who your current role models are. Who are the people you admire? Which people fit the image of what you would like to be? Carefully analyze what characteristics, either personal, intellectual or emotional, you most admire and would like to possess. Often just seeing someone else who did it (went to law school, started her own business, changed careers . . .) can be inspiring.

Don't expect yourself to be your own catalyst without considerable help. Who are your mentors? Has anyone taken a particular interest in helping you reach your personal or professional potential? If there have not been mentors in your past, cultivate them for your future. Often people contacted in the job-hunt process are potential mentors. Was there one person with whom you really had instant rapport? He/she may be interested in applying for the position as your mentor. Often people are flattered and delighted to be sought out for additional advice and help. Often mentors help reinforce your initial, tentative endeavors. They can aid tremendously in counteracting interferences from husbands or friends or children who may have ambivalent feelings about the growth and change you may be experiencing. It is amazing what you will be able to accomplish with someone rooting from the bandstands, cheering you all the way.

Barbara's sister-in-law, Debbie, fulfilled both roles of mentor and role model for Barbara. She was an inspiration to Barbara in many ways. She demonstrated that even though she had a young child it was possible to work full-time, and that it was possible to find acceptable alternative child-care options. She worked in the same field as Barbara, but in a much more stimulating and innovative environment. Consequently, her continuous input of ideas served as a stimulus to Barbara, and they often participated in lively long-distance interchanges that were well worth the cost each month. Debbie was interested in encouraging Barbara to meet her own potential, and in the process Debbie gained new ideas to take back to her own job.

A mentor does not have to be in your field of work. Marilyn had always wanted to work in radio or television, and she got her chance when a woman she had met took an interest in her and suggested that she do an interview program on the college radio station. It was directly in response to the encouragement and support that she received from this woman that Marilyn decided to take a risk and to respond to this new challenge.

Another woman had a close friend who had become an ardent jogger. She began to encourage Jennie, who participated in no other physical exercise, to try jogging. Jennie's response was one of distaste, of wondering why anyone would ever want to put herself through that rigorous, boring activity. She stated unequivocally that she would never run, and did not even want to go once around the track to try it. However, as you may have anticipated, Jennie did try it, and began to feel a definite relationship between her increased energy level and her regular physical activity. Her good friend had served as both mentor and role model, significantly influencing her in her decision to get in shape.

DEAD END

You have been traveling along, and somehow, much to your chagrin, you find yourself at a dead end. Obviously, you need to get back on the main road, headed in a different direction. It may be time to recognize, carefully analyze, and tentatively accept certain weaknesses and shortcomings. Learning what you are *not* skilled at doing, or what you are *not* interested in pursuing, can become a catalyst to discovering alternative directions and pathways. It can be dangerous, however, to make broad generalizations about your future capabilities based on one experience in which you may have had difficulties.

You started that eatery you had always dreamed about, and it was not successful. Analyzing the specifics about this venture can either lead you in totally different directions, or right back into the restaurant business with the knowledge of which mistakes to avoid.

You began a children's bookstore with too little capital, not enough inventory, and lack of expertise in dealing with publishers. You may be disappointed in yourself for not researching the business more accurately. But you may decide to try again, and include toys to offset the struggle of making children's books profitable.

You struggled terribly with statistics in graduate school, barely making a passing grade. You assume you should never do research? Perhaps, but maybe someone else can do the computations, and you can make certain that you have a fundamental understanding of the statistics. You have a job supervising twenty-five people, and are not satisfied with your handling of the work. Maybe supervising is not your particular strength. But maybe you would be terrific at supervising a handful of people, or supervising the supervisors who can attend to the details that frustrate you.

A professor of business at a renowned business school was offered a job as vice-president for a company in another state, a company that he knew well and had worked with on an exchange program for students involved in internships. The increased financial possibilities attracted him and he welcomed the opportunity to put into practice what he had been teaching. He was extremely successful in his new position and decided to make the change a permanent one. He might just as easily have discovered that he preferred the classroom, that he missed the interaction with students and could do without the pressure he began to experience in his new job. If he *had* decided to return to his professorial status, his experience in business would have become a catalyst for renewed investment in his teaching.

A woman who worked as a volunteer arranging flowers at a local hospital was offered a full-time job in a florist shop. Since she could use additional income, she accepted the job offer, but was unhappy in the new position. She did not respond well to the pressure of completing a large number of arrangements each day and lost much of the thrill she had experienced as a volunteer. At first, she was unable to sift through the reason for her dissatisfaction, and she generalized that she just was not talented enough to do the work required at the shop. In reality, it was the time pressure, not her creative potential, that was under scrutiny. She eventually opted to forgo the salary and return to the work environment that had given her so much pleasure.

Another woman volunteered to arrange a house tour for an organization to which she belonged. She quickly discovered that she did not have a penchant for details, and was intolerant of people who did not fulfill their commitments. Consequently, her planning for the tour was fraught with frustration, and not as successful as it might have been under more auspicious circumstances. For her to conclude that she was not a good organizer, however, would not necessarily be accurate. At another time, she could be more careful in choosing co-workers who could complement her strengths and capabilities, and assume the responsibility for the details she disliked handling.

Ellen had gone through a training program to learn to sell life insurance and was challenged by what she had learned and felt she could accomplish. She had become thoroughly knowledgeable about the business of selling insurance and had done well in training. She could hardly wait to begin calling on that huge, untouched market of women not yet tapped. But when she moved from role playing in training sessions to approaching potential clients, she froze. She was quite unsuccessful in those first few months of selling insurance. Was she at a dead end? Was she off the track? She analyzed the situation and pinpointed the problem as stemming from her tremendous difficulty in initiating contact with people she did not know. She remedied the situation by beginning with her friends and acquaintances, and then asking each of them to telephone two of *their* friends or acquaintances to whom they would introduce her. That way, she always had a reference as an introduction to a potential client. The fear and self-consciousness melted away as she began to capably demonstrate her expertise in the field.

You took a photography course, and were all thumbs? Is it a dead end, or perhaps the very early, embryonic stages of learning a new craft. It might be too soon to discern whether or not there exists any artistic talent. If the enthusiasm is still there, take another class. Choose a different instructor. Get a better camera. Find a partner with whom you can work and learn. Set small, tentative goals that are attainable, and give yourself time. Then analyze your capabilities and draw some more accurate conclusions.

HAZARD AHEAD

When you see a sign like Hazard Ahead, don't you wonder what is in store for you? You are cautious. You are alert to possible dangers. But rarely do you decide to turn back or try another road. You anticipate a minimum amount of risk, but rarely feel that the risk is too great. You may feel that if the road is still open, you should be able to cope with any hazards that might lie in wait for you. So you decide that it is worth staying on the road, worth facing possible dangers in order to get to your destination more quickly. And in the end that one road, that risky road, may be your only path to where you want to go. Is the hazard sign going to scare you away or will you chance the risks?

Some successful businesswomen were asked about mistakes they had made and how they had learned from them. Somewhat surprisingly, while the particular mistakes and the specific situations differed, their responses had a common thread. They all agreed that most of their mistakes were the result of *not* taking risks, of not stretching themselves beyond what they knew they could do.

One woman had been very successful in a technical field of medical research. She enjoyed her work and had never considered moving into a supervisory role. Twice she turned down the offered promotion. The first time she turned it down because she had never considered a change from actually carrying out the research problems to that of supervising a number of research projects. The second time she admitted that she doubted her ability to supervise others. But all of her work and interaction with other people in the research department indicated the probability of her success in such a role. She finally agreed to accept the position when she was faced with the possibility of having to be supervised by the person who would be chosen instead of her. (She doubted the other person's capabilities.) She discovered that the move was right for her. Her previous complacency and shortsightedness about her training could have eventually stifled her. Her further career-related choices took into account the things she learned from this experience. She now had much less fear about taking risks.

Another woman discovered that her biggest mistake was not taking the risk of asking questions of other people. She had been afraid of their responses when they found out that she did not know the answer to some of the problems on her new job. She spent many hours poring over old records and accounts to see how the problems had been handled in the past. Finally, there was a point at which she knew that she did not have adequate time to research the problem. She decided to outline what she knew of the problem and how she was considering handling it based on past solutions. She included the ways in which she had handled similar situations, and what she had come to know about company policies, and asked someone she respected to ascertain whether there was something she had not considered. Her colleague was willing to discuss the problem with her, admitting that he found this kind of exchange helpful himself and hoped he might also consult her in the future. She never again allowed herself to *not* take the risk of asking well-thought-out and appropriate questions.

Both of these women developed new personal plans. They began to look for opportunities for new "risks," new situations in which they could take risks that would allow for personal growth, new challenges, and learning from new situations. They no longer viewed risks only in terms of possible *mistakes*, but also in terms of a chance to grow.

When you are anticipating setting out toward a new goal, whether it is an educational one, a career goal, or any other personal planned achievement, list the situations you might consider hazardous on the road to the achievement of your goal. If you are thinking of returning to school or of being retrained in another field, what could hinder your success? Are you concerned about your age, your ability to keep up with others in the class, your writing or math abilities, budgeting your time appropriately? Any of these really could be hazards. But remember that hazards and obstacles are sometimes only potential or partial obstructions. That these hazards do exist, and that you are aware of them, are warnings that you might be better off moving a little more slowly or deciding to better equip yourself for the journey. If you are concerned about your writing or math abilities, you could take a refresher course at a local evening school or get a tutor to help you over the rough spots. You have been forewarned about the dangers so that you might forearm yourself. The experienced backpacker or mountain climber knows that there will be unforeseen hazards. They do research on the area they are going to cover. They inquire about weather conditions at the time of year they will be hiking or climbing. They learn about road or structural changes since the last time they were there. Usually, they do not allow the risks to prevent them from going, although they do want to know what these potential risks could be.

You may never go backpacking or climb a mountain, but your initial setting out toward goals or new challenges may seem fraught with risks that appear to be as personally dangerous to you as those enormous risks taken by explorers of lands and mountains. And those anticipated hazards might eventually confront you. You might come up against roadblocks and have to change your goals. But you can gain strength and proceed with your personal growth by knowing that risks are part of life. Living with their outcome, making new plans, and moving on can all contribute to a rewarding life.

FORK IN THE ROAD

As you are traveling along, you come to an expected fork in the road. You have been advised that one road leads to quite a scenic route, but it is slow traveling on it. The alternate route is a straight highway, and will lead you directly to your destination. Which environment do you want to travel through? How do you want to spend your next two to three hours? Do you have thinking to do, and prefer the highway with its lack of diversions? Or do you prefer to travel quickly, and decrease the tedium of highway driving by listening to your stereo tapes, or listening to the "talking book" that you have recently rented just for times like this? Or would you prefer to travel off the beaten track, hoping to discover an unexpected country inn where you can stop for pie and coffee?

Choose your environment. Research your options by actually putting yourself in various environments and testing out your gut responses. Some of the crucial elements of the environment to consider include: the physical setting, the design of the space, the people, how they are dressed, the lighting, natural light versus artificial light, adequate office space, privacy of office space, proximity to other businesses, and proximity to restaurants.

Deborah was an excellent secretary who had worked, over the years, in a variety of environments. She had worked in a large company with a pool of other secretaries. She had worked in a small company where she had her own office and had a lot more responsibilities and latitude to use her initiative. She had also worked in a doctor's office, where her duties included working with the patients in addition to typing, accounting, and correspondence. She had never been particularly happy until she discovered an environment that stimulated and energized her. Her responsibilities in her new job as secretary to a group of psychologists were similar to her other jobs. But she now had the opportunity to work with professionals in the communications field who listened to her opinions and considered her responses to be valuable; they allowed her to expand the definition of her job as she felt capable of doing so. The physical setting was appealing to her—wide open spaces and modern furnishings and an unusually large number of windows. She had finally discovered an environment she looked forward to entering each morning.

Peggy had outstanding credentials in the educational field of early childhood, and in response to her job-hunting efforts she received three offers that were comparable in pay and benefits. All three were also approximately the same distance from her home. And they were all extremely well thought of in the community. For Peggy, the deciding factor was the difference in environments and her responses to them as she experienced them during the interviewing process. One of the nursery schools was located on a college campus. The space was quite spread out, in an older building with high ceilings, and equipped with plenty of toys and equipment. The second nursery school was almost the exact antithesis in terms of physical setting. It was quite small, to the point where Peggy felt slightly claustrophobic, though she observed the children seemed very happy. The third was a balance of the first two. It was just large enough, very modern, well lit, and made her feel extremely comfortable. Since all other variables were equal, Peggy allowed her responses to the physical setting to determine her decision, and chose the third setting.

Janet was offered an executive position in a large company that was just beginning to hire and promote women into the executive ranks. The grapevine had warned her that the men were resistant to sharing their "turf" with qualified women and that she would probably also encounter resentment from certain women who had been competing for the job she was being offered. Janet decided to accept the challenge, knowing full well that the initial months would be difficult because of the tension and stress resulting from possible interpersonal conflicts. She knew all the facts, and then made the decision that she felt would be right for her at that time in her career. She had carefully assessed the environment and her responses to it in order to come to an appropriate decision.

Sally decided to start her own consulting business and surveyed the area to determine where to open her offices. She knew that the first couple of years would be tough, and that she should be careful not to spend too much on overhead. But she also knew how important location and image were to her potential clients. And finally, she knew herself well enough that she needed to decide on a location that was lovely, afforded a view, but would undoubtedly cost more than she should spend. She made the decision to go ahead and spend more, primarily because she wanted to look forward each morning to going to offices whose location and physical setting (both the external and internal environments) pleased her aesthetically.

RIGHT TURN ON RED

A forty-five-year-old woman begins law school, a career woman decides to breed horses, a secretary enrolls in an undergraduate program, planning to eventually work on a master's in Business Administration. There may be many turns that you need to take on the route you have planned, so stay alert and watch for important signs. Are you bored with what you are doing now? Is there some dream you would like to attain or experience? Do you need to make more money? Your internal mechanisms can provide signals for your need to change. Suddenly a perplexing decision becomes clearer. You decide to apply for that position as supervisor, go back to school, work outside your home. Be aware of your internal barometer. Pay attention to external stimuli that can help guide you. As people live longer and our technology continues to change at a rapid pace, the need for you to follow new pathways may become necessary. So be prepared to turn right on red when it looks like it may be the right time. After all, in most places it is not against the law.

Perhaps you have worked as a beautician, professional dancer, teacher, airline stewardess or engineer and have loved your work. But after some years your needs have changed, new interests have emerged, additional skills have been developed, and your life's circumstances have altered. Should you continue on your original course, or should you heed the turn sign? The decision you make may take you down a road parallel to the one you have been on, or it may lead you to a newly paved road or to one that is still under construction.

Take the time to reevaluate what you are doing now and to assess your own reactions. How are you different from when you first chose your occupation? What has changed? One woman who had chosen the dual career of mother and weaver had for twelve years found these to be compatible home-based jobs. As her children began to focus their interests outside the home, they needed less of her involvement and time. She noticed that she, too, was changing. She was beginning to feel restricted by her solitary endeavors, and wanted to spend more time with other people. She felt ready for new learning experiences and new directions. It was time for her to shift gears.

She was able to identify assets she had that had not been fully utilized in her weaving. She worked well with people, was sensitive and intuitive, could teach others, and had an infinite amount of patience. She began to think of ways to incorporate her love of weaving into a more people-oriented environment. She considered commercial art, high school teaching, fabric design, occupational therapy, and art therapy. After investigating these different options, she decided to explore her interest in art therapy. Because she already had an undergraduate degree in fine arts, she discovered that she was eligible for a master's degree in art therapy, which could be completed in two years. She had discovered a new field for herself that incorporated her artistic talent and her skills in working with people. This new direction seemed to fit well for this time in her life, just as weaving had worked well for her in earlier years.

It is easy to have guilt feelings when you are considering a change. ("People should stay with what they start; they should be loyal workers and have a responsibility to work in the field for which they were trained.") But career decisions do not necessarily need to be "forever" decisions. Identify your needs, generate new ideas, assess, reevaluate—get out your map. Maybe there is an emerging occupation that would be better for you at this point in your life. It may be just the time to set new goals and plan alternate strategies for their attainment.

POOR VISIBILITY AHEAD

When you are moving along at your own individual speed, trying to reach your own destination, it is easy for you to unintentionally become invisible to others, even close friends. Unless you tell them, they will not know what you are doing, what you are interested in, any plans you have made and goals you have set. Do not play the shy "waiting game" hoping that someone will see that you have something to say or observe that you need some help in moving along to the next step toward your goal. If you are looking for a job, let everyone know. You do not necessarily need to know the most important person in the company or institution where you are hoping to secure a job. Letting people at all levels know what your qualifications are, and that you are available and actively seeking a job, will enhance the possibility that you will learn about a job opening. Then you can do the research, decide on the best procedure to use in contacting the company and discover who has the responsibility for hiring someone for that position.

If you are currently employed, it is also important to maintain visibility with appropriate people if you want to receive recognition for your successes and contributions to your company or institution. Let people know that you are capable, interested in your work, and serious about working toward possible advancement. It is not necessary, naturally, to report to your supervisor with every job you have completed or every decision you have made. But at appropriate times, such as department meetings, through quarterly reports, and at annual evaluations and reviews, present the information that points to your progress and contributions. If there is a company or institution newspaper or newsletter, inform them of your participation in community affairs or other contributions you have made to the company, other organizations, or the city.

Your attempts at maintaining visibility might not insure that you are chosen at promotion time. Just as the sign Poor Visibility Ahead can clue you to the possibility of a change in the driving patterns of the people on the road with you, you can try to learn to read the clues that usually precede a change in your company or work setting. You cannot necessarily predict changes that will follow, but you can become more alert to potential changes both in yourself, your family or friends, and also in societal institutions. Your anticipation of change will put you on the alert, and hopefully you will be better able to cope with change, and progress toward your personal and professional goals.

PROCEED WITH EXTREME CAUTION

The road may be quite narrow and winding at this stretch, or icy from the last snow, or slippery because of the pounding rain. It would be foolish not to be careful, not to keep your eyes glued to the road while inching ahead. But it would be as dangerous to stop. And to back up would be unthinkable in almost every case.

It may be hazardous to your own self-confidence *not* to ask for that promotion and raise, and equally as hazardous to accept a promotion with no pay or benefit increases. It can become very frustrating, and often degrading, to be asked to shoulder additional work and responsibilities without being fairly compensated. Laura taught at the college level, was highly respected in her field, and thoroughly enjoyed her work. When a vacancy as chair of the department arose she was asked to take the position. However, she was not offered additional salary or benefits to compensate for the increased time and energy that would be required in her new job. She was told that there were no additional monies available to that department, which was true. However, Laura felt the need for additional compensation and began to peruse the entire job market in search of a salary to match the title.

Claire had to make a decision about whether to take a risk or to play it safe. She had been asked to assume many additional responsibilities in her work without being compensated for these additional tasks. She was hurt and angry. She had to decide if she would begin looking for another job, let her hurt and anger be known (and hope for change) or allow the situation to remain the same. She was concerned that if she made no mention of her legitimate complaint, her supervisors would continue to increase her responsibilities without accompanying pay increases. Claire decided to apply for another job. If she was offered the job, she planned to *then* present her case to her supervisors, saying that she preferred to stay where she was, but felt that a raise or promotion was in order. If they were unwilling—or unable—to offer one, she would then accept the job with the other institution. She knew that it was a clear possibility that her present employers might say, "Go ahead and take the other job." And then she would. For Claire's sense of integrity, and for her own career advancement possibilities, she was willing to take what was for her a risk—that of moving from one job to another.

The code word to this section is "initiate." You may be doing a spectacular job in your position. You may have made inroads in developing new programs, increasing the projected profit for the last two quarters of the year, or improving employee communication and morale. But all the same, you may not be awarded the salary increments you feel to be adequate and fair. You may expect that management will notice, will automatically increase your salary and/or bonus in direct relationship to your accomplishments. But often the waiting to be noticed and compensated can become frustrating.

One woman who became director of computer operations for a large corporation planned carefully for her salary increases. Kristen's strategy included setting goals and behavioral objectives for herself, discussing them with her immediate supervisor, asking for input and criticism on a periodic basis, and setting guidelines with her supervisor about meeting these goals. She built this strategy into the already existing annual salary review system. What Kristen did, in actuality, was to build into a traditional salary review system additional methods for performance appraisal. Kristen did not want to wait until it was time for a salary review to see if her work would be noticed. She did not want to do her job, work hard, produce a lot, and then *hope* that she would be fairly compensated. She took the responsibility of sharing what she expected of herself, asking for input about what was expected of her, and sharing her expectations in terms of monetary increases. Kristen helped insure the fact that she would be dealt with fairly—as fairly as her male counterparts who also had high expectations for salary increments.

In the process of proceeding with extreme caution, Kristen was mentally keeping her options open. She was developing her expertise, earning a reputation as a hard worker who meets her goals, and increasing her level of self-confidence. If she were not fairly compensated, she could never be accused of job hopping or of lack of commitment to her work. She has been honest with herself and her employer about the importance of salary increases both for her sense of accomplishment and for her credibility within the company.

Another area that requires you to proceed with extreme caution is in your response during an interview in which you are being asked questions that are now considered discriminatory. At one time it was common to be asked whether you are married, how many children you have, whether you are planning to have more children, what your husband does, and incredibly, even what kind of birth control you use. Though this line of questioning is illegal and in many cases could be the base of an affirmative action suit against the potential employer, it is often helpful to proceed with extreme caution in your responses. The reasons for the questions are apparent. You might find it better to respond directly to the concerns of job commitment implied in such questions. Some men in a position to hire women still perceive them as unpredictable, flighty dabblers in the business and professional worlds. A response to the question, "How many children do you have?" could be, "It is interesting that you would ask that question. Are you concerned that I would not be free to travel, as this job clearly requires?" In that way, the reason for the question is handled without compromising yourself by answering inappropriate and often illegal questions. And proceeding with caution may not have prevented you from losing the chance at a job for which you might be completely qualified and which you might really like to have.

NO U-TURN

Are there barriers on the path you are traveling? We all meet them on our way. We may stop, turn around, and eventually begin again, looking for a way to get back on track. Learn to view these blocks as a challenge to your problem-solving ability. You want a promotion but they only seem to advance people with degrees. You would like to start a business but you do not have the capital. You want a part-time job, but they are "impossible" to find in your field.

How can you get where you want to go even though the sign says "No U-Turn"? You may believe that the only way to get there is by turning around, but how many other ways can you think of, if you really try? Do not give in to those negative thoughts. ("I could never do it." "They will never choose me." "There is no use in even trying.") Challenge yourself instead to think of one positive step you could take that might cause a positive change. Mothers will often fight selflessly for their children, but give up after a halfhearted try when it comes to their own personal endeavors. When you succumb to negative self-statements or assumptions that things will not work out, you contribute to your sense of powerlessness. If you try to find a way to attain what you want—the promotion, a loan for business, a part-time job in your field—you offer yourself the possibility of success rather than participating in your failure to achieve.

Brainstorm. Look for options. Consider the unlikely, the unusual, the unorthodox. Developing a career, reaching a new personal height, raising a family, aspiring to do anything of consequence, are all going to involve encounters with obstacles. No U-Turn signs can be signals to try to eliminate your negative thoughts and replace them with positive, action-provoking ones. They can serve as a springboard for activating your problem-solving skills.

SLOW: CONSTRUCTION FOR 10 MILES

Why do you always seem to come upon construction work just when you are in a real hurry? You had not anticipated any delay in your trip. Actually, you may come upon construction delays at many other times, but when they do not get in your way or inconvenience you, you may be far less aware of their existence. However, when you are in a hurry, you may get frustrated, anxious, and sometimes even take some risks or make some decisions that are not in your best interest and may even cost you time. You may find yourself racing around the side streets to avoid the construction, but instead be confronted with red lights, stop signs, school crossings, or a recently changed one-way street. In the end, these distractions will cost you more time than you would have lost if you had patiently stayed with the detours or construction adjustments. The unplanned, haphazard efforts to get ahead of the game plan are often more costly in the final analysis. They have not succeeded in effectively solving the problem of getting you to your destination with the least amount of time and effort. And certainly such mistakes of judgment should be reviewed and taken into account the next time you meet a similar obstacle.

The important thing to be learned from any experience in which you have met obstacles and were displeased with the way you handled them, is to do some evaluation and plan ahead regarding how you might contend with similar roadblocks in the future. For example, the person who is opening a small business or has assumed budgeting responsibilities for a job or an organization, is faced with the task of developing an accounting system. If she has had little or no training in accounting, she will probably seek professional advice. One woman who became director of an apartment complex for senior citizens did just that. Her consultant set up a highly technical, computerized system for her use. The problem facing her was that the system did not fit her needs. She only handled about 35 transactions a month, writing five payroll checks and collecting thirty rent checks. The system gave her all kinds of unnecessary information, cross-indexing and subtotaling in various ways. Not having a background in accounting, she was unable to use the system and kept putting off some of the accounting work that needed to be done. Her records were of little help to her when it was necessary to make reports and budget projections. She did learn from that experience and sought another, simpler type of accounting arrangement, suited to the needs of her situation. For the future, when the need arises, she has learned to begin with a simple system and work up to a more complex one.

At a seminar for women who owned their own small

businesses, the main speaker had a number of suggestions for increased efficiency that have possible implications for individuals in their personal lives as well as for people in business. Early in her business career, she had discovered that it was a waste of her time to do things twice. When sorting through mail, it was far more efficient for her to make immediate decisions on many matters. She realized that when she put something aside to think about at a later date, she had rarely reached a better solution, and had often missed deadlines or completely forgotten about the matter. She was referring to the ordinary, daily decisions we all make.

She had also learned to keep a "plan ahead" book or calendar. When a specific thing was to be accomplished in three months, she would break down the job into steps and place them on the calendar at appropriate intervals during the three-month period. She suggested that it would also be wise to have a business plan, with specific goals for the growth or direction of your business. An individual may call this a life plan or long-range goal setting for life accomplishments. She felt that it was important to keep in mind where she wanted her business to go, as well as where it had been. She admitted that she adapted these "business" techniques to her own life, and felt more competent at home as well as in her business life.

ONE-WAY—DO NOT ENTER

You are almost at your destination. The street seems quiet enough at this late evening hour. You just need to go to the fourth house on the left. But there is no denying the fact: the sign clearly says *One-Way—Do Not Enter*. Will you take the extra few minutes to go around the block and enter from the opposite direction? Or will you chance it and count on the lateness of the hour and the quietness of the streets to protect you from any conscientious law enforcement officer who is protecting the streets?

What issues should you consider in making this decision? Do you visit often? If so, will the neighbors draw inaccurate conclusions about you when you ignore the traffic sign? Will they be concerned about the safety of their children on what they *thought* was a protected street? Or will they discard your turning on this one-way street as being of minimal importance? Whatever you decide, the people who observe your actions will surely see you from their own perspective. Their perceptions of you will depend on a variety of factors, including where they live on the street, the darkness of the night, their own feelings about obeying traffic signs, having been in similar situations themselves, how you are dressed, the kind of car you are driving, and the speed with which you are driving. In any case, you have created an image of yourself, in spite of what you had set out to do.

John Molloy wrote a book called *Dress for Success,* and soon followed this immensely successful book with *The Women's Dress for Success Book.* In it he discusses the importance of dress for women in business, and the relationship between attire and acceptance and eventual success. One successful woman in middle management in a large corporation became acutely aware of the importance of her image, including the way she dressed, acted, and responded within her work environment. Her career had not been progressing as rapidly as she had hoped. After reading Molloy's book, she concluded that she did not fit the conservative, predictable corporate image that might be necessary for the kind of success which she sought within the company. She decided to conform more to the corporate image, while still retaining a certain degree of personal style. Her image no longer interfered with management's ability to perceive her in upper management.

We are not suggesting that every woman buy pinstriped suits and conform to a strict dress code. We *are* suggesting, however, that whatever you do, however you decide to dress and act, you become aware that you are creating an image that will affect both your performance and the responses of those with whom you work on a daily basis.

Another woman, an executive in a brokerage company, feels more comfortable wearing dresses, choosing to create a more feminine image than she would present by wearing suits and blazers. She is aware of the relationship between image and success and is certain that her image is not getting in her own way as she develops her career path.

One woman who owned an interior design business decided to hire an employee to work with her, now that her business had passed the one-year mark and was still in operation. She interviewed several promising candidates, and almost instantly formed impressions of these women based on how they had chosen to dress for the interview. In her business, she was extremely conscious of color and design, and she eliminated one well qualified young woman because of the inappropriate color combination of the clothes she had chosen to wear during two separate interviews. She felt that since the woman had a sense of color combinations radically different from her own, she could never be completely confident in the employee's professional decisions about decorating schemes. The applicant had made an important statement about herself simply by the way she had dressed, even before she had said anything. And though she was articulate and had good credentials, she was not hired, due mainly to the visual image that she had created.

One director of a college placement center feels that most recruiters that come to the college make almost instantaneous decisions about potential candidates by the way they dress and carry themselves. He challenged one recruiter to snap his fingers at the point in the interview when he had made a decision about whether to invite the student for a second interview. The recruiter agreed, certain that he would not be snapping his fingers until very near the conclusion of the interview. He was startled when he found himself snapping in the waiting room, when he went to *meet* the potential candidate. Later questioned, he stated that he was negatively impressed by the way the student was slumped in his seat, and the fact that his shirttail was not completely tucked in.

Often college graduates descend on personnel offices wearing clothes that are completely inappropriate for that work environment. Some young women wear high heels and tightly fitting dresses that are more appropriate for the theater and create a negative image from the start. Often these young college graduates may just drop by to pick up an application, dressed in their college attire of jeans and sweaters. Unfortunately, though the contact is brief, the impression informal attire makes is difficult to exclude from memory, even though an applicant may return for an interview more appropriately dressed.

An image does not have to be a façade. It can accurately reflect who you are, and what you want to portray. Different environments foster different expectations. The academic environment is much more casual. A dentist may decide to dress in a sweater in order to create less distance between himself and the children he treats. There is a newly developing field of experts who are trained to anticipate and deal with emotional concerns and anxieties of children in a hospital setting. They encourage hospital personnel to dress informally in order to minimize the impersonality of the hospital environment. It is important to know your audience, and then to make calculated decisions about how you want other people to respond to you. Since you *will* be creating an image, you might as well participate in its creation on a conscious level.

YIELD

Maybe it *is* time to yield to certain realities and try to develop some alternatives. Perhaps it *is* time to try for part-time options, return to education if business is too much pressure, or get out of the stock market and invest in real estate.

If you have been traveling at full speed and the feeling was initially heady, but has deteriorated to dizzy, maybe you have moved from feeling, "I can do anything" to, "I can (should) do everything." This "super-woman" syndrome has become increasingly common among women during career journeys, and can indeed be debilitating.

June decided at age forty to return to school to study interior design. She enrolled in three courses, two of which included laboratories and required a great deal of work. By the end of the semester she felt like a nervous wreck. Her children, ages sixteen, fourteen, and seven, were reacting to the loss of her attention. Her husband was upset and felt threatened, and she felt barely able to keep the threads of her life from unraveling. She decided to yield to the pressure and take some time out from her plans to build a better foundation from which to begin again. June set aside one year to get her life in order and to wean her family from being so dependent on her. She started with herself, by joining an assertive training class, a woman's personal development group, and making plans to organize her home so that maintenance would be easier. With time, patience, and persistence, her children became more independent and confident in their abilities to depend on themselves. Her husband grew to understand and accept her need to go to school and develop a life separate from her family. And she has become much clearer about her own priorities.

This fall, June not only enrolled in design courses, but also located a scholarship for which she was eligible. She has applied to graduate school in architecture, hoping to fulfill a lifelong dream. She feels refueled now, and better able to continue her journey.

Jordana has been working in her job at the university for six years, ever since she married. The decision to start a family propelled her into a state of ambivalence. Should she stay at home after her baby is born? Would she be jeopardizing her job if she stayed home for a year rather than the three months maternity leave that was university policy? Wanting to enjoy her baby and get her child off to a good start was a pressing need, as was the reality that she enjoyed a job in which she had built up seniority. As the baby grew inside of her, so did her sense of ambivalence and anxiety. At first, the only alternatives she could think of were to quit her job or to stay home for only three months. One evening she and her husband sat down to brainstorm some other possibilities. She could try to convince her employers to give her a six- or twelve-month leave. She could arrange to work two days a week in her present job, as someone already did in another department on campus. She could use this time at home with her baby to attend classes part-time in other areas that interest her. She could take her leave, and then decide at the end of that time what she wanted to do, based on her experience of being at home. Jordana felt relieved when she realized that her route was not necessarily as fixed and unswerving as she had thought it to be. She could yield to situations that arose by planning her own itinerary based on many possible choices.

REST AREA AHEAD

Since women have begun exploring the career paths men have traditionally followed, they are encountering one of the road-blocks that is often present on the road to success, that of stress. Terry had been pushing herself forward in tremendous strides. Because her family was cooperative, she felt free to assume increasingly greater responsibilities and new projects. She was working three-fourths time and pursuing a Ph.D. in her field when she decided to participate in an interesting six-month project. She organized, planned, worked, and worried, barely making it through the next six months. When it was over, she felt satisfied with what she had accomplished, but she was physically and mentally exhausted. She decided to acknowledge the fact that she needed to slow down, and take time off by herself without feeling guilty. She vacationed alone at her parents' summer home near the ocean, spending four days on rest and relaxation. She luxuriated in the feeling of having no responsibilities and only her own needs to consider. When she returned home she felt refreshed, happy to see her family, and ready to resume her responsibilities.

There are pressures and realities in everyone's life that are impossible to ignore. Yielding requires acknowledging your feelings. It means recognizing and taking into account those situations which may have consequences which will negatively affect your ultimate goal. It is important to find ways to deal with these situations, to stop moving quickly, gain some perspective and then return to your road when you are ready.

Should you stop here or push on to the next rest area, which is eighty miles ahead? You feel all right, albeit a little slow and sluggish. You do not want to break your rhythm, and you feel like pushing on. You really want to get to where you are going. However, maybe you will feel more alert if you do stop just for a little while. Maybe you will handle the driving better after you take a short rest.

When you are goal oriented, you may sometimes find it difficult to allocate time for the necessary rest periods. Your mind may be racing ahead, as you are reviewing and evaluating certain projects in your head. At times like these you might also become physically less resilient. Or you might not have a specific goal in mind but have the feeling that you *should* have one, that you should be "doing something." Your energies might, in turn, be dissipated from this lack of direction. It is important to use times of rest to reenergize yourself, and to reorient yourself to your tasks and goals. In calisthenics, the warm-up exercises we all did in gym class, the momentary rests for our muscles were a necessary part of total muscle toning.

Most of us do believe rest to be necessary. How frequently have you said, "I need some rest," or, "Just give me a minute's rest, and then I will be fine and ready to go again." However, you may not use periods of rest as effectively as possible, as a time to revitalize yourself. You may need to learn what type of rest is most appropriate to your individual situation. Society encourages you to make every moment count, to strive constantly, to always be better than your competition, whether that competition is the owner of a rival store, the other English teacher, the housewife next door, or the tennis player on the other side of the net. Perhaps this continuous striving is appropriate in order to eventually succeed, but it should be put into its proper perspective.

If your job or your daily activities are ones of high pressure or competition, then the type of activities in which you are involved during your times of rest or leisure might more effectively be noncompetitive types of activities. You do not have to be in high pressure sales to feel in competition; each time you try to reason with a child, or look for a better way of teaching a skill, creating a dinner, designing a room, or solving a chemical equation, you may feel the stress resulting from competitive feelings. During your lunch hour you might become revitalized by spending time at the ballet barre, or on a walk in the park, rather than from a game of racquet ball. If you do engage in a potentially competitive game, you may decide to let your opponent work herself into a state of frenzy, while you take it easy. If, on the other hand, much of your day is spent in routine, noncompetitive situations, you may need to energize yourself by matching wits and skills with another.

Of prime importance is deciding which type of activity will give you needed respite from your usual duties and responsibilities and which will allow you to tackle your work with renewed energy. One top-level executive relaxed by learning to play the piano. This endeavor was so far removed from her daily work that it provided the kind of rest that resulted in the renewed energy she needed to deal with difficult problems that faced her at work.

Another woman who had chosen to stay home with her small children found that jogging competitively (she enters at least ten runs a year) and being in regular tennis tournaments was energizing for her. In this way she was able to be active, stay alert, and match wits and skills with others in ways that were good alternatives and balances to the work she did in the home.

ALL VEHICLES MUST EXIT: ROAD ENDS

Your job is being terminated. Your school is closing. Your company is merging with another and your job has become redundant. You can clearly see that within a year's time your job will have become obsolete, and you will need to move in a new career direction. Your husband lost his job or you recently got a divorce, and you must return to work quickly. You feel as though you have been deceived; you were lured into a field that cannot absorb you, no matter how competent you may prove yourself to be. You are angry at your teachers, your parents, your advisers—all of whom should have had the foresight to prevent this from having happened.

But perhaps you did not pay close enough attention to the signs along the road. There may have been an earlier warning that the highway was not yet completed. Perhaps it had been written about in the newspaper or discussed on the news. After all, you knew that the population of school-aged children was declining in your district. You saw the writing on the wall that claimed the end of teaching being a secure profession. But you were so comfortable in your work, had developed such a high level of expertise, and had reached an acceptable salary level, and so you decided to stay and hope that you would remain employed. The business world seemed a little too foreign, too unrelated to your experience, to venture out there unless absolutely necessary.

Sharon was a remedial-reading specialist in an excellent school system. When she had gone to college, she was urged to specialize in reading in order to insure a secure niche for herself. So she specialized. And what happened to her niche? Just at the point of possible tenure, she was terminated. She had no choice; she had to get off "the road." The question to ask herself now was whether to search for a similar job in another district or take the opportunity to change jobs completely. She considered returning to graduate school, but was unsure of what area to pursue. She launched a campaign to discover her options. She developed a network, wrote letters, telephoned people, inventoried her skills, and researched her interests. Within a few months' time she was offered a job in training at a local company with a significant salary increase and better fringe benefits than she had ever had before.

Anita was a secretary who worked for an executive in a company that she discovered was going out of business. She loved her work, but took the opportunity to search for an environment that had less pressure. She took inventory. Ultimately she decided that she would love to relocate and identified a writer's collective that wanted to employ a secretary. She was able to combine her love of reading with her expert secretarial skills in a work environment which would have significantly less pressure than her previous job. One road had ended and another had begun. Anita felt great pride in having been able to identify the characteristics of the job she wanted, and to actually find a job that fit these characteristics.

ROAD CONSTRUCTION AHEAD

Significant changes or alterations in your ways of thinking and acting will affect the important people in your life. There may be no way to prevent the disruption inside yourself that accompanies change, but you can be prepared for it, plan for it, anticipate it. Put up clear markers and blinking yellow lights to communicate to those around you what is happening and what they can expect from you. When you are open about what is happening, it is easier for others to understand and accept your changes, regardless of whether they are in total agreement with you. Often the comment, "She/he is not the person I married" is heard. Of course not. We are all continuously changing as a result of growing older, experiencing more, and reevaluating our wants and needs. Unfortunately, two people in a relationship may be changing at different rates or in different directions. It can take determination and fortitude to maintain a balance in the relationship and a respect for each other's individuality.

How does your changing—wanting to be knowledgeable about family finances, leaving a job to have children, taking on a job that involves traveling—affect your relationships with your family? How much of what you "suppose" your husband or children think has actually been checked out with them? New routines, different priorities, and less time to spend together can be unsettling. Good communication can be the first step toward facilitating and easing the process of change. Wanting to begin a new career may only be the observable source of conflict.

Changes in you, however, may actually go much deeper. Perhaps you have undergone a basic rethinking of your role, your life style, of what you can be or what you would like to become. This metamorphosis took time to develop and surface in you. It is unreasonable to expect your spouse or children to become aware of and sympathetic with your emerging "self" if you have not previously shared your internal changes with them. It is also unlikely that they will be able to assimilate your new ideas immediately. Often by the time you have openly communicated your ideas and plans they have been simmering for a long time within yourself. But your family may be caught totally unaware, hearing them for the first time. Their initial responses may include feelings of being surprised or threatened. At this point, conflicts often erupt. It is important to be able to listen to (and *hear*) each person's concerns and fears that are a response to your changing. In a family, a change in one person's life pattern is bound to have a ripple effect on all family members. Our experiences with women going through this same process have demonstrated that relationships can often adapt to accommodate change.

If you are beginning a new venture, it may take quite a bit of energy to handle obstacles and challenges along the way. It will be much easier to tackle these endeavors if you have your family's cooperation. You can begin to gain their respect for what you are doing by taking your work seriously and valuing it yourself. If you say, "It is *just* a part-time job," then they may adopt that attitude. If you consider your work important, then they, also, will treat it with high regard. Whether you are volunteering, going to school, or in the paid labor force, talk to them about what you are doing, what you would like to do in the future and how you plan to go about it. Express your fears, hopes, and desires. If you are terrified about your first day on a college campus ("What if I say the wrong thing, or cannot find the library, or can't keep up with the other students?") share these fears with your family. What child has not experienced those same feelings at one time? Your husband may remember how he felt the first time he conducted a meeting, was evaluated, or faced a difficult situation at work.

Your family's interest in you and support of your new endeavors can be significant in helping you through those moments of self-doubt. Your experiences can provide learning opportunities for those around you. When your family sees you trying out new behaviors, they can learn that it is acceptable to try something, even when they are scared or unsure. They can learn about risk taking from you, and about taking chances on the future. This open sharing can facilitate family communication and help prevent serious disruption that sometimes accompanies change.

NO PARKING: VIOLATORS TOWED AT OWNER'S EXPENSE

There are places designed for parking: lots, rest areas, garages, or spaces in front of your own house. There are also places that are clearly not designed for parking. If you want to stop or to rest, then seek the places that allow you to do so without causing problems for yourself. But when you are interested in "keeping your engine running," then keep yourself moving, place yourself in situations in which it is necessary that you keep your "mental motor" turned on. You do not have to put yourself on a busy highway where people are racing in all directions if you don't want to keep up with the fast pace of the traffic. But you may want to keep yourself in gear and move along at your own pace on a less busy street.

When you are not actively involved in a field for which you have been trained, it takes effort to be aware of the changes taking place in that field. You may be interested, but if you are not actively involved, there are many other people, interests, and responsibilities that demand your time and attention. And before too long you may have lost contact with that field and find yourself choking and sputtering, both mentally and verbally, when you attempt to discuss it with others. Now the field may *actually* have changed very little. But you do not know that. You *feel* out of tune and others will pick up your feelings of uncertainty.

You can keep current in your field in a number of ways, with a minimal expenditure of time. You can maintain your membership in organizations that send newsletters, even if you are not active in the organization. Newsletters are a quick way of keeping you aware of the major concerns in your field of interest, whether it is fashion or bioenergetics. Organization newsletters are more specific than are general magazines for the lay public.

Keep in touch with one or two people who share your interests and your special training. They do not have to be actively employed in the field, but it would help. Your common interests will encourage both of you to be better informed and to maintain a high level of awareness. You can volunteer to work in your field once or twice a month or you may offer your "professional" services to organizations and institutions that need them but depend on volunteer help. For example, if your training has been in writing or journalism, you might volunteer your skills to your church, your children's school, your neighborhood association, or to a community newspaper. A physical therapist might volunteer to the visiting nurses association, the local hospital or to community senior citizen organizations. Salespeople might find that the local scouting groups or the athletic association might be able to use their expertise.

We have only touched on some of the possible ways to remain active in your field at a reduced rate of speed. But the benefits of continuing your contact will far outweigh the time and effort you have spent in doing so. It will be much less likely that you'll be "towed away" when seeking employment in your field. And more importantly, you will have a sense of accomplishment in maintaining your ties with an area of interest and training separate from the other areas of responsibility that occupy your time. You will maintain a sense of identity apart from the others in your life, which can, in turn, enhance your relationship with them.

You do not necessarily need to have left your field in order to lose contact with the changes, trends and developments taking place. You may assure yourself that since you are employed in your field, you are certainly aware of what is taking place. Not necessarily so. You may become complacent, stop reading in the field, drop membership in organizations, and avoid discussions about your field. If you try changing jobs, you may get a good idea of what this letting your "homework" slide may have cost you in terms of job opportunities.

You may become so busy taking care of details or with daily responsibilities or concerns that, unless you actively seek to do so, you may lose touch with advanced techniques, current findings, and new ideas. The same techniques we suggested for the person *not* currently employed are also applicable to the employed person. Set aside a specific time to read, and find a person or two with whom you can consistently discuss your field. In addition to reading the journals in your field and organizational newsletters and magazines, you can also get catalogs of new publications from publishing houses that specialize in your field. Reading the summaries of new publications will keep you aware of what topics are being written about and discussed. You might also arrange for a more formalized discussion group with four or five others. You could decide on articles, books, or topics that you would all read and then discuss. Or invite area professionals to meet with you and share their thoughts on new or related developments. Whether or not you are employed in your field of interest, it is important to make conscious efforts to keep your mind moving along so that you will not be "towed in" in violation of the No Parking signs.

MERGE SLOWLY

When you begin a new project, you may be filled with energy and enthusiasm, eager to get quickly under way. But it may be more beneficial to you and to your project to "merge slowly," to gradually build up pressure and steam, rather than to tackle the project full tilt and either antagonize others or burn up your own energy too quickly. The suggestion to move slowly in uncertain situations also applies to situations where you may feel that you have been inappropriately excluded or overlooked. You may find it more advantageous to take your time and plan your strategy carefully. Hopefully, this strategy will lead to your eventual inclusion on that committee, or to receiving that desired promotion.

When Beth began her new job as training director for a company who was still uncertain about their commitment to having their own training program, she felt anxious about creating programs that may not have support within the company. She had not worked in a company training department before, but she had developed excellent teaching and training skills. After doing considerable research, she developed many ideas about what was needed in this company. But she did not want to initiate some of those programs that she felt would be appropriate until she had built a support system within the company.

Although waiting to do what she felt was important caused her to feel anxious, she spent her time getting to know as many people as possible and familiarizing herself with their departmental responsibilities. She spoke informally with them about her ideas, and asked many of them what they considered necessary and important areas for her to develop. She gained a much better understanding of which programs would have the best chance for early success, and which programs needed to be offered after people had grown more comfortable about the introduction of the new department. She had also built a personal support system within the company. She had opened the lines of communication between herself and the other employees. Now the chances were greater that she would be approached by other employees when the need was felt for training programs. She became part of the company, not just a new idea the company wanted to try.

Sandy also decided to move slowly when she found herself excluded from a committee on which she felt she should have been included. Her job responsibilities were eventually supposed to include supervision of the program created by that committee. Rather than directly approaching the chairman of the committee, whom she did not know, she approached a number of people whom she felt would support her inclusion on the committee. She discussed her concerns about not being involved in the initial planning of the program, but having eventual responsibility for its supervision. These people did support her joining and requested that she be added to the committee; she was added and well accepted by the chairman and the other committee members.

MINIMUM 40 MPH/MAXIMUM 55 MPH

Now you are traveling at a comfortable pace toward your destination. There are other travelers on the road going at a faster clip. There are also some going slower than you. Choose your own speed, within reasonable parameters. Think for yourself. Choose to use your automatic speed control only if you are comfortable doing so, and if you want your progress to be stabilized. Pass the car on your left if you want to. If not, stay in the right lane. Do not allow any "back seat" or "front seat" drivers to determine your speed or your progress. Only *you* can know what speed is just right for you.

One woman attended a career exploration class, partially as a result of society's pressure to "be doing something important"—something "worthwhile." She was well protected financially and would not need to work even in the event of her husband's death. The course instilled in her a renewed confidence that she was exactly where she wanted to be, that she did not want to return to the paid work force. But she was now able to enjoy her freedom and affluence without feeling guilty or defensive because of negative responses from other people.

Cathy was in her middle thirties and was a highly respected drama consultant to nursery schools and day-care centers. She had had extensive training in early childhood development as well as in theater, and had recently written and published several plays for very young children to participate in. In spite of all these qualifications and her fine reputation in the community, Cathy was worried about her future. She had recently become concerned about the lack of earning power she had in this field, and was thinking about redirecting herself into a more lucrative field in the near future. She felt certain that she would need to return to college for more degrees, for further credentials in another field.

In reality, Cathy would probably have had no difficulty securing a job that would be more lucrative for her without taking any more courses. The key factor, however, was how necessary she felt these additional credentials to be and how these feelings impacted both her perception of herself and the jobs she would seek. She felt insecure in comparison to other financially independent women with whom she had contact. The work world outside of her very specialized field, and that of her husband's, was not very familiar to her. So it was important for Cathy to do whatever she felt necessary in order to be ready to sell herself into a job that would be more congruent with her growing financial expectations. She was indeed going at her own speed, working to develop her special unique life/work pattern.

Designing your own future will be easier than creating a map or a chart, because there are a number of guides and markers that you can follow and professionals with whom you can consult. The challenge is to recognize the clues and markers as only *guides*, not as definite indications of which road or path that you should take. It is also a challenge to continue to see yourself as an individual woman, not just someone who has been affected by the woman's movement and now wants to get in on the act.

With the social and economic changes that are taking place in this country and around the world, women will not only be joining the labor force, they will eventually become a necessary part of it at some point in their lives if not during most of their lives.

Use this easy traveling time to brainstorm, to be creative, to try out new directions. Try to get a job without an M.B.A. Start the business in your home that you have always dreamed about. Ask for a job you do not think you will get, and accept it if it is offered to you and feels right. Buy that house you have thought about restoring, then sell it for a profit. Purchase apartment houses, and learn how to make secure investments. Teach weaving in your home. Develop a cooking class for children in the neighborhood. Develop a column and sell the idea to the newspaper. (You don't need to have formal, journalistic training in every case.) Test out how far your enthusiasm will get you. Discover your best speed. Listen to yourself. Pay attention to the beat of your own drum. What direction is it coming from? How fast is it approaching? With what intensity? Does it frighten you or excite you? Where will it lead you? Only you can decide.

You Can Count on Change: A Look at Present and Future Trends

❧

As women, you are traveling on previously uncharted courses, experimenting with new ideas and roles, combining old ones in new ways and coming to terms with your personal definitions of work. You are participating in and experimenting with the creation and development of your unique life and work patterns. You are planning, forecasting, analyzing, and evaluating where you have been and what your future directions will include. Your feelings regarding the changes taking place in our society and in our lives range from angry and confused, ambivalent and unsure, to exhilarated and powerful. Though decisions about your life and work patterns will not be clear-cut or easy to make, many of you are feeling stronger as a result of having participated in a self-directed and self-determined change.

We personally have observed a large range of life and work

patterns while working with women over the last five years. In 1979, 50 percent of the labor force was female, but we go even further and agree with the person who once said, "All women are working women." For ease of description, however, we will talk about those women who work in the paid labor force separately from those who do not.

Within each category, there are many variations in how those women have chosen to adapt that particular pattern for themselves. We wanted to find out just how kaleidoscopic the possibilities for life and work patterns are. In other words, in how many ways have women succeeded in integrating work, learning, and leisure time into the fabric of their lives?

VISIBLE PATTERNS

First Pattern: The pattern of the woman who marries in her early twenties, but consciously defers having children in order to use her twenties to develop her career. The significant difference between this woman and the one who deferred having children while supporting her husband through graduate school or medical school is that the reason for waiting to have a family is due to the emphasis placed on "her" career or "their" careers rather than only on his.

Second Pattern: The woman who does not plan to marry until her late twenties. This woman, instead, prefers to use these early and middle twenties to establish a comfort level with her independence, develop her interests, learn to support herself, and develop her career. This pattern has become a much more viable option with the dissipation of the "old maid" stereotype which pressured young women into seeking husbands and beginning families.

Third Pattern: The woman who chooses to remain single. As alternative life styles have developed, and opportunities for women to become economically independent have increased, many women are choosing a single life style. This may entail a committed living-together arrangement, living alone, living with another woman or women, or participating in some type of communal situation. She may or may not choose to have children. Pursuing meaningful work is often an important focus for the single woman, and she may devote a great deal of energy to developing her career path.

Fourth Pattern: The woman who marries, chooses to work, and tentatively decides to remain child-free. An important focus for her becomes the development of meaningful work in her life. Sometimes, as she nears the end of her childbearing years, she reevaluates her decision not to have children and changes her mind. Consequently, she may return to work after a maternity leave, work part-time, or take some time out. But in most cases she is determined to retain her professional identity and commitment to integrate work into her family life in a way that feels right to her.

Fifth Pattern: Women who have careers, leave their careers for an indefinite period of time to have and raise children, but continue to keep current in their field. Many of these women had traditionally female jobs such as teacher or nurse, and originally planned to return to their chosen work. Often, however, in the interim years they develop new career interests and begin to develop alternate paths for themselves as a result of their new interests and changing societal patterns.

Sixth Pattern: Women who have chosen "career motherhood" while their children are in the home and make significant contributions to their communities through volunteer work and work in their children's schools. These women may or may not have had college educations. Often they have taken courses at local community colleges and have begun to strengthen new interests. Usually their income is not absolutely necessary to the family money pot. They feel firmly committed to using their energies to support their husbands and raise their children. They are becoming increasingly concerned with the need to be financially aware and to plan for the possibility that they may have to work in the future.

Seventh Pattern: Women who have combined their careers and motherhood by creating and maintaining a home-based occupation. These women are attempting to remain available to their children, but also to face the economic realities confronting their families by generating additional income outside their homes. Often they must leave their homes periodically during the day, but they are independent and flexible in their decisions regarding leaving the home.

Eighth Pattern: Women who are participating in a dual-career family, a "two-paycheck" family, in which responsibilities for the home and for the children are shared equally. Though many families are recipients of two paychecks, this woman has a partner who emotionally supports the development of her career and who shares both physically and emotionally in the necessary responsibilities of running a home and caring for children. Often this woman has a fairly clear-cut career plan, and very often her income is not significantly lower than her husband's.

Ninth Pattern: The woman who does not want to earn her money by being tied to a traditional job requiring forty hours a week for fifty weeks a year. She may be committed to participating in the paid labor force, but is dedicated to developing a more autonomous, higher paying, sometimes close-to-full-time work. Perhaps she is an insurance saleswoman, or a sales representative or the founder of a small business that allows her flexible scheduling or independence. Or perhaps she has been able to negotiate a three-quarters-time job, and can be home when her children arrive from school.

Tenth Pattern: The woman who is aware of the importance of work in her life, who is continuously building her skills and taking pride in following through on certain projects, but who has not developed a defined career path. On the other hand, she is mentally connected to the development of options for women and is successful in developing options for herself which may not have an *obvious* continuing thread.

Eleventh Pattern: The woman who only recently has begun to think about integrating work into her life. She married early, may have worked for a couple of years, but did not find work to be her first priority. She has responded to the women's movement and to a growing realization that she needs her own work in order to be "happy." Or she may have begun to realize that in order to combat inflation she has no choice but to find ways in which she can generate income. She is a "reentry" woman, one with great capacities and capabilities for making contributions, but who needs support and direction. She is anxious to begin developing a career path that would be satisfying and income-producing.

Twelfth Pattern: The woman who has had a family and who has become proficient in a job but who sees the need to plan for a career change. This woman may have been trained to teach or to do secretarial work when these were the principal options open to women. As times change, as affirmative action makes its impact, as she becomes aware that there are considerably more options open to her, she may begin to look for new opportunities. She may plan to return to school, to change jobs without additional formal education, to enter a training program, to try to attain a personal dream that had always remained dormant. She is just beginning to plan for her future career, to reach out, to take risks, and to create new alternatives for herself.

The emergence of these patterns that we have seen most often, and of other less common alternative life/work patterns, is significantly impacted by changes in population trends, the family, the economy, availability of education, increase of leisure time, and the blurring of the distinction between work, learning, and leisure. These variables with which futurists have begun to concern themselves will significantly affect future decisions women will make about their emerging life/work patterns.

In the fiftieth anniversary issue of *Business Week*, Frederick R. Brodzinski, an educator who is the vice-president of the New York chapter of the World Future Society, states that fifty years from now a person will change her/his *career* three times, rather than changing *jobs* three times as is presently predicted. It is helpful to explore the variables that will impact our changing opportunities resulting both from advanced technology and the explosion of work opportunities fifty years from now.

CHANGES IN POPULATION TRENDS

Business Week reports that by the year 2029 Americans will live an average of ten to fifteen years longer than now due to tremendous advances in the prevention and cure of disease. Consequently more than 20 percent of the population will be over sixty-five years old, spurring the growth of the specialization of products and services for the aged. Many of these older Americans will be totally capable of participating in the work force and will need to be absorbed.

The "baby boom" began in 1946 and ended in the 1960s. It was followed by the "baby bust," which is already resulting in fewer young entries into the labor market. Consequently the projections are that the unemployment rate will decrease, and a wealth of job opportunities will face both men and women in 2029.

CHANGES IN THE FAMILY

Will family life survive in its present forms, or disappear? How will what happens to families affect the unique life and work patterns that women design for themselves? Or to ask the question in reverse, how will the life/work pattern that women create affect the design of their family life?

Jane Howard, author of *Families*, spent three years visiting, observing, and participating in families across the country. She concludes that "families aren't dying; what families are doing in flamboyant and dumbfounding ways is changing their size, their shape, and their purpose." She reports that at this point in the late 1970s only 16.3 percent of America's 56 million families live in a conventional "nuclear" arrangement which includes children, husband as the provider, and wife as the homemaker.

The composition and flavor of families have been shaped through the years by conflicting societal pressures. Economic factors are a strong influence on the development of family patterns. Louise Kapp Howe, editor of *The Future of the Family*, suggests that the family alters to meet the needs of the economy. As a nation we have moved from agricultural to industrial to a post-industrial economy, which is reflected in our shifts from rural to urban to suburban living. The rising divorce rate, the invention of contraceptives, the changing demands placed on men and women have all contributed to changes in family composition. As a result, the definition of nuclear families has changed to include different forms, including dual-career families, single-parent families, blended families, communal families, and other combinations.

Political forces also have an impact. Spurred by the women's movement, legislation has been passed that strives toward equalizing economic and employment opportunities for women. Women's increasing abilities, desires, and often *needs* to be economically independent have also had major effects on family life. Women are deciding to stay single, choosing divorce, marrying and pursuing a career of their own, all options which change the way they live and the way they integrate work and families into their lives. This integration is not an easy one, and not everyone is doing it successfully. But from this trial and error will come ways of doing it successfully—ways which strengthen, not weaken, family life.

CHANGES IN THE ECONOMY

The bicentennial assessment of the future economic structure by the magazine *Business Week* delineates many significant changes in our economy and our society. These changes will have untold but far-reaching effects on the work and career patterns of both men and women within the next fifty years. The projections are based on hundreds of interviews with professionals in many fields whose business it is to predict the future. Naturally, they are educated guesses, projections which could be altered by unforeseeable factors that have not been anticipated.

– Some of the changes projected by *Business Week* which will result in a different employment pattern are:

- a solution to the energy crunch by the year 2000
- discovery of alternate, synthetic forms of energy
- many major producers of consumer goods will have disappeared in their present forms
- tremendous growth in the service industries
- manufacturing will grow from 24 percent of the gross national product to 50 percent
- 80 to 90 percent of the work force will be operating in jobs that involve the accumulation and processing of information (according to futurist Earl C. Joseph)
- tremendous growth in the communications industries
- introduction of robots to do routine production jobs
- diagnosis of health problems electronically
- growth of agriculture, but industrialization of the farm almost completely eliminating the family farm
- raising and harvesting of fish rather than hunting and capturing
- advances in prevention and cure of disease
- assumption by corporations of day-care facilities
- home-based electronic entertainment centers
- growth of waste management-industrial specialization in collection and processing of waste and distribution of recovery products
- basic metals production moved to lower-cost nations
- shipbuilding nonexistent in this country
- computers and communications will digitize the world

Though these changes will not take place overnight, anticipating their arrival can influence the directions of our career paths. It seems obvious that technology will have a major impact on our roles in the work world, and will speed job obsolescence. Much of the population will have to seek new careers, and many people may become overwhelmed by the enormous number of options available to them. It has even been suggested that career planning programs will be needed to help *restrict* options, a thought that is difficult to imagine. By the year 2029 it is anticipated that barriers to equal employment for women and minorities will be almost nonexistent, and that most women will have found a way to integrate career and family. While a prediction for the year 2029 may not mean much to most of us, remember that we are all participating right now in the process that will yield that result.

CHANGES IN EDUCATION AND LEISURE TIME

It is predicted that education will be perceived in a broader context and become more available to everyone. It will be necessary for people to retrain and reeducate themselves in the face of job obsolescence. There will continue to be a proliferation of alternative educational opportunities, private training institutes, apprenticeships, "free schools," and so on. The potential for a "learning society" is growing. Fred Best, in *The Future of Work*, believes that jobs of the future will be interrelated with continuous learning and that advanced education will become a common preparation for work. According to Marshall McLuhan (author of the phrase "the medium is the message") the worker of tomorrow will become increasingly concerned with "learning a living."

In *The Future of Work*, Best projects a significant increase in the leisure hours available to the average worker. Today's worker has about 1,200 hours a year more free time than his historical counterpart of 1890, and that number of leisure hours is going to continue growing, particularly in the face of modern medical advances that prolong life spans. An interesting and beneficial use of this newly accrued free time could be in retraining, reassessing, and redirecting one's career path, or in many cases, choosing a new path. Though it may seem, at first, that the need to retrain and change careers would be a burden, the process may be made easier by the addition of more available leisure time and the increased educational opportunities which are also evolving.

ADDITIONAL PROJECTED LIFE AND WORK PATTERNS

Only time will tell how many of these predictions and projections will actually come to fruition, but looking into the potential of the future can have a significant effect on the development of our own life and work patterns. The coming changes may generate feelings which range from excitement and exhilaration to ones of awe and concern. But the fact of change, and learning to anticipate and take change for granted, can help free us to create and develop alternative life/work plans beyond those with which we have commonly come in contact.

Paul Dickson, in *The Future of the Workplace: The Coming Revolution in Jobs*, discusses the beginning stages of new ways to integrate work into our lives. They include:

- paired or partnership work: two people filling one full-time job
- shared work: two people dividing a job with each taking responsibility for half the work
- split-location work: the work is done at the office *and* at home
- split-level work: one job is analyzed into components and divided up
- specialist: a person specializes in one aspect of a job and works part-time for an employer or several employers

Fred Best also discusses emerging alternative work-week patterns, such as:

- the forty-hour, four-day week
- four days on, four days off
- flexible work hours: can arrive and leave during a range of hours
- group jobs: hiring a group to assume ongoing responsibility for an entire task job, such as running a restaurant

The Center for Leisure in Tampa, Florida, envisions the extension of flexible scheduling to monthly or even yearly time spaces. It has been suggested that routine jobs might be more palatable with more frequent and longer time periods away from work.

One final trend that is in the incipient stages is the decision of some working couples to each work half-time or two-thirds time so that they will have more time at home with children or simply to develop themselves further. This is partially dependent, of course, on the economic feasibility of this plan. But it is also dependent on both spouses feeling secure enough in themselves that their identities have not become wrapped up in the cloak of their jobs.

The most important thing for which you must prepare yourself is to learn to cope with the reality that life is and will continue to be everchanging. Change is the one constant upon which you can count. You can wait for it to seek you out, or you can encourage its visitation. You will be the designer of your own life if you participate in the changes that undoubtedly will affect your life. It will be fulfilling to feel and discover that you have been able to help shape the direction of your work and its integration into your total life plan.

Bibliography

BOOKS

Allport, Gordon W. *Patterns and Growth in Personality.* New York: Holt, Rinehart and Winston, 1961.

Baltes, Paul and Schaie, K. Warner (eds.). *Life Span Developmental Psychology: Personality and Socialization.* New York: Academic Press, 1973.

Bardwick, Judith M., Douvan, E., Horner, M. & Gutmann, D. *Feminine Personality and Conflict.* Belmont, California: Brooks/Cole Publishing, 1970.

Best, Fred (ed.). *The Future of Work.* Englewood Cliffs, New Jersey, 1973.

Bernard, Jessie. *Women, Wives, Mothers: Values and Options.* Chicago: Aldine-Atherton, 1974.

Bolles, Richard Nelson. *What Color Is Your Parachute?* Berkeley, California: Ten Speed Press, 1979.

Bolles, Richard Nelson and Crystal, John. *Where Do I Go From Here With My Life?* Berkeley, California: Ten Speed Press, 1978.

Buhler, Charlotte & Massarik, Fred (eds.). *The Course of Human Life: A Study of Goals In the Humanistic Perspective.* New York: Springer, 1968.

Coup, R. T., Green, S. & Gardner, B. B. *A Study of Working Class Women in a Changing World.* Chicago: Social Research Associates, 1973.

Daniels, Pamela and Ruddick, Sara (eds.). *Working It Out: 23 Women Writers, Artists, Scientists, and Scholars Talk About Their Lives and Work.* New York: Pantheon Books, 1978.

DeRosis, Helen. *Women and Anxiety.* New York: Delacorte Press, 1979.

Dickson, Paul. *The Future of the Work Place: The Coming Revolution in Jobs.* New York: Weybright and Talley, 1975.

Eisdorfer, Carl and Lawton, M. P. (eds.,). *Psychology of Adult Development and Aging.* Washington D.C.: American Psychological Association, 1973.

Epstein, Cynthia F. *Woman's Place. Options and Limits In Professional Careers.* Berkeley, California: University of California Press, 1970.

Erikson, Erik H. *Childhood and Society* (2nd edition). New York: Norton, 1963.

————. *Identity and the Life Cycle.* Selected papers. New York: International Universities Press, 1967.

Gardner, John W. *Self-Renewal: The Individual and the Innovative Society.* New York: Harper Colophon Books, 1965.

Ginzberg, Eli & Associates. *Life Styles of Educated Women*. New York: Columbia Press, 1966.

Harmon, Lenore, Birk, J. M., Fitzgerald, L. E. and Tanney, M. F. *Counseling Women*. Monterey, California: Brooks/Cole Publishing, 1978.

Harragan, B. L. *Games Mother Never Taught You: Corporate Gamesmanship for Women*. New York: Warner Books, 1977.

Heyward, Du Bose. *The Country Bunny and the Little Gold Shoes*. Oviedo, Florida: Sandpiper Press Inc., 1974.

Howard, Jane. *Families*. New York: Simon and Schuster, 1978.

Howe, Louise Kapp (ed.). *The Future of the Family*. New York: Simon and Schuster, 1973.

Janeway, Elizabeth. *Between Myth and Morning: Women Awakening*. New York: William Morrow, 1975.

Jung, Carl G. *The Stages of Life*. The Collected Works of C. G. Jung (Vol 8). New York: Pantheon Books, 1960.

Kanter, Rosabeth Moss. *Men and Women of the Corporation*. New York: Basic Books, Inc., 1979.

Loeser, Herta. *Women, Work and Volunteering*. Boston: Beacon Press, Inc., 1975.

Loring, Rosalind K. and Otto, Herbert A. *New Life Options*. New York: McGraw-Hill Company, 1976.

Lowenthal, Marjorie F., Thurnher, M. & Chiriboga, D. *Four Stages of Life: A Comparative Study of Women and Men Facing Transition*. San Francisco: Jossey-Bass Inc., 1975.

Lynn, David. *Daughters and Parents: Past, Present, and Future*. Belmont, California: Wadsworth Publishing, Inc., 1979.

Maslow, Abraham. *Motivation and Personality*. New York: Harper and Row, Inc., 1970.

May, Rollo. *Psychology and the Human Dilemma*. New York: J. Norton Publishing, 1978.

Medsger, Betty. *Women at Work. A Photographic Documentary*. Mission, Kansas: Andrews & McMeel, Inc., 1975.

Meier, Gretl. *Job Sharing: A New Pattern for Quality of Work and Life*. The W. E. Upjohn Institute for Employment Research. Kalamazoo, Michigan, 1978.

Merriam, Eve. *Mommies at Work*. New York: Scholastic Book Services, 1973.

Miller, Jean Baker. *Toward A New Psychology of Women*. Boston: Beacon Press, Inc., 1977.

Molloy, John T. *Dress for Success*. New York: David McKay Co., 1975.

———. *The Women's Dress for Success Book*. New York: Warner Books, 1978.

Neugarten B. L. (ed.). *Middle Age and Aging.* Chicago: University of Chicago Press, 1968.

Osborn, Ruth H. *Developing New Horizons for Women.* New York: McGraw-Hill Book Company, 1977.

Reich, Charles. *The Greening of America: How the Youth Revolution Is Trying to Make America Liveable.* New York: Random House, 1970.

Rogers, Carl. *Carl Rogers On Personal Power. New York: Delacorte Press, 1977.*

Sheehy, Gail. Passages: Predictable Crises of Adulthood. New York: Dutton, 1976.

Shook, Robert L. *Greatest Salespersons: What They Say About Selling.* New York: Harper and Row, Inc., 1978.

Simon, Sidney B., Howe, L. W., and Hirschenbaum, H. *Values Clarification: A Handbook of Practical Strategies for Teachers and Students.* New York: Hart Associates, 1972.

Smith, D. and Bierman, E. L. (eds.). *The Biologic Ages of Man.* Philadelphia: W. B. Saunders Company, 1973.

Temple, D. (ed.) *Seen and Not Heard: A Garland of Fancies For Victorian Children.* New York: Dial Press, 1970. (Originally published in 1846.)

Troll, L. *Early and Middle Adulthood.* Monterey, California: Brooks/Cole Publishing, 1975.

———. *The Middle Adult Years.* Monterey, California: Brooks/Cole Publishing, 1975.

Tyler, Leona E. *Individuality: Human Possibilities and Personal Choice in the Psychological Development of Men and Women.* San Francisco: Jossey-Bass, Inc, 1978.

Wax, Judith. *Starting in the Middle.* New York: Holt, Rinehart & Winston, Inc., 1979.

Wethersby, Terry. *Conversations: Working Women Talk About Doing A Man's Job.* Millbrae, California: Les Femmes Publishing, 1977.

ARTICLES AND PUBLICATIONS

———. "The Future: How U. S. Business Will Change in the Next 50 Years," *Business Week* (September 3, 1979)

Campbell, D. P. *SVIB-SCII manual.* Stanford, California: Stanford University Press, 1973.

Elder, G. H. "Role Orientations, Marital Age, and Life Patterns in Adulthood," *Merril-Palmer Quarterly of Behavior and Development* (1972), 18, 3-24.

Farmer, H. S. "What Inhibits Achievement and Career Motivation In Women?" *Counseling Psychologist* (1976), 6, 2 II, 12-14.

Gass, G. A. "Counseling Implications of Woman's Changing Role," *Personnel and Guidance Journal* (1959), 37, 482-487.

Lipman-Bluman, J. "How Ideology Shapes Women's Lives," *Scientific American* (1972), 226-34-42.

Lopata, H. Z. "The Life Cycle of the Social Role of Housewife," *Sociology and Social Research* (1967), 51, 5-22.

Roche, Gerald, R. "Much Ado About Mentors," *Harvard Business Review* (January-February, 1979), 14-28.

Schiff, Jacqui L. "Passivity," *Transactional Analysis Journal* (January, 1971) 1:1.

Index

Perspective, changing, 55–74
  age, myths about, 68–70
  career women, examination
    of, 59
  failure, myths about, 63–64
  housewife-turned-career wo-
    man, stereotypes,
    70–71
  marriage, myths about,
    64–68
  myths as barriers to, 59–70
  personal stereotypes, 71–74
    quiz to determine, 72–74
  selfishness, myths about,
    61–63
  single working women and,
    58
  stereotypes, becoming con-
    scious of, 55–61
  working-class housewives,
    57–58
Power, 18–23
  defined, 9, 18
  "Fortunately/Unfortunately"
    (exercise), 22–23
  marital attitudes and, 18–22
Preparedness, 138–80
  assuming control, 150–52
  barriers to, 154–67
  career changing, 146–50
  competition, 154–56
  "creative" envy, 156–58
  delegating responsibility,
    163–64
  emergencies, planning for,
    164
  goal-directed consciousness,
    167
  interviewing, 152–54
  as a mind set, 138–40
  options, expanding, 152

organization, 162–63
  sales and, 151–52
  skills, transferability of,
    140–46
  skills-analysis sheets, 175–76
  time, management of, 158–62
  time wasters, identifying,
    164–67
  volunteer work and, 167
Progress, evaluation of, 232–65
  alternatives and options,
    253–54
  caution and, 245–48, 262–63
  change affecting others,
    258–60
  changes of direction, 242–44
  contacts, need for, 233
  dead ends, 235–38
  dress and, 251–53
  environments, selection of,
    240–42
  initiation, importance of, 246
  losing a job, 257–58
  mistakes, learning from,
    238–39
  new ventures, 259–60,
    262–63
  other women, interaction
    with, 233–35
  pace, 263–65
  planning ahead, 248–50
  problem-solving, 248
  reevaluation, periodic need
    for, 242–44
  responsibility, acceptance of,
    232–35
  rest periods, necessity for,
    254–56
  "super-woman syndrome,"
    253–54
  visibility, 244–45